COLIN DRURY

Management and cost accounting
STUDENTS' MANUAL

Van Nostrand Reinhold (UK)

First published in 1985 by
Van Nostrand Reinhold (UK) Co. Ltd
Molly Millars Lane, Wokingham, Berkshire,
England

Reprinted 1986

Typeset by Doyle Photosetting Ltd, Tullamore, Ireland

Printed and bound in Great Britain by
J.W. Arrowsmith Ltd, Bristol

Library of Congress Cataloging in Publication Data

Drury, Colin.
    Management and cost accounting: Students' manual

    (The VNR series in accounting and finance)
    Includes bibliographies and index.
    1. Managerial accounting.   2. Cost accounting.
I. Title.   II. Series.
HF5635.D798   1985   658.1′511   85-3266
ISBN 0-442-30638-5

British Library Cataloguing in Publication Data

Drury, Colin
    Management and cost accounting.—(The VNR
    series in accounting and finance)
    Students' manual
    1. Managerial accounting
    I. Title
    658.1′511   HF5635

ISBN 0-442-30638-5

Management and
cost accounting
STUDENTS' MANUAL

Preface

This manual is complementary to the main textbook, *Management and Cost Accounting*. Throughout the main book I have kept the illustrations simple to enable the reader to understand the principles involved in designing and evaluating management and cost accounting systems. More complex problems are provided at the end of each chapter so that the student can pursue certain topics in more depth, and concentrate on the application of principles. The objective of this manual is to provide solutions to the problems which have an asterisk beside the question number and, where necessary, to supplement the main text with a discussion of the additional issues raised by the questions.

The solutions given in this manual are my own and not the approved solution of the professional body setting the question. Where an essay question is asked and a full answer requires undue repetition of the book, either references are made to the appropriate sections of the main book, or an answer guide or outline is provided. You should note that there will be no 'ideal' answer to questions which are not strictly numerical. Answers are provided which, it is felt, would be generally acceptable in most contexts.

Where possible the questions are arranged in ascending order of difficulty. A short description of each question is given at the beginning of each chapter of this manual. The reader should select questions which are appropriate to the course which is being pursued. As a general rule questions designated as ACCA Level 1, ACCA Foundation, ICMA Cost Accounting 1 and 2 are appropriate for a first year course. These questions are mainly concerned with cost accounting which is covered in Part II of the main text. Questions designated as ICMA Management Accounting, ICAEW Management Accounting, ACCA Level II Management Accounting and ACCA Professional Two Management Accounting are appropriate for a second year course.

Finally I would like to thank, once again, the Institute of Chartered Accountants in England and Wales, the Association of Certified Accountants and the Institute of Cost and Management Accountants for permission to reproduce questions which have appeared in past examinations.

v

Index to solutions

Cost and revenue classification

The following is a summary of the questions:

2.1 to 2.3   Short questions which can be used to test your understanding of cost classification.

2.4 to 2.6   These are more demanding, time-consuming, professional foundation level questions on cost classification.

2.7   Calculation of a product cost for cost-plus pricing.

2.8   Illustrates how accounting information can be used for decision-making using cost–volume–profit relationships.

2.9   A useful discussion question emphasising that fixed costs should not be ignored for decision-making and cost control. You may prefer to delay this question until Chapter 8 has been completed.

2.10 to 2.13   Questions set at post foundation level suitable for either first or second year courses. 2.12 and 2.13 are essay questions where a variety of different answers are possible.

Answers to problem 2.1

(a) SV (or variable if direct labour can be matched exactly to output)

(b) F

(c) F

(d) V

(e) F (Advertising is a discretionary cost. See Chapter 16 for an explanation of this cost.)

(f) SV

(g) F

(h) SF

(i) V

Answers to problem 2.2

Controllable c, d, f

Non-controllable a, b, e, g, h

Answer to problem 2.4

(a)(i)

	Schedule of Annual Mileage Costs			
	5,000 miles £	10,000 miles £	15,000 miles £	30,000 miles £
Variable costs:				
Spares	100	200	300	600
Petrol	380	760	1,140	2,280
Total variable cost	480	960	1,440	2,880
Variable cost per mile	0.096	0.096	0.096	0.096
Fixed costs				
Depreciation (1)	2,000	2,000	2,000	2,000
Maintenance	120	120	120	120
Vehicle licence	80	80	80	80
Insurance	150	15ᴄ	150	150
Tyres (2)	—	—	75	150
	2,350	2,350	2,425	2,500
Fixed cost per mile	0.47	0.235	0.162	0.083
Total cost	2,830	3,310	3,865	5,380
Total cost per mile	0.566	0.331	0.258	0.179

Notes

(1) Anual depreciation $= \dfrac{£5,500 \text{ (cost)} - £1,500 \text{ (trade-in price)}}{2 \text{ yrs}} = £2,000$

(2) At 15,000 miles per annum tyres will be replaced once during the 2 year period at a cost of £150. The average cost per year is £75. At 30,000 miles per annum tyres will be replaced once each year.

Comments

Tyres are a semi-fixed cost. In the above calculations they have been regarded as a step fixed cost. An alternative approach would be to regard the semi-fixed cost as a variable cost by dividing £150 tyre replacement by 25,000 miles. This results in a variable cost per mile of £0.006. For a discussion of the alternative treatment of semi-fixed costs see Chapter 2.

Depreciation and maintenance cost have been classified as fixed costs. They are likely to be semi-variable costs but in the absence of any additional information they have been classified as fixed costs.

(ii)

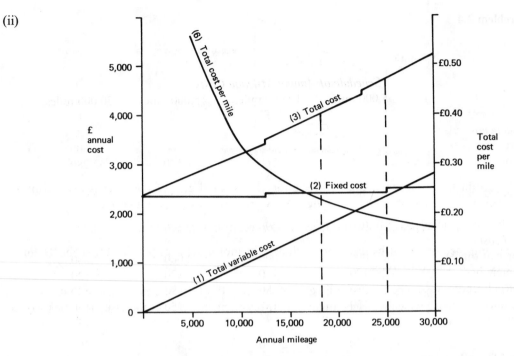

The step increase in fixed cost is assumed to occur at an annual mileage of 12,500 miles and 25,000 miles because tyres are assumed to be replaced at this mileage

(iii) The respective costs can be obtained from the vertical dashed lines in the graph.

(b) The *cost per mile* declines as activity increases. This is because the majority of costs are fixed and do not increase when mileage increases. However, *total cost* will increase with increases in mileage.

Answer to problem 2.5

(a)

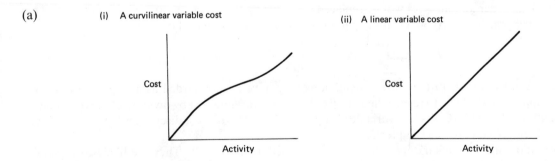

(b) See Chapter 2 for an explanation of a semi-variable cost and a stepped fixed cost. An example of a semi-variable cost is machine maintenance where part of the cost consists of a fixed element (preventive maintenance) and a variable element which varies according to the intensity of use. Supervision is an example of a stepped fixed cost. See Figure 2.6 in Chapter 2 for a diagram of a stepped fixed cost. The following is a diagram of a semi-variable cost.

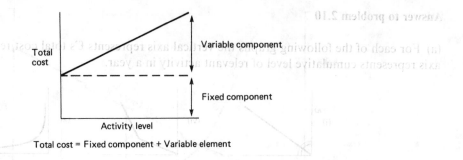

Total cost = Fixed component + Variable element

(c)(i) With the production unit method of depreciation the original cost of the asset is divided by the estimated number of units produced during its life. The depreciation charge for a period is:

$$\text{Number of units produced} \times \text{depreciation rate per unit}$$

The production unit method might be used for machinery or motor vehicles provided that the decline in value of these assets is related to usage.

(ii) Depreciation does not provide funds for asset replacement. If a firm wishes to ensure that funds are provided, an amount of cash which will accumulate to the replacement value of the asset must be invested.

Answer to problem 2.6

(a) The statement is incorrect. Total fixed costs do not decline as output increases. Total fixed costs remain constant as output increases. They may increase in steps (See Chapter 2) as output is expanded. It is fixed cost per *unit* that declines as output increases.

(b)(i) This cost is graphed as a stepped fixed cost.
  (ii) If depreciation is on a machine hour basis then it will be graphed as a variable cost.
  (iii) This is a semi-variable cost.

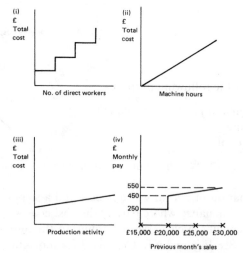

Answer to problem 2.10

(a) For each of the following graphs the vertical axis represents £'s total cost/revenue and the horizontal axis represents cumulative level of relevant activity in a year.

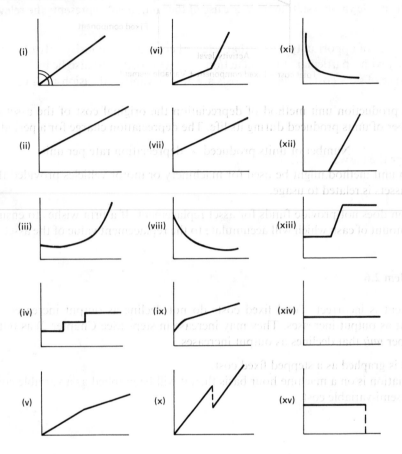

Answer to problem 2.11

Cost information is required for the following purposes;

    (a) Costs for stock valuation and profit measurement;
    (b) Costs for decision-making;
    (c) Costs for planning and control.

For the alternative measures of cost which might be appropriate for each of the above purposes see Chapter 2.

Answer to problem 2.12

(i) See Chapter 2 for a definition of opportunity cost and sunk cost.

(ii) *Opportunity cost*: If scarce resources such as machine hours are required for a special contract then the cost of the contract should include the lost profit that would have been earned on the next best alternative. This should be recovered in the contract price.

   Sunk cost: The original cost of equipment used for a contract is a sunk cost and should be ignored. The change in the resale value resulting from the use of the equipment represents the relevant cost of using the equipment.

(iii) The significance of opportunity cost is that relevant costs do not consist only of future cash outflows associated directly with a particular course of action. Imputed costs must also be included.

   The significance of sunk costs is that past costs are not relevant for decision-making.

Answer to problem 2.13

See Chapter 2 for the answer to this question.

Accounting for materials and labour

All the questions in this chapter are at foundation level. The following is a summary of the questions.

3.1	A description of various documents used in a material control system.
3.2 to 3.6	Computations for various stores pricing methods. With the exception of question 3.6 these questions are not difficult. 3.6 requires that output is expressed in terms of equivalent production. It will, therefore, be necessary to refer to Chapter 6 for an explanation of this term.
3.7	This question consists of two parts: stores pricing and labour cost accounting.
3.8	A simple problem which is useful for illustrating some of the issues to be considered when introducing an incentive scheme.
3.9 to 3.11	These are more difficult questions which focus on the effect of introducing incentive schemes. For an additional question on labour cost accounting see 5.7.
3.12	A useful question for reinforcing your understanding of a material control system.

Answer to problem 3.1

(a)(i) *Perpetual inventory:* A perpetual inventory system involves the recording of each stock movement on a bin card or computerised record so that the balance of every item in stock is always available. This system allows the quantities of goods in stock to be ascertained without physical counting.

(ii) *Continuous stocktaking:* Continuous stocktaking is carried out in order to check the accuracy of the perpetual inventory records. The system involves the physical counting of a few items of stock each day which are then compared with the balance shown on bin cards. The objective is to check each item of material in stock at least once per year and avoid the need for a periodic stocktaking. End of period stock valuations are based on quantities shown in the perpetual inventory records.

(b)(i) *Goods received note:* ICMA terminology definition is: 'A form recording all details relating to the receipt of materials from an outside source'.
Source: Receiving Department
Purpose: To provide documentary evidence of proof of receipt of materials and to compare with invoices before payment to suppliers are made. Documentation for entry of receipts in stores records.

(ii) *Material transfer note:* ICMA terminology definition is 'A document which records the transfer of material from one store to another, from one cost centre to another, or from one cost unit to another'.
Source: A cost centre no longer requiring the material that has been issued.
Purpose: To record movements of materials between cost centres or cost units.

(iii) *Purchase requisition:* Document requesting purchasing department to purchase goods.

Source: Normally stores department, or head of department requiring those goods which are not kept in the stores.

Purpose: Authorisation to purchasing department to place an order for the supply of goods.

(iv) *Materials returned note:* ICMA terminology definition is 'A document which records the return of unused materials to stores'.

Source: A cost centre returning materials to stores.

Purpose: To provide the documentation to reverse the accounting entries for a previous stores issue.

(c)

Materials Returned Note				
Credit Issuing Dept. . . . . Job No. . . . . Serial No.				
Debit Stores Ledger Account . . . . Bin No. . . . . Date				
Code No.	Description	Quantity or Weight	Unit Cost £	Value £
Authorised by . . . . Received by				

Answers to problems 3.2

(a)(i)   *Stores record of K using FIFO*

		Receipts		Issues		Balance		
Date	Quantity	Price £	Amount £	Quantity	Price £	Quantity	Price £	£
April	1,000	1.00	1,000			1,000	1.00	1,000
				500	1.00	500	1.00	500
May	500	1.20	600			500	1.00⎫	1,100
						500	1.20⎭	
				500	1.00			
				250	1.20	250	1.20	300
June	1,000	1.00	1,000			250	1.20⎫	1,300
						1,000	1.00⎭	
July				250	1.20			
				350	1.00	650	1.00	650
August	500	1.20	600			650	1.00⎫	1,250
						500	1.20⎭	
				650	1.00	500	1.20	600
September	500	1.30	650			500	1.20⎫	1,250
						500	1.30⎭	
				500	1.20			
				100	1.30	400	1.30	520
			3,850					

Stores record of L using LIFO

Date	Receipts Quantity	Price £	Amount £	Issues Quantity	Price £	Balance Quantity	Price £	£
April	1,000	1.00	1,000			1,000	1.00	1,000
				500	1.00	500	1.00	500
May	500	1.20	600			500	1.00)	
						500	1.20)	1,100
				500	1.20			
				250	1.00	250	1.00	250
June	1,000	1.00	1,000			1,250	1.00	1,250
July				600	1.00	650	1.00	650
August	500	1.20	600			650	1.00)	
						500	1.20)	1,250
				500	1.20			
				150	1.00	500	1.00	500
						500	1.00)	
September	500	1.30	650			500	1.30)	1,150
				500	1.30			
				100	1.00	400	1.00	400
			3,850					

Stores record of M using 6 months weighted average

Date		Receipts Quantity	Price £	Amount £	Issues Quantity	Balance Quantity
April	...	1,000	1.00	1,000	500	500
May	...	500	1.20	600	750	250
June	...	1,000	1.00	1,000		1,250
July	...				600	650
August	...	500	1.20	600	650	500
September	...	500	1.30	650	600	400
		3,500		3,850		

Weighted average price per sack = £3,850 ÷ 3,500 = £1.10

(a)(ii) Valuation of closing stocks:

> K 400 sacks @ £1.30 = £520
> L 400   ,,   @ £1.00 = £400
> M 400   ,,   @ £1.10 = £440

Profit resulting from each pricing method

	K(FIFO)		L(LIFO)		M(Average)
	£		£		£
Sales (3,100 × £1.50)		4,650		4,650	4,650
Purchases	3,850		3,850		3,850
Less closing stock	520	3,330	400	3,450	440	3,410
Total Profit		1,320		1,200	1,240
Profit per student		440		400	413.33

(a)(iii) See 'Stores Pricing' in Chapter 3 for the answer to this question.

(b) The sentence in this statement implies that stocks and WIP should be valued at production cost and this should include overheads that accrue on a time basis (i.e. fixed production overheads). In other words for financial reporting, stocks should be valued at absorption cost and not variable cost. For a discussion of this statement see 'External and Internal Reporting' in Chapter 8.

Answer to problem 3.4

(a)   *Stores Account—Component X*

	£		£
Opening Stock (440 units at £5)	2,200	2/11 WIP A/c (300 at £5)	1,500
8/11 Creditors (400 at £4.50)	1,800	9/11 Factory Overhead A/c (50 at £5)	250
15/11 Creditors (400 at £5.50)¹	2,200	13/11 WIP A/c $\left(\begin{array}{l}90 \text{ at } £5 \\ 210 \text{ at } £4.50\end{array}\right)$	1,395
21/11 WIP A/c (40 at £5.50)	220		
22/11 Creditors A/c (400 at £6)	2,400	16/11 WIP A/c $\left(\begin{array}{l}190 \text{ at } £4.50 \\ 310 \text{ at } £5.50\end{array}\right)$	2,560
		20/11 Plant and Equipment (20 at £5.50)	110
		28/11 Scrap A/c (30 at £5.50)	165
		30/11 Closing Stock $\left(\begin{array}{l}40 \text{ at } £5.50 \\ 400 \text{ at } £6\end{array}\right)$ (given)	2,620
		30/11 P & L A/c—Stock Loss (40 at £5.50) (See Note 1)	220
	8,820		8,820

Note
(1) The closing stock is given but there is a balancing figure in the account of 40 units. This is assumed to be the difference between the book stock and the physical stock. Therefore the 40 units are written off as a stock loss to the P & L account.

(b) For the answer to this question see 'Pricing the Issues of Raw Materials' in Chapter 3.

Answer to problem 3.5

(a) See 'Materials Control Procedure' in Chapter 3 for the answer to this question.

(b)(i)

Stores account

Receipts	Kilos	£	Issues	Kilos	£
Opening stock	650	1,300	Work in progress A/c (2)	3,200	6,400
Purchases (see note 1)	4,000	8,000	Purchase returns	300	600
			Stock loss written off to		
			stock losses account	250	500
			Closing stock	900	1,800
	4,650	9,300		4,650	9,300

Notes
(1) Calculation of purchases:

Creditors account

	£		£
Cash	7,200	Opening balance	3,800
Purchase returns	600	Purchases (difference)	8,000
Closing balance c/fwd	4,000		
	11,800		11,800

(2) The balancing difference in the account is assumed to represent issues to work in progress.

(b)(ii) The following are possible reasons for the stock loss:
Breakages
Evaporation
Pilfering
Incorrect recording of receipts, issues and balance
Incorrect physical count
Incorrect opening stock
Timing differences

Answer to problem 3.6

(a)

Stores ledger account: timber (LIFO basis)

	£		£
Opening balance: 40,000 at £1.40	56,000	April 12: 80,000 units at £1.50 (1)	120,000
April 5: 125,000 units at £1.50	187,500	April 26: 70,000 units at £1.70 (2)	119,000
April 19: 70,000 units at £1.70	119,000	30,000 units at £1.50	45,000
		Balance: 15,000 at £1.50	
		40,000 at £1.40	78,500
	362,500		362,500

Notes
(1) On a LIFO basis issues will be at £1.50. Therefore 80,000 units are issued (£120,000 ÷ £1.50).
(2) On a LIFO basis 70,000 units will be issued at £1.70 = £119,000. The remaining issues will be at £1.50 per unit. Total issues are £164,000. Therefore the number of units issued at £1.50 per unit will be:

$$\frac{£164,000 - £119,000}{£1.50 \text{ per unit}} = 30,000 \text{ units}$$

Stores ledger account: varnish (FIFO basis)

	£			£
Opening balance: 1,600 litres at £1.20	1,920	April 12: 1,000 litres at £1.20 (1)		1,200
April 5: 400 litres at £1.10	440	April 26: 600 litres at £1.20	720	
April 19: 1,800 litres at £1.30	2,340	400 litres at £1.10	440	
		300 litres at £1.30	390	1,550
		Balance 1,500 litres at £1.30		1,950
	4,700			4,700

Notes
(1) On a FIFO basis issues will be at £1.20 per litre. Therefore 1,000 litres are issued (£1,200 ÷ £1.20).
(2) On a FIFO basis the total issues will add to £1,550 consisting of:
   600 litres at £1.20 (Unused opening balance)
   400 litres at £1.10 (April 5 purchase)
The balance of £390 (£1,550 − £1,160) will be issued at £1.30. This will result in 300 litres being issued at £1.30 (£390/£1.30).

Comparison of book stocks and physical stocks

	Timber (units)	Varnish (litres)
Physical stock	55,000	700
Book stock	55,000	1,500
Difference	—	800

(b) The calculation of the number of desks *completed* during the period is as follows:

Quantity sold	4,600
Closing stock	925
Total output	5,525
Less opening stock	650
Completed desks	4,875

Comparison of material which should have been consumed and material actually consumed

	Timber	Varnish
Desks completed	4,875	4,875
Less opening WIP equivalent production (1)	200 ($\frac{2}{3} \times 300$)	75 (300 × $\frac{1}{4}$)
	4,675	4,800
Add closing WIP equivalent production (1)	120 ($\frac{3}{4} \times 160$)	60 ($37\frac{1}{2}\%$ × 160)
Equivalent production (1)	4,795	4,860
Consumption per desk	30 sq. ft.	0.47 litres
Total estimated consumption	143,850 sq. ft.	2,284 litres
Actual consumption (2)	180,000 sq. ft.	3,100 litres $\left(\begin{array}{l}\text{2,300 issues plus}\\ \text{800 stock loss}\end{array}\right)$
Excess usage	36,150 sq. ft.	816 litres

Note

(1) The objective is to ascertain the material that should have been used for production in the *current period*. Therefore opening stock equivalent production is deducted to ascertain production in the *current period*.

(2) Physical quantity issued per stores ledger account plus 800 litres stock loss for varnish.

(c) It appears that stores records for timber are accurate but the consumption of material once it has been issued, is not adequately controlled as actual consumption is approximately 25% greater than estimated consumption. There is a stock loss of 800 litres for varnish suggesting that the storekeeping for this material is not under control. However, the consumption of varnish is under control once it has been issued from store. The possible reasons for the differences are as follows:

Timber	*Varnish*
Inaccurate usage estimates	Inaccurate stock records of receipts and issues
Excess waste/scrap	Inaccurate stock counts
Pilfering in factory	Pilferage in stores
Inaccurate estimate of degree of completion	
Inaccurate record of stock of finished goods	

Answer to problem 3.9

(a) *Calculations*
Minimum Output = 450 units (given)
Current Maximum Output = 900 units (600 hours available ÷ $\frac{2}{3}$ hour)
Incentive Scheme
    Maximum Output = 1,200 units (600 hours available ÷ $\frac{1}{2}$ hour)

Revenue accounts—Current wages scheme

	Minimum output (450 units) £	Maximum output (900 units) £
Sales	4,050	8,100
Cost of sales:		
Materials	(900)	(1,800)
Labour (1)	(1,200)	(2,000)
Variable overhead (2)	(900)	(1,800)
Fixed overheads	(1,200)	(1,200)
Profit/(Loss)	(150)	1,300

Notes

(1) 450 units = 10 workers × 40 hours × £3 per hour = £1,200

    900 units = 600 hours at £3 per hour + overtime premium (200 hours at £1) = £2,000.

(2) Variable overheads vary with hours worked. For an output of 450 units the hours worked are 300 (450 units × $\frac{2}{3}$ hour). Therefore variable overhead is 300 hours at £3.

Revenue accounts—Proposed wages scheme

	Minimum output (450 units)	Current max. output (900 units)	Proposed max. output (1,200 units)
Sales	4,050	8,100	10,800
Cost of sales:			
Materials	(900)	(1,800)	(2,400)
Labour (1)	(1,200)	(1,850)	(2,600)
Variable overhead (2)	(675)	(1,350)	(1,800)
Fixed overhead	(1,200)	(1,200)	(1,200)
Profit/(Loss)	75	1,900	2,800

Notes

(1) 450 units: Minimum wage payment

    900 units: 450 hours worked ($\therefore$ Overtime premium of 50 hours at £1 is paid)

        Total payment is 900 units at £2 plus overtme premium.

    1,200 units: 1,200 units at £2 plus overtime premium of 200 hours at £1.

(2) 450 units: Hours worked (225) at £3 per hour

    900 units: Hours worked (450) at £3 per hour

    1,200 units: Hours worked (600) at £3 per hour

At the minimum output level profits are higher with the incentive scheme because of the reduction in variable overheads. Variable overheads vary with hours worked and the introduction of the incentive scheme results in a reduction of 75 hours. Therefore variable overheads are reduced by £225 (75 hours at £3) when the incentive scheme is introduced. At an output of 1,200 units improved labour efficiency also results in an extra output of 300 units. Therefore profits are increased by the additional sales revenue less the additional costs resulting from the extra output.

(b)(i) The 100 hours lost by the dispute will not result in any lost output. Idle time will be reduced by 100 hours. If the guaranteed wage rate does not apply to the hours lost then there will be a saving of £300 (100 hours at £3 per hour).

(ii) If demand exceeds the supply then sales will be reduced by 200 units (100 hours ÷ $\frac{1}{2}$ hour per unit). The lost profits resulting from the lost sales is as follows:

		£
Lost Sales (200 × £9)		1,800
Less saving in costs:		
Materials	400	
Variable Overhead	300	
Labour	400	1,100
Reduction in profit		700

If the overtime is reduced by 100 hours then there will be an additional saving in the overtime premium of £100. Consequently profits will be reduced by £600.

Answer to problem 3.10

(a)

Calculation of gross wages

	Direct £	Indirect £
Ordinary Hours	15,228 (4,230 × £3.60)	1,848 (880 × £2.10)
Overtime Premium	756 (630 × $\frac{1}{3}$ × £3.60)	56 (80 × $\frac{1}{3}$ × £2.10)
	15,984	1,904

Total wages = £17,888 (£15,984 + £1,904)

Allocation of gross wages
                  £

	£
Direct Workers Production Time: 3,525 hours (2,400 + 1,125) at £3.60 =	12,690
Direct Workers' Non-Production Down Time: 705 hours at £3.60 =	2,538
Direct Workers' Overtime Premium	756
Indirect Workers' gross wages	1,904
Wages charged to production overhead	5,198

Wages control account

	£		£
Cash (net wages paid per question)	12,864 }	WIP A/c	12,690
	1,420 }	Production overhead A/c	5,198
Employees deduction account			
(Balance)	3,604		
	17,888		17,888

(b)(i) The effect of the proposed scheme is examined by comparing the previous week's earnings for the direct workers with the earnings that would have been earned if the proposed scheme had been in operation:

Proposed scheme:

	£
Type 1 receiver (4,800 units at £1.90)	9,120
Type 2 receiver (1,500 units at £2.85)	4,275
Non-productive down time (see note 1)	1,410
	14,805

Present scheme:

Direct wages paid per part (A)	£15,984

Note

(i) Calculation of allowed hours for the previous week's production:

Type 1	4,800 units × 24 minutes	1,920 hours
Type 2	1,500 units × 36 minutes	900 hours
		2,820 hours

Non-Productive down time $= 20\% \times 2,820$ hours $\times £2.50 = £1,410.$

Conclusion

It appears that the proposed incentive scheme will reduce the wages cost but the factors outlined in (Bii) must be examined before a final decision is made. The above analysis assumes that the company will pay only for the hours worked by the direct operatives. If hours which are surplus to requirements are paid then the results of the proposed scheme should be adjusted as follows:

	hours
Total productive hours per note (1) above	2,820
Allowance for non-productive time (20%)	564
	3,384
Ordinary time for direct operatives	3,600
Shortfall	216

Assuming that the 216 hours are paid at £2.50 or £3.60 then the cost of the incentive scheme will be increased by the appropriate amount. However, the proposed scheme is still cheaper than the present scheme.

(b)(ii) Additional factors to be examined are:

(a) How will any surplus plus labour capacity (as in bi) be dealt with?

(b) Will the opportunity for the direct workers to earn a higher wage be a source of grievance with the indirect workers and workers in other departments?

(c) Will product quality be affected?

(d) Will less supervision be required?

(e) Will the scheme result in increased administration costs?

(f) Will future output be significantly increased and can it be sold? An estimate of future output with the incentive scheme and output without the incentive scheme is required. Cost and revenue comparison should then be made for the different output levels.

(g) Will variable overheads be affected? Do they vary with direct labour hours of input?

Accounting for overhead expenditure

With the exception of 4.14, all questions are at foundation level (although some have been set in the professional examinations at post-foundation level).
The questions are summarised as follows:

4.1 and 4.2	Discussion questions which can be used to test your understanding of the relevant topics in Chapter 4.
4.3 to 4.5	Apportionment of overheads and the preparation of overhead analysis statements (4.4 applies to a non-profit making organisation).
4.6 and 4.7	Calculation of overhead absorption rates and the under and over recovery.
4.8 and 4.10	Combination of an analysis of overheads by departments (not including a detailed overhead analysis) and the calculation of overhead absorption rates. 4.8 and 4.9 are not difficult but students might find 4.10 difficult.
4.11	Requires the calculation of overhead absorption rates and the extraction of the variable cost for a make or buy decision. This question is useful for emphasising the decision-making aspects at this stage. Alternatively you might prefer to defer this problem until make or buy decisions have been studied in Chapter 10.
4.12 and 4.13	Reapportionment of service department costs based on reciprocal service charges. 4.13 is the most difficult question.
4.14	An excellent question for providing a consolidation of Chapter 4. Part A of the question requires the calculation of overhead absorption rates and includes the reciprocal allocation of service department overheads. Part B requires the provision of relevant cost information (including the abstraction of variable overheads) for decision-making. This question serves as an introduction to decision-making.

Answer to problem 4.1

(a) For the answer to this question see 'Pre-Determined Overhead Rates' in Chapter 4.

(b) A lower production overhead rate does not necessarily indicate that factory X is more efficient than factory Y. The reasons for this are:

(i) Factory Y's operations might be highly mechanised resulting in large depreciation costs whereas factory X's operations might be labour intensive. Consequently products produced in factory Y will incur higher overhead and lower labour costs whereas products produced in factory X will incur lower overhead and higher labour costs.

(ii) Factory Y may have invested in plant with a larger operating capacity in order to meet future output. This will result in larger fixed costs and a higher overhead rate.

(iii) Both factories may use different denominators in calculating the overhead rates. For example, if factory Y uses normal capacity and factory X uses maximum practical capacity then factory Y will have a higher overhead rate.

(iv) Current budgeted activity might be used by both firms to calculate the overhead rate. The level of budgeted activity. The lower overhead rate of factory X might be due to a higher sales volume rather than efficient factory operations.

(v) Different cost classification might result in different overhead rates. Factory X might treat all expenditure as a direct cost wherever possible. For example employers' costs might be charged out by means of an inflated hourly wage rate. Factory Y may treat such items as overhead costs.

Answer to problem 4.2

(a) For the answer to this question see 'Blanket Overhead Rates and Departmental Overhead Rates' in Chapter 4.

(b) For the answer to this question see Appendix 2 of Chapter 4.

Answer to problem 4.3

(a)

Overhead analysis sheet

Item of expense	Basis of apportionment	Total	Machining Dept.	Assembly Dept.	Finishing Dept.	Stores	Occupancy
		£	£	£	£	£	£
Indirect wages	Actual Allocation	34,000	9,000	15,000	4,000	6,000	
Indirect materials	,, ,,	2,400	400	1,400	600		
Maintenance	,, ,,	2,100	1,400	600	100		
Power	,, ,,	2,200	1,600	400	200		
Rent	,, ,,	2,000					2,000
Rates	,, ,,	600					600
Insurance on building	,, ,,	200					200
Lighting and heating	,, ,,	400					400
Cleaning of factory	,, ,,	800					800
Depreciation on plant and equipment	Plant and equipment cost	16,700	14,000	2,000	600	100	
Wage related costs	Total wages	28,200	8,320	16,440	2,240	1,200	
Factory administration and personnel	No. of employees	7,100	2,000	4,000	1,000	100	
Insurance on plant and equipment	Plant and equipment cost	1,670	1,400	200	60	10	
Occupancy costs reapportioned	Area in sq. feet	—	1,200	1,800	800	200	(4,000)
Stores costs reapportioned	No. requisitions	—	1,680	5,090	840	(7,610)	
		98,370	41,000	46,930	10,440	—	—
Direct labour hours			32,000	4,000			
Direct labour overhead rates			£1.47	£2.61			
			Ans. (b)	(i)	(ii)		

(b)(i) £1.47 per hour (See overhead analysis sheet).
(ii) £2.61 per hour (See overhead analysis sheet).

(c)(i) *Depreciation and insurance of plant* is likely to be related to value of plant.
(ii) *Wage related costs* are likely to vary with total wages paid.
(iii) *Factory administration and personnel costs*—Personnel costs are likely to be related to number of employees. It is difficult to select a basis of apportionment which is closely related to factory administration costs. It is assumed that the greater the number of employees the greater the administration costs but this is difficult to justify. Probably administration costs are related to several variables and no single method of apportionment is likely to be satisfactory.
(iv) *Occupancy costs reapportionment*. These costs are related to area.
(v) *Stores reapportionment*. The benefits which each production department receive from stores are likely to be related to the number of requisitions issued by each department.

(d) Depreciation and insurance might be related to replacement cost rather than historical cost. Therefore the replacement cost of assets is a better method of apportionment. It would be preferable to reapportion stores costs on the basis of the amount of time stores staff devote to each department.

Answer to problem 4.6

(a) Overhead rate $= \dfrac{\text{Budgeted overhead}}{\text{Budgeted direct wages}} \times 100$

$\phantom{\text{(a) Overhead rate}} = \dfrac{£225,000}{£150,000} \times 100 = 150\%$

		£
(b)	Direct materials	190
	Direct wages	170
	Production overhead (150% × £170)	255
	Production cost	615
	Gross profit ($\frac{1}{3}$ × £615)	205
		820

(c)(i) Each department incurs different overhead costs. For example the overhead costs of Department A are considerably higher than the other departments. A blanket overhead rate is only appropriate where jobs spend the same proportion of time in each department. See 'Blanket Overhead Rates and Departmental Overhead Rates' in Chapter 4 for an explanation of why departmental overhead rates are preferable.
(ii)

$$\text{Department A machine hour overhead rate} = \frac{£120,000}{40,000 \text{ machine hours}}$$
$$= £3 \text{ per machine hour}$$

A machine hour rate is preferable because machine hours appear to be the dominant activity. Also most of the overheads incurred are likely to be related to machine hours rather than direct labour hours. Possibly one worker operates 4 machines since the ratio is 40,000 machine hours to 10,000 direct labour hours. If some jobs do not involve machinery, but others do, then two separate cost centres should be established (one related to machinery and the other related to jobs which involve direct labour hours only).

$$Department\ B\ Direct\ Labour\ Hour\ Overhead\ Rate = \frac{£30,000}{50,000\ direct\ labour\ hours}$$
$$= £0.60\ per\ labour\ hour$$

Because direct labour hours are five times greater than machine hours a direct labour hour overhead rate is recommended. A comparison of direct labour hours and direct wages for budget, actual and job 657 for department B suggests that wage rates are not equal throughout the department. Therefore the direct wages percentage method is inappropriate.

$$Department\ C\ Direct\ Labour\ Hour\ Overhead\ Rate = \frac{£75,000}{25,000\ direct\ labour\ hours}$$
$$= £3\ per\ direct\ labour\ hour$$

This method is chosen because it is related to time and machine hours are ruled out. A comparison of budgeted direct wages and labour hours for budget, actual and job 657 for department C suggests that wage rates are equal at £1 per hour throughout the department. Therefore direct labour hours or direct wages percentage methods will produce the same results.

(d) Department A: 40 machine hours × £3 =120
     Department B: 40 labour hours × £0.60= 24
     Department C: 10 labour hours × £3 = 30
                              174

(e) (i)

Current rate (actual wages × 150%)

	Absorbed	Actual	Over/(under) absorbed
	£000	£000	£000
A	45	130	(85)
B	120	28	92
C	45	80	(35)
	210	238	(28)

(ii)

Proposed Rates

	Absorbed	Actual	Over/(under) absorbed
	£000	£000	£000
A	135	130	5
B	27	28	(1)
C	90	80	10
	252	238	14

Answer to problem 4.8

(a)

	Machine Shop £	Assembly Shop £	Canteen £	Total £
Allocated Overhead	68,000	39,000	16,000	123,000
Reapportionment of Canteen (1)	10,000	6,000	(16,000)	—
	78,000	45,000	—	123,000

Overhead Absorption Rates

$$\text{Machine shop machine hour rate (2)} = \frac{£78,000}{26,000 \text{ hours}} = £3 \text{ per machine hour}$$

$$\text{Assembly shop machine direct labour hour rate (2)} = \frac{£45,000}{18,000 \text{ hours}} = £2.50 \text{ per direct labour hour}$$

A direct labour hour rate is used for the assembly department because the time expended on products in this department is mainly labour based. Because wage rates are constant the direct wages percentage method is equally applicable. In the machining department a machine hour rate is used because a considerable proportion of overheads will be incurred as a result of machine running time.

Notes
(1) Reapportioned on the basis of number of employees.
(2) The calculation of the budgeted hours is as follows:

	Product A	Product B	Total
Budgeted production	2,000 units	2,500 units	
Machine shop hours per unit	3	8	
Total machine shop hours	6,000	20,000	26,000
Assembly dept. direct labour hours per unit	4	4	
Total assembly direct labour Hours	8,000	10,000	18,000

Budgeted cost per unit

		A £		B £
Materials		8		5
Direct labour: machine shop	15		18	
assembly	8	23	8	26
Overheads: machine shop	9		24	
assembly	10	19	10	34
Total cost		50		65

(b) Sales and variable costs will increase if production is 300 units higher than budget. The variable overhead absorption rates are:

Machine shop: £1 per machine hour (£26,000 ÷ 26,000 machine hours)
Assembly dept.: £0.50 per direct labour hour (£9,000 ÷ 18,000 direct labour hours)

The variable overhead cost per unit for product A is £36 and is calculated as follows:

	£
Materials	8
Labour	23
Variable overhead: Machine shop (3 × £1)	3
assembly dept. (4 × £0.50)	2
Total unit variable cost	36

Sales and production of an extra 300 units will increase profits by £7,200.
The calculation is as follows:

	£
Additional sales revenue (300 × £60)	18,000
Less additional variable costs (300 × £36)	10,800
	7,200

Answer to problem 4.11

(a) The calculation of the overhead absorption rates are as follows:

Forming department machine hour rate = £6.15 per machine hour $\left(\dfrac{\pounds602,700}{98,000 \text{ hours}}\right)$

Finishing department labour hour rate = £2.25 per labour hour $\left(\dfrac{\pounds346,500}{154,000 \text{ hours}}\right)$

The forming department is mechanised and it is likely that a significant proportion of overheads will be incurred as a consequence of employing and running the machines. Therefore a machine hour rate has been used. In the finishing department several grades of labour are used. Consequently the direct wages percentage method is inappropriate and the direct labour hour method should be used.

(b) The decision should be based on a comparison of the incremental costs with the purchase price from an outside supplier if spare capacity exists. If no spare capacity exists then the lost contribution on displaced work must be considered. The calculation of incremental costs requires that the variable element of the total overhead absorption rate must be calculated. The calculation is:

Forming department variable machine hour rate = £2.05 $\left(\dfrac{\pounds200,900}{98,000 \text{ hours}}\right)$

Finishing department variable direct labour hour rate = £0.75 $\left(\dfrac{\pounds115,500}{154,000 \text{ hours}}\right)$

The calculation of the variable costs per unit of each component is:

	A	B	C
	£	£	£
Prime cost	24.00	31.00	29.00
Variable overheads: Forming	8.20	6.15	4.10
Finishing	2.25	7.50	1.50
Variable unit manufacturing cost	34.45	44.65	34.60
Purchase price	£30	£65	£60

On the basis of the above information component A should be purchased and components B and C manufactured. This decision is based on the following assumptions:
 (i) Variable overheads vary in proportion to machine hours (Forming department) and direct labour hours (Finishing department).
(ii) Fixed overheads remain unaffected by any changes in activity.

(iii) Spare capacity exists.
For a discussion of make or buy decisions see Chapter 10.

(c) Production overhead absorption rates are calculated in order to ascertain costs per unit of output for stock valuation and profit measurement purposes. Such costs are inappropriate for decision-making and cost control. For an explanation of this see 'Overheads for Decision-Making' and 'Overhead for Control' in Chapter 4.

Answer to problem 4.12

(a)   *Overhead analysis (£) (by repeated distribution method)*

	Production departments				Canteen	Boiler house
	1	*2*	*3*	*4*		
Allocation per overhead analysis	200,000	500,000	300,000	400,000	50,000	100,000
Allocation of boiler house	20,000	10,000	30,000	20,000	20,000	(100,000)
	220,000	510,000	330,000	420,000	70,000	—
Allocation of canteen	7,000	21,000	14,000	21,000	(70,000)	7,000
	227,000	531,000	344,000	441,000	—	7,000
Allocation of boiler house	1,400	700	2,100	1,400	1,400	(7,000)
	228,400	531,700	346,100	442,400	1,400	—
Allocation of canteen	140	420	280	420	(1,400)	140
	228,540	532,120	346,380	442,820	—	140
Allocation of boiler house (1)	35	17	53	35	—	(140)
Allocation to production departments	228,575	532,137	346,433	442,855	—	—

Note
(1) Apportioned in the ratio 20 : 10 : 30 : 20 and no reallocation to canteen. Alternatively the simultaneous equation method can be used:
    Let X = Total overheads for canteen after boiler house charges have been allocated.
    Let Y = Total overheads for boiler house after canteen charges have been allocated.
    $X = 50,000 + 0.2Y$
    $Y = 100,000 + 0.1X$
    Rearranging the above equations
    $X - 0.2Y = 50,000 \ldots \ldots (1)$
    $-0.1X + Y = 100,000 \ldots \ldots (2)$
    Multiply equation (1) by 5 and equation (2) by 1

$5X - Y = 250,000$

$-0.1X + Y = 100,000$

Adding the above equations

$4.9X = 350,000$

$$\therefore X = \frac{350,000}{4.9} = \underline{£71,428.6}$$

Substituting for X in equation (1)

$71,428.6 - 0.2Y = 50,000$

$21,428.6 = 0.2Y$

$\therefore Y = 107,143$

We now apportion the values of X and Y to the production departments in the agreed percentages.

	Production departments			
	1	2	3	4
	£	£	£	£
Allocation as per overhead analysis	200,000	500,000	300,000	400,000
Allocation of canteen (£71,429)	7,143	21,429	14,286	21,429
Allocation of boiler house (£107,143)	21,429	10,714	32,143	21,429
	228,572	532,143	346,429	442,858

(b) The problems associated with apportioning service department costs to production departments are:
  (1) Difficulty in determining suitable bases for apportionment of service department costs to production. The base selected should be one that exerts a major influence on the costs of the service departments.
  (2) When there are several service departments working for each other the analysis can become complex. The simultaneous equation and repeated distribution methods cannot be used when complex interrelationships occur. Matrix algebra can be used for complex problems. Alternatively computers can easily deal with reciprocal service department apportionments.

SOLUTIONS TO CHAPTER 5 PROBLEMS

Accounting for a job costing system

The details of the questions are as follows:

5.1 and 5.2 Preparation of ledger accounts for an integrated accounting system. 5.1 includes a material price variance.

5.3 Preparation of ledger accounts for a non-integrated accounting system.

5.4 and 5.5 Preparation of the cost ledger accounts when extracts from the financial accounts and the reconciliation of the costing and financial accounting profit are given in the question.

5.6 Preparation of ledger accounts from incomplete information so as to estimate the cost of the closing stock of materials destroyed by a fire.

5.7 Labour cost accounting and the preparation of the relevant labour accounts. This question refers to aspects of labour cost accounting covered in Chapter 4.

5.8 Preparation of a Production Overhead Account including the measurement of output in standard hours.

5.9 to 5.11 Construction of contract accounts.

Answer to problem 5.1

(a)   (*All figures £000*)

Land and buildings A/c

April 1 Balance b/f	500

Plant, machinery and office equipment A/c

April 1 Balance b/f	800

Provision for depreciation, plant, machinery and office equipment A/c

	April 1 Balance	200
	30 Production overhead	20
	Administration	5
		225

Stores ledger control A/c

April 1 Balance b/f	80	April 30 Material price variance	5
30 Creditors	50	Work-in-progress	40
		Production overhead	8
		Balance c/f	77
	130		130

25

Work-in-progress A/c

April	1	Balance b/f	40	April	30	Finished goods	110
	30	Wages and salaries	40			Balance c/f	90
		Stores Ledger	40				
		Production overhead	80				
			200				200

Finished goods stock A/c

April	1	Balance b/f	20	April	30	Cost of sales	112
	30	Work-in-progress	110			Balance c/f	18
			130				130

Debtors A/c

April	1	Balance b/f	260	April	30	Bank	190
	30	Sales	160			Balance c/f	230
			420				420

Creditors A/c

April	30	Bank	70	April	1	Balance b/f	100
		Balance c/f	80		30	Stores ledger	50
			150				150

Bank A/c

April	30	Debtors	190	April	1	Balance b/f	50
		Balance c/f	70		30	Creditors	70
						Wages and salaries	80
						PAYE and NI	30
						Production overhead	20
						Administration	10
			260				260

Share capital A/c

				April	1	Balance b/f	1,100

Share premium A/c

				April	1	Balance b/f	200

Profit and loss appropriation A/c

April	30	Profit and Loss	20	April	1	Balance b/f	35
		Balance c/f	15				
			35				35

PAYE and National Insurance A/c

April 30	Bank	30	April 1	Balance b/f	15
	Balance c/f	25	30	Wages and salaries	30
				Production overhead	5
				Administration overhead	3
				Selling overhead	2
		55			55

Wages and salaries A/c

April 30	Bank	80	April 30	Work-in-progress	40
	PAYE and NI	30		Production overhead	20
				Administration overhead	30
				Selling overhead	20
		110			110

Production overhead A/c

April 30	Wages and salaries	20	April 30	Work-in-progress	80
	Bank (expenses)	20		$(200\% \times 40)$	
	Provision for depreciation	20			
	PAYE and NI	5			
	Stores Ledger	8			
	Profit and Loss a/c	7			
	(over absorption)				
		80			80

Administration overhead A/c

April 30	Wages and salaries	30	April 30	Profit and Loss A/c	48
	Bank	10			
	Provision for depreciation	5			
	PAYE and NI	3			
		48			48

Selling overhead A/c

April 30	Wages and salaries	20	April 30	Profit and Loss A/c	22
	PAYE and NI	2			
		22			22

Material price variance A/c (See note 1)

April 30	Stores Ledger	5	April 30	Profit and Loss A/c	5

Sales A/c

April 30	Trading A/c	160	April 30	Debtors	160

Cost of sales A/c

April 30 Finished goods	112	April 30 Trading A/c	112

(B)   *Trading and profit and loss A/c*

April 30 Cost of sales	112	April 30 Sales	160
Gross profit c/f	48		
	160		160
Administration overhead	48	Gross profit b/f	48
Selling overhead	22	Production overhead	
Material price variance	5	(over-absorbed)	7
		Net loss —	
		Appropriation A/c	20
	75		75

(C)   *Trial balance at 30th April, 2980*

	Dr	Cr
Land and buildings	500	
Plant, machinery and office equipment	800	
Provision for depreciation		225
Material stores	77	
Work-in-progress	90	
Finished goods stock	18	
Debtors	230	
Creditors		80
Bank		70
Share capital		1,100
Share premium		200
Profit and Loss appropriation		15
PAYE and NI		25
	£1,715	£1,715

Note

(1) An explanation of the accounting entries for a standard costing system is presented in Chapter 18.

Answer to problem 5.4

(a)(i)   *Raw materials stock account*

	£		£
Opening stock (110 less 7)	103	Issues (difference)	578
Purchases	640	Returns (to supplier)	20
		Closing stock (130+15)	145
	743		743

(ii)

Work in progress account

	£		£
Opening stock (25+3)	28	Finished goods A/c (Difference)	984
Raw materials A/c	578	Closing stock (27 less 5)	22
Direct labour (220+20)	240		
Production overhead absorbed			
(240 at $66\frac{2}{3}\%$)	160		
	1,006		1,006

(iii)

Finished goods account

	£		£
Opening stock (82 less 9)	73	Cost of sales A/c (Difference)	989
Work in Progress A/c	984	Closing stock (72 less 4)	68
	1,057		1,057

(iv)

Profit and loss account

	£		£
Sales returns A/c	30	Sales A/c	1,530
Cost of sales A/c	989		
Gross profit c/d	511		
	1,530		1,530
Production overheads		Gross profit b/d	511
underabsorbed	2		
Administration expenses	200		
Net profit	309		
	511		511

The reconciliation statement indicates that discounts, selling expenses and debenture interest are not included in the cost accounts. Therefore these items are not included in the Costing Profit and Loss Account.

(b) Interest on capital tied up in stocks should be taken into account for decision-making and cost control purposes. This is because the interest on capital tied up in stocks represents an opportunity cost (in terms of the lost interest) which would have been earned if the money tied up in stocks had been invested.

Interest on capital tied up in stocks should not be included in product costs for stock valuation purposes per SSAP 9. Therefore the cost accumulation system will not include notional costs for stock valuation purposes. Nevertheless it is essential that all *relevant* costs (including opportunity costs) are included in cost statements for the purpose of decision-making and cost control.

Answer to problem 5.6

(a) The closing stock of raw materials is found by preparing the appropriate control accounts (starting with Finished Goods) and ascertaining WIP transfer and material issues as follows:

Finished goods stock account

	£		£
Opening balance	5,490	Variable cost of sales (1)	57,600
Work in Progress Account	60,880	Closing balance (given)	8,770
(Difference)			
	66,370		66,370

Work in progress account

	£		£
Opening balance (given)	17,500	Transfer to finished goods account	60,880
Direct Wages (given)	16,200	Closing balance (given)	22,160
Overhead Control Account (2)	12,960		
Material issued to WIP	36,380		
(Difference)			
	83,040		83,040

Stores control account

	£		£
Opening balance (given)	16,740	Materials issued per WIP A/c	36,380
Purchases	44,390	Closing balance (difference) (3)	24,750
	61,130		61,130

Notes

(1) Sales $= 166\frac{2}{3}\%$ of variable cost of sales

$\therefore$ Variable cost of sales $= \dfrac{£96,000 \times 100}{166\frac{2}{3}} = £57,600$

(2) Overhead charged to production $= 80\%$ of Direct wages
$$= 80\% \times £16,200 = £12,960$$

(3) Question states all material issues are charged to production. Therefore the stores control account will not include any issue of indirect materials. Consequently the balance of the control account represents the closing stock of materials destroyed by fire.

(b)(i) The original purchase price is a sunk and irrelevant cost. The cost of the fire is not the purchase price of the stock destroyed but the cost of placing the company back into the position it occupied before the fire; to do this requires purchasing materials at current replacement costs.

(ii) For a discussion of the implications of charging material issues to production using replacement costs see 'Pricing the Issues of Raw Materials' in Chapter 3.

(c) For a discussion of the implications of valuing work-in-progress and finished goods using the variable cost approach see Chapter 8.

Answer to problem 5.7

(a)   *Calculations*

(1) *Calculation of wages*

		Direct workers	Indirect workers	Total
		£	£	
Attendance time		1,200 (800 × £1.50)	350 (350 × £1)	
Overtime premium		75 (100 × £0.75)	20 (40 × £0.50)	
Shift premium		150	50	
Group bonus		160	70	
Gross wage		1,585	490	2,075
Employees' deductions:				
Income tax	250		100	
National insurance	75	325	35	135
Net wage		1,260	355	

(2) *Analysis of direct workers gross wage*

		Direct	Indirect
		£	£
Production time		885 (590 × £1.50)	315 (210 × £1.50)
Overtime premium		15 (20% × £75)	60 (80% × £75)
Shift premium			150
Group bonus			160
		900	685

(3) *Analysis of indirect workers*

		Direct	Indirect
		£	£
Attendance time*		8 (8 × £1)	342 (342 × £1)
Overtime premium*		4 (20% × £20)	16 (80% × £20)
Shift premium			50
Group bonus			70
		12	478

*20% of the 40 hours overtime was incurred at the specific request of the customer and is charged directly to the job.

(4) *Charges to WIP and Production Overhead A/c*

   Total charged to WIP A/c £912 (900 + 12)
   Total charged to Production Overhead A/c £1,163 (685 + 478).

Wages Control Account

	£		£
Cash (see calculation 1)	1,260	Work in Progress A/c	
Cash (see calculation 1)	355	(see calculation 4)	912
Income Tax A/c	250	Production O/H A/c	
Income Tax A/c	100	(see calculation 4)	1,163
National Insurance A/c	75		
National Insurance A/c	35		
	2,075		2,075

Production Overhead Control Account

	£	
---	-----	
National Insurance A/c (Employer's contribution 125+55)	180	
Wages Control A/c (see calculation 4)	1,163	

Work in Progress Account

	£	
-------------------------------------	---	
Wages Control A/c (see calculation 4)	912	

Cash and Bank Account

			£
	-	--------------------	-----
		Wages Control A/c	1,260
		Wages Control A/c	355

Income Tax Account

	£		£
Balance C/f	350	Wages Control A/c (D. Workers)	250
		Wages Control A/c (Ind. Workers)	100
	350		350

National Insurance Account

	£		£
Balance C/f	290	Wages Control A/c (D. Workers)	75
		Wages Control A/c (Ind. Workers)	35
		Production O/H A/c (Employer's contribution)	180
	290		290

(b)(i) Employment costs have been regarded as manufacturing overheads. These costs will be charged to jobs by means of overhead absorption rates. For an explanation of the treatment see 'Employment Costs' in Chapter 3.

(ii) If the bonus earnings can be traced to individual batches then the group bonus should be regarded as a direct cost. The group bonus has been charged to production overhead account since it is assumed that the bonus cannot be traced to individual batches.

(iii) The overtime premium has been charged to production overhead, with the exception of 20%, which was incurred specifically at the request of a customer. For an explanation of the treatment see 'Accounting Treatment of Various Labour Cost Items' in Chapter 3.

Answer to problem 5.10

(a)   *Contract Accounts (for the previous year)*

	MNO £000's	PQR £000's	STU £000's		MNO £000's	PQR £000's	STU £000's
Cost of contract to date				Wages accrued B/Fwd		2	
B/Fwd		190	370	Plant Control A/c		8	
Materials on site B/Fwd			25	Materials on site C/Fwd	8		
Plant on site B/Fwd		35	170	Plant on site C/Fwd	70		110
Materials Control A/c	40	99	180	Prepayment C/Fwd			15
Wages Control A/c	20	47	110	Cost of work not			
Sub-contractors A/c			35	certified C/Fwd			26
Salaries	6	20	25	Cost of work certified			
Plant Control A/c	90	15		(Balance)	82	411	786
Wages accrued C/Fwd		5					
Apportionment of							
construction services							
(see note 1)	4	10	22				
	160	421	937		160	421	937
Cost of work certified				Value of work certified	90	390	950
B/Fwd	82	411	786	Loss taken*		21	
Profit taken this period*			114				
Profit taken previous							
periods*			15				
Profit not taken	8		35				
	90	411	950		90	411	950
Cost of work not				Wages accrued B/Fwd		5	
certified B/Fwd			26				
Materials on site B/Fwd	8						
Plant on site B/Fwd	70		110				
Prepayment B/Fwd			15				

*See (b)(i) for calculation

Note
(i) Costs incurred by Construction Services Department

	£000's
Plant depreciation (12−5)	7
Salaries	21
Wages paid	8
	36

Wages incurred by each department are:

	£000's	
MNO	20	
PQR	50	(47+5−2)
STU	110	
	180	

The costs apportioned to each contract are:

	£000's	
MNO	4	$(\frac{20}{180} \times £36)$
PQR	10	$(\frac{50}{180} \times £36)$
STU	22	$(\frac{110}{180} \times £36)$
	36	

(b)(i)

Contract MNO

Nil

Contract PQR	£
Cost of contract to date (see part (A))	411,000
Value of work certified	390,000
Recommended loss to be written off	21,000

Contract STU	£
Cost of work certified	786,000
Cost of work not yet certified	26,000
Estimated costs to complete	138,000
Estimated cost of contract	950,000
Contract price	1,100,000
Anticipated profit	150,000

The profit taken to date is calculated using the following formula:

$$\frac{\text{Cash received to date (£950,000)}}{\text{Contract price (£1,100,000)}} \times \text{Estimated profit from the contract (£150,000)}$$

$$= £129,545 \text{ (say £129,000)}$$

The profit taken for the current period is £114,000 consisting of the profit to date of £129,000 less the profit previously transferred to the profit and loss account of £15,000.

(b)(ii)

Contract MNO: This contract is at a very early stage and it is unlikely that the outcome can be reasonably foreseen. It is therefore prudent not to anticipate any profit at this stage.

Contract PQR: This contract has incurred a loss and applying the prudence concept this loss should be written off as soon as it is incurred.

Contract STU: Applying the prudence concept a proportion of the profit $\dfrac{\text{Cash received to date}}{\text{Contract price}}$ is recognised in this period. The proportion of profit that is recognised is arbitrary and very much a matter of opinion. Alternative apportionments applying the concept of prudence could have been applied.

SOLUTIONS TO CHAPTER 6 PROBLEMS

Process costing

Details of the questions are as follows:

6.1 and 6.2 Preparation of process accounts when there is no opening or closing WIP. Consequently the problem of equivalent production does not arise. Both questions require the preparation of abnormal loss and gain accounts.

6.3 to 6.8 Calculation of the average cost per *equivalent unit* using the *average cost* basis. 6.3 does not include any losses in process. 6.4 and 6.5 assume that losses in process are *not* allocated to the closing WIP whereas the loss is allocated to closing WIP with 6.6 and 6.7; 6.8 assumes that losses occur part way through the process.

6.9 to 6.12 Calculation of the cost per equivalent unit using the FIFO basis. With the exception of 6.10 these questions include losses in process. 6.12 is the most difficult question in the chapter.

6.13 Cost control question requiring the preparation of a performance report using equivalent production calculations.

For more difficult questions on process costing see 7.9 and 7.11 in Chapter 7.

Answer to problem 6.1

(a) For an explanation of normal and abnormal losses and the accounting treatment see 'Normal and Abnormal Losses' in Chapter 6.

(b)
Process 1

	Kilos	£ per kilo	£		Kilos	£ per kilo	£
Materials	5,000	0.5	2,500	Process 2	3,800	1.15	4,370
Labour			800	Normal Loss	1,000	0.30	300
Production overhead			1,600	Abnormal Loss	200	1.15	230
	5,000		4,900		5,000		4,900

$$\text{Cost per unit} = \frac{\text{Cost of Production less scrap value of normal loss}}{\text{Expected Output}}$$

$$= \frac{£4,900 - £300}{4,000 \text{ kilos}} = £1.15 \text{ per kilo}$$

36

Process 2

	Kilos	£ per kilo	£		Kilos	£ per kilo	£
Transferred from Process 1	3,800	1.15	4,370	Finished goods			
Materials	4,000	0.80	3,200	Stock	7,270	1.50	10,905
Labour			1,753	Normal Loss	780	0.70	546
Production Overhead			1,753				
			11,076				
Abnormal Gain	250	1.50	375				
	8,050		11,451		8,050		11,451

$$\text{Cost per unit} = \frac{£11{,}076 - £546}{7{,}800 - 780} = £1.50$$

Finished Goods Stock Account

	£	
Process 2	10,905	

Abnormal Loss Account

	£		£
Process 1	230	Normal Loss A/c (200 × £0.30)	60
		P. & L. A/c	170
	230		230

Abnormal Gain Account

	£		£
Normal Loss A/c (250 × £0.70)	175	Process 2 A/c	375
P. & L. A/c	200		
	375		375

Normal Loss Account (Income Due)

	£		£
Process 1 (Normal Loss)	300	Abnormal Gain	175
Process 2 (Normal Loss)	546	Balance or cash	
Abnormal Loss	60	received	731
	906		906

Answer to problem 6.4

(a) *Statement of Input and Output (Units)*

Input
Opening WIP   3,200 units
Current period input   24,800 units
                            _____
                            28,000

Output
Completed Units   25,000 units
Closing WIP   2,500 units
Normal Loss   500 units
                            _____
                            28,000

Statement of Cost per Unit

Element of Cost	Opening WIP £	Current Cost £	Total Cost £	Completed Units	Normal Loss	WIP Equiv. Units	Total Equiv. Units	(a) Cost per Unit £
Direct Materials	14,000	96,000	110,000	25,000	500	2,500	28,000	3.9286
Conversion Cost	19,500	177,375	196,875	25,000	500	1,250	26,750	7.3598
			306,875					11.2884

		£	£
Value of Work in Progress:			
Direct Materials 2,500 units × £3.9286		9,822	
Conversion Cost 1,250 units × £7.3598		9,200	19,022 (C)
Completed Units: 25,000 units at £11.2884		282,210	
Add Normal Loss (500 × £11.2884)		5,643	287,853
			306,875

(b) Total cost of production transferred to finished stock = £287,853.

Note
The question does not indicate at what stage in the process the normal loss occurs. It has been assumed that losses are detected at the completion stage. Consequently the cost of the normal loss is charged to completed production only.

Answer to problem 6.6

(a)
Calculation of Input for Process 1

	Litres	£
Opening Stock	4,000	10,800
Receipts	20,000	61,000
Less Closing Stock	(8,000)	(24,200)
Process Input	16,000	47,600

Output	*Litres*
Completed units	8,000
Closing WIP	5,600
Normal Loss (15% of input)	2,400
	16,000

Because input is equal to output there are no abnormal gains or losses.

Calaculation of Cost per Unit (Process 1)

It is assumed that the loss occurs at the point of inspection. Because WIP has passed the inspection point the normal loss should be allocated to both completed units and WIP.

(1)	(2)	(3)	(4)	(5)	(6) Total Equiv. Units	(7) Cost per Unit	(8) WIP (5 × 8)
Element of Cost	*£*	*Completed Units*	*Normal Loss*	*Closing WIP*			
Materials	47,600	8,000	2,400	5,600	16,000	£2.975	£16,660
Conversion Cost (1)	21,350	8,000	1,800	4,200	14,000	£1.525	£6,405
	68,950					£4.50	£23,065

(1) Conversion Cost = Direct Labour (£4,880) + Direct Expenses (£4,270) + Overhead (250% × £4,880)

Cost of Normal Loss:	£
Materials 2,400 × £2.975 =	7,140
Conversion Cost 1,800 × £1.525 =	2,745
	9,885

The apportionment of Normal Loss to completed units and WIP is as follows:

	Completed Units	*WIP*
Materials	8,000/13,600 × £7,140 = £4,200	5,600/13,600 × £7,140 = £2,940
Conversion Cost	8,000/12,200 × £2,745 = £1,800	4,200/12,200 × £2,745 = £ 945
	£6,000	£3,885

The cost of completed units and WIP is as follows:

		£	£
Completed Units:	8,000 units × £4.50 = 36,000		
	Share of Normal Loss	6,000	42,000
WIP:	Original Allocation	23,065	
	Share of Normal Loss	3,885	26,950
			£68,950

For an explanation of the above procedure see Appendix to Chapter 6. *Where the normal loss is apportioned to WIP and completed units a simpler approach is not to include the normal loss in the unit cost statement.* The calculation is as follows:

Element of Cost	£	Completed Units	Closing WIP	Total Equiv. Units	Cost per Unit	WIP
Materials	47,600	8,000	5,600	13,600	£3.50	£19,600
Conversion Cost	21,350	8,000	4,200	12,200	£1.75	£ 7,350
					£5.25	£26,950

Completed Units 8,000 × £5.25 = £42,000

Process 1 Account—May 1979

	Litres	£		Litres	£
Materials	16,000	47,600	Transfers to Process 2	8,000	42,000
Labour		4,880	Normal Loss	2,400	—
Direct Expenses		4,270	Closing Stock C/f	5,600	26,950
Overheads Absorbed		12,200			
	16,000	68,950		16,000	68,950

With process 2 there is no closing WIP. Therefore it is unnecessary to express output in equivalent units. The cost per unit is calculated as follows:

$$\frac{\text{Cost of production less scrap value of normal loss}}{\text{Expected output}} = \frac{£54,000 \ (1)}{(90\% \times 8,000)} = £7.50$$

(1) Cost of production = Transferred in cost from process 1 (£42,000) + Labour (£6,000) + Overhead (£6,000).

Process 2 Account—May 1979

	Litres	£		Litres	£
Transferred from Process 1	8,000	42,000	Finished Goods Store		
Labour		6,000	(Note 2)	7,500	56,250
Overheads Absorbed		6,000	Normal Loss	800	
Abnormal Gain (Note 1)	300	2,250	Closing Stock	—	—
	8,300	56,250		8,300	56,250

Finished Goods Account

	Litres	£			
Ex Process 2	7,500	56,250			

Abnormal Gain Account

	£		Litres	£
Profit & Loss A/c	2,250	Process 2 A/c	300	2,250
	2,250			2,250

Notes

(1) Input = 8,000 litres Normal Output = 90% × 8,000 litres = 7,200 litres
   Actual Output = 7,500 litres ∴ Abnormal Gain = 300 litres × £7.50 per litre = £2,250

(2) 7,500 litres at £7.50 per litre

(b) If the material can be replaced then the loss to the company will consist of the replacement cost of the materials. If the materials cannot be replaced then the loss will consist of the lost sales revenue less the costs not incurred as a result of not processing and selling the 100 litres.

Answer to problem 6.8

The physical input and output to the process is as follows:

		Units
Input:	Opening WIP	3,000
	Introduced during period	20,000
		23,000
Output:	Completed Production	15,000
	Closing WIP	4,000
	Abnormal Loss	
	(Opening WIP)	3,000 22,000
	Difference = Normal Loss	1,000
		23,000

The cost per unit (CPU) is calculated as follows:

Cost element	OP WIP £	Current cost £	Total cost £	Comp. units	CL. WIP	Norm. loss (1)	Abn. loss (2)	Total Equiv.	CPU £	WIP £
A	12,600	84,000	96,600	15,000	4,000	1,000	3,000	23,000	4.20	16,800
B	2,400	16,000	18,400	15,000	4,000	1,000	3,000	23,000	0.80	3,200
C	—	19,200	19,200	15,000	—	1,000	—	16,000	1.20	—
Conversion cost	2,880	88,800	91,680	15,000	2,000	900	1,200	19,100	4.80	9,600
	17,880	208,000	225,880						11.00	29,600

Notes

(1) All of the material will have been added at the 90% stage. Therefore materials are 100% complete as regards normal loss.

(2) The opening WIP which is spoilt is 40% complete. Material C is not added until the 60% stage but materials A and B will already have been added.

		£
Closing WIP		29,600

Comp. Prodn. 15,000 × 11.00 =		165,000	
Normal loss 1,000 × 4.20 = 4,200			
1,000 × 0.80 = 800			
1,000 × 1.20 = 1,200			
900 × 4.80 = 4,320	10,520	175,520	

Abnormal loss 3,000 × 4.20 = 12,600		
3,000 × 0.80 = 2,400		
1,200 × 4.80 = 5,760	20,760	
	£225,880	

Process Account

Opening WIP	17,880	Completed production	175,520
A	84,000	Abnormal loss	20,760
B	16,000	Closing WIP	29,600
C	19,200		
Conversion cost	88,800		
	£225,880		£225,880

Answer to problem 6.9

(a)	*Production Statement*	
Input		*Blocks*
Opening WIP		400
Transfer from previous		
process		4,500
		4,900

Output		
Closing stock		500
Loss		300
Completed units (Balance)		4,100
		4,900

Statement of equivalent production and calculation of cost and completed production

	Current costs £	Completed units less opening WIP equiv. units	Abnormal loss	Closing WIP equiv. units	Current total equiv. units	Cost per unit £
Previous process costs	9,000	3,700 (4,100 − 400)	300	500	4,500	2.0
Materials	4,360	3,780 (4,100 − 320)	180 (60%)	400 (80%)	4,360	1.0
Labour and overhead	2,125	3,860 (4,100 − 240)	90 (30%)	300 (60%)	4,250	0.50
	15,485					3.50

Cost of completed production: £ £
   Opening WIP (Given)   1,000
   Previous process cost (3,700 × £2)   7,400
   Materials (3,780 × £1)   3,780
   Labour and overhead (3,860 × £0.50)   1,930   14,110

Cost of closing WIP:
   Previous process cost (500 × £2)   1,000
   Materials (400 × £1)   400
   Labour and overhead (300 × £0.50)   150   1,550

Cost of abnormal loss:
   Previous process cost (300 × £2)   600
   Materials (180 × £1)   180
   Labour and overhead (90 × £0.50)   45   825

Process 3 account

	Blocks	£		Blocks	£
Opening WIP	400	1,000	Abnormal loss	300	825
Transfer from process 2	4,500	9,000	Completed production transferred to		
Current cost:			finished stock	4,100	14,110
Materials		4,360	Closing WIP	500	1,550
Labour and overhead		2,125			
		16,485			16,485

Abnormal Loss Account

	£		£
Process 3 A/c	825	Cash/Bank	300
		Profit and loss A/c	525
	£825		£825

(b) Closing stocks are valued in order that costs can be matched with revenue for profit measurement purposes. The costs attached to the closing WIP represent the unexpired costs of the process for the period.

Answer to problem 6.13

(a)

Cost Element	Opening WIP Value £	Current Cost £	Total Cost £	Completed units	WIP equiv. units	Total equiv. units	Cost per unit £	WIP value £
Direct								
Materials	17,400	162,600	180,000	8,200	800	9,000	20	16,000
Conversion								
Cost	10,000	173,920	183,920	8,200	160	8,360	22	3,520
			363,920				42	19,520

Completed units 8200 × £42 =   344,400

Total cost   363,920

Process Account

	Units	£		Units	£
Opening WIP	1,000	27,400	Process B	8,200	344,400
Materials	8,000	162,600	Closing WIP c/d	800	19,520
Conversion cost		173,920			
		363,920			363,920

(b)   *Calculation of equivalent production produced during current period*

	Total equivalent units	Opening WIP equivalent units	Equivalent units produced during period
Materials	9,000	1,000	8,000
Conversion cost	8,360	400	7,960

Performance report

	Standard cost £	Actual cost £	Difference £
Materials	160,000 (8,000 × £20)	162,600	2,600 A
Conversion cost	183,080 (7,960 × £23)	173,920	9,160 F
			6,560 F

SOLUTIONS TO CHAPTER 7 PROBLEMS

Joint product and by-product costing

Questions 7.1 to 7.8 are suitable for a first year course whereas 7.9 to 7.11 are appropriate for a second year course. Details are as follows:

7.1 to 7.2   Preparation of a process account and the apportionment of joint costs to products. 7.2 is also concerned with the accounting treatment of by-products.

7.3 to 7.7   Apportionment of joint costs and decisions on whether or not joint products should be further processed. Question 7.7 is the most difficult question.

7.8   Calculation of missing items from incomplete information.

7.9 to 7.11   Questions set at advanced level requiring the apportionment of joint costs and the presentation of cost information for decision-making. 7.11 is the most difficult question in the chapter requiring approximately two hours preparation.

Answer to problem 7.1

(a)   *Process 1 Account*

	Units	Unit Cost	£		Units	Unit Cost	£
Direct materials	25,000	4.0	100,000	Normal loss	2,500		5,000
Direct labour			62,500	Transferred to			
Overheads			45,000	process 2	23,000	9.0	207,000
Abnormal gain	500	9.0	4,500				
			212,000				212,000

The calculation of the cost per unit is as follows:

$$\frac{\text{Cost of production less scrap value of normal loss}}{\text{Expected output}} = \frac{£207,500 - £5,000}{22,500} = £9$$

Normal Loss Account

	£		£
Process 1 A/c	5,000	Cash/Bank A/c ($2000 \times £2$)	4,000
		Abnormal Gain A/c	1,000
	5,000		5,000

Abnormal Gain Account

	£		£
Normal Loss A/c	1,000	Process 1 A/c	4,500
Costing Profit & Loss A/c	3,500		
	4,500		4,500

(b)

Cost of process 2:	£
Transferred from process 1	207,000
Direct labour	69,000
Overheads	69,000
	345,000

(i)   *Apportionment according to weight of output*

	Product A	Product B	Product C
	£	£	£
Sales	216,000 (9,000 × £24)	144,000 (8,000 × £18)	72,000 (6,000 × £12)
Joint costs (1)	135,000	120,000	90,000
Profit/(Loss)	81,000	24,000	(18,000)

Note

(1) The joint product costs are apportioned as follows:

Product A $\dfrac{9,000}{23,000} \times £345,000 = £135,000$

Product B $\dfrac{8,000}{23,000} \times £345,000 = £120,000$

Product C $\dfrac{6,000}{23,000} \times £345,000 = £90,000$

(ii)   *Apportionment according to sales value*

	Product A	Product B	Product C	Total
	£	£	£	£
Sales	216,000	144,000	72,000	432,000
Joint costs (1)	172,500	115,000	57,500	
Profit/(Loss)	43,500	29,000	14,500	

Note

(1) The joint product costs are apportioned as follows:

Product A $\dfrac{£216,000}{£432,000} \times £345,000 = £172,500$

Product B $\dfrac{£144,000}{£432,000} \times £345,000 = £115,000$

Product C $\dfrac{£72,000}{432,000} \times £345,000 = £57,500$

(c) Apportionment of joint costs is necessary for stock valuation purposes although it is impossible to accurately apportion joint costs to products. For decision-making purposes joint cost apportionments are inappropriate. For example, product C makes a loss when joint costs are apportioned by weight whilst a profit is made when costs are apportioned on the basis of sales value. For a discussion of the limitation of joint cost allocation for decision-making purposes see Chapter 7.

Answer to problem 7.3

(a)   *Operating Statement for October, 1979*

	£	£
Sales: Product A (80,000 × £5)=400,000		
Product B (65,000 × £4)=260,000		
Product C (75,000 × £9)=675,000	1,335,000	
Operating costs	1,300,000	
Less closing stock (1)	200,000	
	1,100,000	
Profit	235,000	

Note
(1) Production for the period in kilos:

	A	B	C	Total
Sales requirements	80,000	65,000	75,000	
Closing stock	20,000	15,000	5,000	
Production	100,000	80,000	80,000	260,000

$$\text{Cost per kilo} = \frac{£1,300,000}{260,000 \text{ kilos}} = £5 \text{ per kilo}$$

∴ Closing stock = 40,000 kilos at £5 per kilo

(b)   *Evaluation of Refining Proposal*

	A	B	C	Total £
Incremental revenue per kilo (£) (see note 1)	12	10	11.50	
Variable cost per kilo (£)	4	6	12.00	
Contribution per kilo (£)	8	4	(0.50)	
Monthly production (kilos)	100,000	80,000	80,000	
Monthly contribution (£)	800,000	320,000	(40,000)	1,080,000
Monthly fixed overheads (specific to B)		360,000		360,000
Contribution to refining general fixed costs (£)	800,000	(40,000)	(40,000)	720,000
Refining general fixed overheads				700,000
Monthly profit				20,000

Comments

(1) It is more profitable to sell C in it's unrefined state and product B is only profitable in it's refined state if monthly sales are in excess of 90,000 kilos (£360,000 fixed costs ÷£4 contribution per unit).

(2) If both products B and C are sold in their unrefined state then the refining process will yield a profit of £100,000 per month (£800,000 product A contribution less £700,000 fixed costs).

(3) The break-even point for the refining process if only product A was produced is 87,500 kilos (£700,000 fixed costs ÷£8 contribution per unit). Consequently if sales of A decline by $12\frac{1}{2}\%$ the refining process will yield a loss.

Answer to problem 7.6

(a) See Chapter 7 for the answer to this question.

(b)(i) It is rational to undertake a common process if the total revenue from the sale of the products from the joint process exceed the joint costs plus further processing costs of those products which are further processed. Consider the following example:

A joint process costs £600 and joint products A, B and C emerge. The further processing costs and sales revenue from the finished products are as follows:

Products	Additional finishing costs	Sales revenue from finished product
	£	£
A	300	600
B	400	800
C	500	1,000
	1,200	2,400

In the above example total revenue (£2,400) is greater than joint costs (£600) plus the additional costs of further processing (£1,200). Therefore it is rational to undertake the joint process.

(ii) It is rational to 'finish off' each of the products from the joint process if the additional revenues from further processing exceed the additional costs of further processing. For an illustration of this statement see Example 7.1 in Chapter 7.

Answer to problem 7.7

(i) Reference to the diagram indicates that the relative sales value of each product is as follows:

	Boddie (£000's)	Soull (£000's)	Total (£000's)
Total sales	8,400	36,000	44,400
Plus NRV of three keys		2,170(1)	2,170
	8,400	38,170	46,570

(1) (280,000 litres × £8)−£70,000 delivery costs.

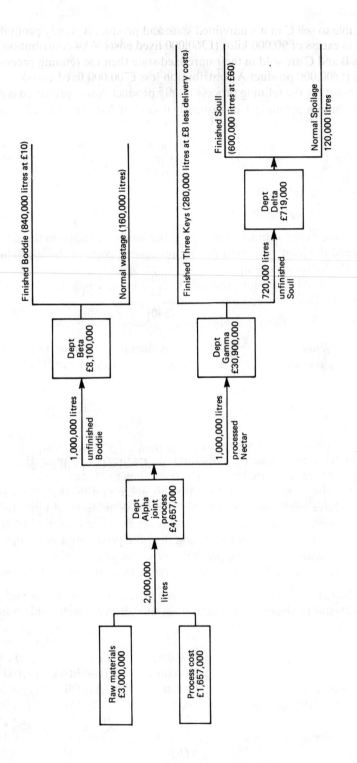

Allocation of joint costs:

$$\text{Boddie} = £840,000 \left(\frac{8,400}{46,570} \times £4,657,000 \right)$$

$$\text{Soull} = \frac{£3,817,000}{4,657,000} \left(\frac{38,170}{46,570} \times £4,657,000 \right)$$

(ii)   *Profit and loss statement*

	Boddie (£000's)	*Soull* (£000's)	*Three keys* (£000's)	*Total* (£000's)
Sales	8,400	36,000	2,240	46,640
Less specifically attributable costs:				
Dept beta	8,100			
Dept gamma		30,900		
Dept delta		719		
Delivery costs			70	
Contribution to joint costs	300	4,381	2,170	6,851
Less apportioned joint costs	840	3,817		4,657
Profit/(Loss)	(540)	564	2,170	2,194

(iii) The incremental revenues are in excess of the incremental costs for all three products. In other words each product provides a contribution towards the joint costs. Consequently all three products should be produced.

Answer to problem 7.9

(a) The profits shown in the process accounts do not indicate the relative profitability of the three products. This is because the profits are calculated after the apportionment of the joint costs which are common and unavoidable to all the joint products. Therefore the loss arising on product Y may be due to the way in which the joint costs have been apportioned. An alternative method of apportionment may result in product Y showing a profit. Because the incremental revenues of process Y (30,000 units at £0.40) are in excess of the incremental costs of further processing then the production of product Y will increase total company profits. To compare the relative profitability of the joint products it is necessary to compare the incremental profits (incremental revenues less incremental costs) for each product.

(b) To determine whether or not a product should be further processed it is necessary to compare the incremental costs with the incremental revenues from further processing. This information is presented in the following schedule:

	Process 2	*Process 3*	*Process 4*
Output	50,000 litres	30,000 litres	20,000 litres
Sales value at split-off point	£40,000	£9,000	£26,000
Sales value after further processing	60,000	21,000	35,000
Incremental revenue	£20,000	£12,000	£9,000
Incremental expense (processing expense)	13,333	9,000	14,000
Incremental profit or (loss)	£6,667	£3,000	(£5,000) loss

The above schedule suggests that process 4 should be closed down and the output from the joint process (product Z) sold at the split-off point. This analysis assumes that all of the processing expenses represent incremental costs. If the processing expenses include more than £5,000 unavoidable costs such as apportionment of administration expenses then the process should not be closed down. This is because incremental revenues will be in excess of incremental costs. *Note that opening and closing stocks are identical. Therefore they will not affect the analysis.*

(c) The sales values at split-off point are:

Process 2	Process 3	Process 4	Total
£40,000 (50,000 × 80p)	£9,000 (30,000 × 30p)	£26,000 (20,000 × £1.30)	£75,000

Joint costs of £50,000 are apportioned to the processes. The apportionments are:

Process 3   £6,000 (£9,000/£75,000 × £50,000)
Process 4   £17,333 (£26,000/£75,000 × £50,000)

Because the opening and closing stocks are identical it is unnecessary to restate them for the purpose of calculating profits. The monetary value of the stock movements will be zero. Therefore the revised profit calculations will be as follows:

	Process 3 £	Process 4 £
Sales	21,000	35,000
Input from process 1	(6,000)	(17,333)
Process expense	(9,000)	(14,000)
Profit	6,000	3,667

(d)

Process 1

	Litres	£		Litres	£
Opening work in progress	4,000	1,200	Production transferred		
Direct material	99,000	9,900	X to process 2	50,000	40,000
Processing expense		39,500	Y to process 3	30,000	9,000
Profit to profit and loss			Z to process 4	20,000	26,000
account		25,000	Closing work in progress	3,000	600
	103,000	£75,600		103,000	£75,600

Process 4

	Litres	£		Litres	£
Opening work in			Sales revenue	20,000	35,000
progress (1)	2,000	3,300	Loss to profit and		
Input from process 1	20,000	26,000	loss account		5,000
Processing expense		14,000	Closing work in		
			progress (1)	2,000	3,300
	22,000	£43,300		22,000	£43,300

Notes

(1) The additional input costs to process 4 are £16,000 (£26,000 − £10,000) or £0.80 per unit. Therefore the 2,000 units in stock will be increased by £1,600 resulting in a revised stock valuation of £3,300 (£1,700 + £1,600).

(e) Joint cost allocation procedures are of little use for decision-making purposes. The main use is for stock valuation and profit measurement purposes. In this respect the relative sales value method of apportionment is preferable. For an explanation of this see section on 'Methods of Apportioning Joint Costs to Joint Products' in Chapter 7. Neither of the cost-allocation methods discloses that process 4 is unprofitable. One solution is to use market values at split-off point as a transfer price and to regard process 1 as a profit centre (see Chapter 23 for a discussion of profit centres). This approach does indicate that process 4 makes a loss but because market prices are used it may not be acceptable for financial accounting purposes. This is because the stocks will be valued at market values rather than cost. The market value method is preferable for decision-making purposes.

Absorption costing and variable costing

Questions 8.1 to 8.8 require absorption and variable costing profit calculations and stock valuations. These questions are appropriate for a first year course. Questions 8.9 to 8.11 test similar principles but at a more advanced level.

Answer to problem 8.1

See Chapter 8 for the answer to this question.

Answer to problem 8.2

(a)(i) With an absorption costing system all production costs are charged to products whereas only variable production costs are charged to products with a marginal (variable) costing system. Fixed production overhead is charged as a period cost with a marginal costing system.
(ii) Each unit in stock is valued at total manufacturing cost per unit with an absorption costing system. With a marginal costing system stocks are valued at variable production cost per unit.

(b) Fixed overhead absorption rate $= \dfrac{\text{£200,000 fixed overheads}}{\text{400,000 units normal activity}}$

$= \text{£0.50 per unit}$

(i) Overhead absorbed by B in first quarter $= 110,000 \times \text{£0.50} = \text{£55,000}$
$\therefore$ Answer $=$ Item 4

(ii) Overhead absorbed $\qquad = \text{£55,000}$
Overhead incurred per quarter $= \text{£50,000}$ (£200,000 $\div$ 4)
Over-absorption $\qquad \underline{\text{£5,000}}$

Answer $=$ Item 2

Absorption costing and marginal costing profit calculations

	Absorption costing		Marginal costing	
	£	£		£
Sales (80,000 units × £5)		400,000		400,000
Production costs				
Variable (110,000 × £2)	220,000		220,000	
Fixed (110,000 × £0.50)	55,000		—	
	275,000			
Less closing stock (30,000 × 2.50)	75,000	200,000	60,000 (30,000 × 2)	160,000
		200,000		240,000
Over-absorption of fixed overhead	(5,000)			
Variable selling overheads				
(80,000 × £1)	80,000		80,000	
Fixed selling overheads				
(300,000 ÷ 4)	75,000	150,000	75,000	
Fixed production overheads		—	50,000	205,000
Profit		50,000		35,000

(iii) Answer = Item 2
(iv) Answer = Item 1

Answer to problem 8.3

Variable costing profit statements

	Q1	Q2	Q3	Q4
	£	£	£	£
Opening stock	—	—	180,000	60,000
Production at £6 per unit	900,000	1,020,000	840,000	900,000
Less closing stock (1)	—	180,000	60,000	—
Cost of sales	900,000	840,000	960,000	960,000
Sales at £10 per unit	1,500,000	1,400,000	1,600,000	1,600,000
Gross profit	600,000	560,000	640,000	640,000
Fixed factory overheads	150,000	150,000	150,000	150,000
Fixed selling and administration overheads	100,000	100,000	100,000	100,000
Net profit	350,000	310,000	390,000	390,000

Total profits = £1,440,000

Absorption costing profit statements

	Q1	Q2	Q3	Q4
	£	£	£	£
Opening stock	—	—	210,000	70,000
Production at £7 per unit	1,050,000	1,190,000	980,000	1,050,000
	1,050,000	1,190,000	1,190,000	1,120,000
Under/(over) recovery (2)	—	(20,000)	10,000	—
	1,050,000	1,170,000	1,200,000	1,120,000

	Q1 £	Q2 £	Q3 £	Q4 £
Less closing stock (3)	—	210,000	70,000	—
Cost of sales	1,050,000	960,000	1,130,000	1,120,000
Sales	1,500,000	1,400,000	1,600,000	1,600,000
Gross profit	450,000	440,000	470,000	480,000
Selling and administration overheads	100,000	100,000	100,000	100,000
Net profit	350,000	340,000	370,000	380,000

Total profits = £1,440,000

Notes
(1) Quarter 2 = 30,000 units at £6 and Quarter 3 = 10,000 units at £6.
(2) 20,000 units in excess of normal activity were produced in Quarter 2 resulting in an over recovery of £20,000. In Quarter 3 output was 10,000 units less than normal activity resulting in an under recovery of £10,000.
(3) Quarter 2 = 30,000 units at £7 and Quarter 3 = 10,000 units at £7.

(b) Comments are as follows:
   (i) Both systems yield the same profits (Quarter 1) when production = sales.
   (ii) When production volume is in excess of sales volume (Quarter 2) absorption costing yields the higher profits.
   (iii) When sales volume is in excess of production volume (Quarters 3 and 4) variable costing yields the higher profits.
   (iv) Sales volume remains unchanged in Quarters 3 and 4 but with the absorption costing system changes in profit occur. Profit does not change with the variable costing system.
   (v) Both systems yield identical profits over the four quarters.

Answer to problems 8.5

Preliminary workings
Normal level of activity = 10,000 units (£1,000,000 sales ÷ £100 selling price)
Year ending 1981: Sales = 8,000 units (80% of normal level of activity)
           Production = 10,000 units (100% of normal level of activity)
         Closing stock = 2,000 units
Year ending 1982: Opening stock = 2,000 units
                Sales = 10,000 units (100% of normal level of activity)
            Production = 8,000 units (80% of normal level of activity)

Costs per unit

Direct materials	30 (£300,000 ÷ 10,000)
Direct wages	20 (£200,000 ÷ 10,000)
Variable production overhead	5 (£50,000 ÷ 10,000)
Variable production cost	55
Fixed production overhead	20 (£200,000 ÷ 10,000)
Total production cost	75

(a)(i) *Budgeted profit and loss statement (absorption costing)*

	1981			1982		
	Units	*Per unit*		*Units*	*Per unit*	
		£	*£000*		*£*	*£000*
Sales	8,000	100	800	10,000	100	1,000
Production cost of sales						
Opening stock	—		—	2,000	75	150
Production costs absorbed	10,000	75	750	8,000	75	600
Closing stock	(2,000)	75	(150)	—		—
	8,000		600	10,000		750
Under-absorbed overhead (see note 1)			—	2,000	20	40
			600			790
Administration overhead			100			100
Selling overhead			50			50
Total cost			750			940
Net profit			£50			£60

(a)(ii) *Budgeted profit and loss statement (marginal costing)*

	1981			1982		
	Units	*Per unit*		*Units*	*Per unit*	
		£	*£000*		*£*	*£000*
Sales	8,000	100	800	10,000	100	1,000
Opening stock	—		—	2,000	55	110
Variable production cost	10,000	55	550	8,000	55	440
Closing stock	(2,000)	55	(110)	—		—
Variable cost of sales	8,000		440	10,000		550
Contribution			360			450
Fixed costs (see note 2)			350			350
Net profit			10			100

Notes

(1) Production for 1982 is 8,000 units resulting in fixed overheads of £160,000 (8,000 units at £20)being charged to production. Therefore there is an under-absorption of fixed overheads of £40,000 (2,000 units at £20).

(2) Fixed overhead = Production overhead (200,000) + Administration overhead (100,000) + Selling overhead (50,000).

(b) The differences in profits and stock movements are as follows:

	1981		1982	
	Increase/(Decrease)		*Increase/(Decrease)*	
	in Stocks	*Profits*	*in Stocks*	*Profits*
	£	*£*	*£*	*£*
Absorption costing	150,000	50,000	(150,000)	60,000
Marginal costing	110,000	10,000	(110,000)	100,000
Difference	40,000	40,000	(£40,000)	(£40,000)

In 1981 £40,000 of the fixed overheads are included in the stock valuation with the absorption costing system. This reduces 1981 cost of sales and makes absorption costing profit £40,000 more than marginal costing profit. Note that production exceeds sales in 1981. In 1982 where sales exceed production (i.e. stocks are declining) the marginal costing system shows the higher profit. This is because the absorption costing opening stock includes the £40,000 fixed overheads. Also £200,000 fixed overheads is charged as an expense in 1982 with the absorption costing system resulting in £240,000 fixed overhead being expensed. With a marginal costing system fixed overheads of £200,000 are charged in 1982.

Answer to problem 8.9

(a) It is assumed that opening stock valuation in 1982 was determined on the basis of the old overhead rate of £2.10 per hour. The closing stock valuation for 1982 and the opening and closing valuations for 1983 are calculated on the basis of the new overhead rate of £3.60 per hour. In order to compare the 1982 and 1983 profits it is necessary to restate the 1982 opening stock on the same basis as that which was used for 1983 stock valuations.

We are informed that the 1983 closing stock will be at the same physical level as the 1981 opening stock valuation. It should also be noted that the 1982 opening stock was twice as much as the 1981 equivalent. The 1981 valuation on the revised basis would have been £130,000 resulting in a 1982 revised valuation of £260,000. Consequently the 1982 profits will be £60,000 (£260,000 – £200,000) lower when calculated on the revised basis.

From the 1982 estimate you can see that stocks increase and then decline in 1983. It appears that the company has over-produced in 1982 thus resulting in large opening stocks at the start of 1983. The effect of this is that more of the sales demand is met from opening stocks in 1983. Therefore production declines in 1983 thus resulting in an under-recovery of £300,000 fixed overheads which is charged as a period cost. On the other hand the under-recovery for 1982 is expected to be £150,000.

The reconciliation of 1982 and 1983 profits is as follows:

	£
1982 profits	128,750
Difference in opening stock valuation for 1982	(60,000)
Additional under-recovery in 1983	(150,000)
Budgeted loss for 1983	(81,250)

(b) To prepare the profit and loss accounts on a marginal cost basis it is necessary to analyse the production costs into the fixed and variable elements. The calculations are:

	1981	1982	1983
	£	£	£
Total fixed overheads incurred	600,000	600,000	600,000
Less under-recovery	300,000	150,000	300,000
Fixed overheads charged to production	300,000	450,000	300,000
Total production cost	1,000,000	975,000	650,000
Proportion fixed	3/10	6/13 (450/975)	6/13
Proportion variable (balance)	7/10	7/13	7/13

Profit and loss accounts (marginal cost basis)

	Actual 1981		Estimated 1982		Budget 1983	
	£	£	£	£	£	£
Sales		1,350,000		1,316,250		1,316,250
Opening finished goods stock at marginal cost	70,000 (1)		140,000 (1)		192,500 (2)	
Variable factory cost	700,000 (1)		525,000 (2)		350,000 (2)	
	770,000		665,000		542,500	
Closing finished goods stock at marginal cost	140,000 (1)	630,000	192,500 (2)	472,500	70,000 (2)	472,500
		720,000		843,750		843,750
Fixed factory cost	600,000		600,000		600,000	
Administrative and financial costs	220,000		220,000		220,000	
		820,000		820,000		820,000
Profit/ (Loss)		(£100,000)		£23,750		23,750

Notes

(1) 7/10 × absorption cost figures given in the question.
(2) 7/13 × absorption cost figures given in the question.

(c) The underabsorption of overhead may be due to the fact that the firm is operating at a low level of activity. This may be due to a low demand for the firm's products. The increase in the overhead rate will cause the product costs to increase. When cost-plus pricing is used the selling price will also be increased. An increase in selling price may result in a further decline in demand. Cost-plus pricing ignores price/demand relationships. For a more detailed discussion of the answer required to this question see section on 'Limitations of Cost-Plus Pricing' in Chapter 11.

(d) For an answer to this question see section on 'Reasons for Using Cost-Based Pricing Formulas' in Chapter 11 and 'Some Arguments in Support of Absorption Costing' in Chapter 12. Note SSAP9 requires that absorption costing (full costing) is used for external reporting.

SOLUTIONS TO CHAPTER 9 PROBLEMS

Cost–volume–profit analysis

The quantitative questions in this chapter are arranged in ascending order of difficulty. Details are:

9.1 to 9.4   Construction of break-even or profit–volume graphs. These questions are not difficult.
9.5   A Simple problem which can be used to illustrate the product mix assumption in CVP analysis.
9.6 to 9.14 These questions consist of a variety of CVP problems using a non-graphical approach. 9.6 and 9.7 are the least difficult. Part (a) of 9.9 tests your ability to interpret a break-even graph. 9.10 introduces CVP analysis under conditions of uncertainty and 9.12(b) is related to CVP analysis in a nursing home. 9.13 distinguishes between profit contribution and cash contribution. 9.14 is related to various aspects of cost and management accounting including CVP analysis; a useful question for revision at this stage.
9.15 to 9.18 Discussion questions on CVP analysis.

Answer to problem 9.2

Preliminary Calculations

	Sales (Units)	Profit/(Loss)
November	30,000	£40,000
December	35,000	£60,000
Increase	5,000	£20,000

An increase in sales of 5,000 units increases contribution (profits) by £20,000. Therefore contribution is £4 per unit. Selling price is £10 per unit (given) and variable cost per unit will be £6.

$$\text{Contribution—Fixed costs} = \text{Profit}$$
$$\text{At 30,000 units sales: £120,000— ?} = £40,000$$
$$\therefore \text{Fixed Costs} = £80,000$$

The above information can now be plotted on a graph. A break-even chart or a profit–volume graph could be constructed. A profit–volume graph avoids the need to graph the fixed costs since the information can be read directly from the graph. See page 60 for a break-even chart and a profit–volume graph.

(a)(i) Fixed Costs = £80,000.
   (ii) Variable Cost per unit = £6.

   (iii) $\text{Profit–Volume Ratio} = \dfrac{\text{Contribution per unit (£4)}}{\text{Selling price per unit (£10)}} \times 100 = 40\%.$

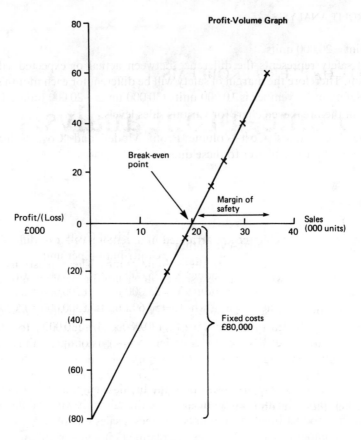

Profit-Volume Graph

Profit/(Loss) £000

Break-even point

Margin of safety

Sales (000 units)

Fixed costs £80,000

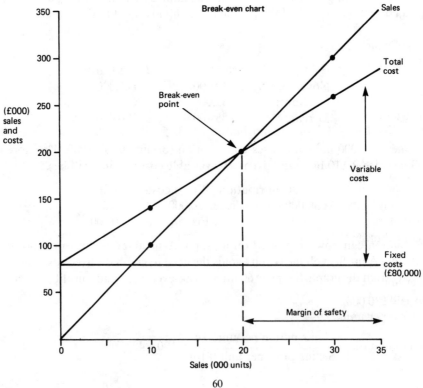

Break-even chart

(£000) sales and costs

Sales

Total cost

Break-even point

Variable costs

Fixed costs (£80,000)

Margin of safety

Sales (000 units)

(iv) Break-even point = 20,000 units.
(v) The margin of safety represents the difference between actual or expected sales volume and the break-even point. Therefore the margin of safety will be different for each month's sales. For example the margin of safety in November is 10,000 units (30,000 units – 20,000 units). The margin of safety can be read from the breakeven chart for various sales levels.

(b) and (c) See 'The Accountants' Cost–Volume–Profit Model' and 'Cost–Volume–Profit Analysis Assumptions' in Chapter 9 for the answer to these questions.

Answer to problem 9.5

$$\text{Break-even point} = \frac{\text{Fixed Costs}}{\text{Contribution per unit}}$$

Product X = 25,000 units (£100,000 ÷ £4)
Product Y = 25,000 units (£200,000 ÷ £8)
Company as a whole = 57,692 units (£300,000 ÷ £5.20*)

$$*\text{Average contribution per unit} = \frac{(70,000 \times £4) + (30,000 \times £8)}{100,000 \text{ units}}$$

$$= £5.20$$

The sum of the product break-even points is less than the break-even point for the company as a whole. It is incorrect to add the product break-even points because the sales mix will be different from the planned sales mix. The sum of the product break-even points assumes a sales mix of 50% to X and 50% to Y. The break-even point for the company as a whole assumes a planned sales mix of 70% to X and 30% to Y. CVP analysis will yield correct results only if the planned sales mix is equal to the actual sales mix.

Answer to problem 9.6

Original Budget

Contribution per unit = £31.25 (£2,500,000 ÷ 80,000 units)
Selling price per unit = £50 (£31.25 unit contribution + £18.75 unit variable cost)
Output = 80,000 units
Profit = Contribution (£2,500,000) – Fixed Costs (£2,100,000) = £400,000

Proposal 1

Contribution per unit = £26.25
Output = 100,000 units
Profit = Total contribution (£2,625,000) – Fixed Costs (£2,175,000) = £450,000

Proposal 2

Contribution per unit = £36.25
Output = 90,000 units
Profit = Total contribution (£3,262,500) – Fixed Costs (£2,545,000) = £717,500

Proposal 3

Revised Fixed Costs = £2,502,000

$$\text{Required unit contribution} = \frac{\text{Required Total Contribution } (£2,502,000 + £600,000)}{\text{Units Sold } (80,000 + 10\%)}$$

$$= £35.25$$

∴ Required selling price = £35.25 (Unit contribution) + £18.75 (unit variable cost)

$$= £54$$

Proposal 4

Revised Sales = £4,800,000 (96,000 units × £50)
Revised Profit = £720,000 (15% on sales)
Revised Fixed Costs = £2,165,000
   (without advertising increase)
Total Variable Costs = £1,800,000 (96,000 units × £18.75)
Total Contribution = £3,000,000
∴ Total Contribution − (Revised Fixed Costs + Increased Advertising) = Profit
∴ £3,000,000 − (£2,165,000 + Increased Advertising) = £720,000
∴ Additional expenditure on advertising = £115,000

Proposal 5

The contribution to yield an additional profit of £275,000 (£675,000 − £400,000) and to cover additional fixed costs of £50,000 will be £325,000. Therefore the contribution per unit sold is £16.25 (£325,000 ÷ 20,000 units). Hence the selling price is £35 (£16.25 unit contribution + £18.75 unit variable cost) and a special discount of 30% could be given.

Answer to problem 9.7

(a) *Analysis of semi-variable costs (1)*

$$\text{Method A: Variable element} = \frac{\text{Increase in Costs}}{\text{Increase in Activity}} = \frac{£10,000}{100,000 \text{ copies}} = £0.10 \text{ per copy}$$

   Fixed element = Total semi-variable cost (£55,000) − variable costs (£35,000) at an activity
      level of 350,000 copies
   ∴ Fixed element = £20,000

$$\text{Method B: Variable element} = \frac{\text{Increase in Costs}}{\text{Increase in Activity}} = \frac{£5,000}{100,000 \text{ copies}} = £0.05 \text{ per copy}$$

   Fixed element = Total semi-variable cost (£47,500) − variable costs (£17,500) at an activity
      level of 350,000 copies
   ∴ Fixed element = £30,000

Note

(1) The analysis is based on a comparison of total costs and activity levels at 350,000 and 450,000 copies
   per year.

Contribution per copy of new magazine

	Method A	Method B
	£	£
Selling price	1.00	1.00
Variable cost (given)	(0.55)	(0.50)
Variable element of semi-variable cost	(0.10)	(0.05)
Lost contribution from existing magazine	(0.05)	(0.05)
Contribution	0.30	0.40

Calculation of Net Increase in Company Profits

	Method A			Method B		
Copies sold	500,000	400,000	600,000	500,000	400,000	600,000
Contribution per copy	30p	30p	30p	40p	40p	40p
Total contribution	£150,000	£120,000	£180,000	£200,000	£160,000	£240,000
Fixed costs (1)	£100,000	£100,000	£100,000	£150,000	£150,000	£150,000
Net increase in profit	£50,000	£20,000	£80,000	£50,000	£10,000	£90,000

Note

(1) Method A = Specific fixed costs (£80,000) + Semi-Variable element (£20,000) = £100,000
   Method B = Specific fixed costs (£120,000) + Semi-Variable element (£30,000) = £150,000

(b) Break-even point = $\dfrac{\text{Fixed costs}}{\text{Contribution per unit}}$

Method A = £100,000 ÷ 0.30 = 333,333 copies
Method B = £150,000 ÷ 0.40 = 375,000 copies
The margin of safety is the difference between the anticipated sales and the break-even point sales:
Method A = 500,000 − 333,333 = 166,667 copies
Method B = 500,000 − 375,000 = 125,000 copies

(c) Method B has a higher break-even point and a higher contribution per copy sold. This implies that profits from Method B are more vulnerable to a decline in sales volume. However, higher profits are obtained with Method B when sales are high (see 600,000 copies in (a)).

The break-even point from the sale of the existing magazine is 160,000 copies (£80,000 ÷ £0.50) and the current level of monthly sales is 220,000 copies. Therefore sales can drop by 60,000 copies before break-even point is reached. For every 10 copies sold of the new publication, sales of the existing publication will be reduced by one copy. Consequently if more than 600,000 copies of the new publication are sold the existing magazine will make a loss. If sales of the new magazine are expected to consistently exceed 600,000 copies then the viability of the existing magazine must be questioned.

Answer to problem 9.10

(a)(i) The opportunity costs of producing cassettes are the salary foregone of £1,000 per month and the rental foregone of £400 per month.

 (ii) The consultant's fees and development costs represent sunk costs.

(b) The following information can be obtained from the report.

	£10 selling price 7,500–10,000 units	£9 selling price 12,000–18,000 units
Sales quantity	7,500–10,000 units	12,000–18,000 units
Fixed costs (1)	£13,525	£17,525
Profit at maximum sales (2)	£3,975	£4,975
Profit/(loss) at minimum sales (3)	(£400)	(2,525)
Break-even point (4)	7,729 units	14,020 units
Margin of safety:		
Below maximum	2,271 units	3,980 units
Above minimum	229 units	2,020 units

Notes
(1) Fixed production cost +£1,400 opportunity cost
(2) (10,000 units × £1.75 contribution)—£13,525 fixed costs = £3,975 profit
    (18,000 units × £1.25 contribution)—£17,525 fixed costs = £4,975 profit
(3) (7,500 units × £1.75 contribution)—£13,525 fixed costs = £400 loss
    (12,000 units × £1.25 contribution)—£17,525 fixed costs = £2,525 loss
(4) Fixed costs ÷ contribution per unit

Conclusions
(1) The £10 selling price is less risky than the £9 selling price. With the £10 selling price the maximum loss is lower and the break-even point is only 3% above minimum sales (compared with 17% for a £9 selling price).
(2) The £9 selling price will yield the higher profits if maximum sales quantity is achieved.
(3) In order to earn £3,975 profits at a £9 selling price we must sell 17,200 units (required contribution of 17,525 fixed costs plus £3,975 divided by a contribution per unit of £1.25).

Additional information required
(1) Details of capital employed for each selling price.
(2) Details of additional finance required to finance the working capital and the relevant interest cost so as to determine the cost of financing the working capital.
(3) Estimated probability of units sold at different selling prices.
(4) How long will the project remain viable?
(5) Details of range of possible costs. Are the cost figures given in the question certain?

Answer to problem 9.15

(a) The selling price is in excess of the variable cost per unit thus providing a contribution towards fixed costs and profit. At point (A) sales are insufficient to generate a contribution to cover the fixed costs (difference between total cost and variable cost lines in the diagram). Consequently a loss occurs. Beyond the break-even point, sales volume is sufficient to provide a contribution to cover fixed costs, and a profit is earned. At point (B) the increase in volume is sufficient to generate a contribution to cover fixed costs and provide a profit equal to the difference (represented by the dashed line) between the total revenue and cost line.

(b) See Chapter 9 for the answer to this question.

Answer to problem 9.16

The comparisons of CVP models represented in management accounting and economic theory is presented in the first half of Chapter 9. Additional points include the following:

(i) Both models are concerned with explaining the relationship between changes in costs and revenues and changes in output. Both are a simplification of cost and revenue functions because variables other than output affect costs and revenues.

(ii) The value of both models is reduced when arbitrary cost allocation methods are used to apportion joint costs to products or divisions.

(iii) The economic model indicates two break-even points whereas the management accounting model indicates one break-even point.

(iv) Both models are based on single value estimates of total costs and revenues. It is possible to incorporate uncertainty into the analysis using the methods outlined in the section 'CVP Analysis Under Conditions of Uncertainty' in Chapter 12.

(v) The model based on economic theory provides a theoretical presentation of the relationship between costs, revenues and output. The model is intended to provide an insight into complex inter-relationships. The management accounting model should be seen as a practical decision-making tool which provides a useful approximation for decision-making purposes if certain conditions apply (e.g. relevant range assumption).

Answer to problem 9.17

(a) See 'Cost–Volume–Profit Analysis Assumptions' in Chapter 9 for the answer to this question.

(b) Examples of the circumstances where the underlying assumptions are violated include:

(i) *Variable cost per unit remaining constant over the entire range:* This assumption is violated where quantity discounts can be obtained from the purchase of larger quantities. Consequently the variable cost per unit will not be constant for all output levels. However, over a restricted range, or several restricted ranges, a linear relationship or a series of linear relationships may provide a reasonable approximation of the true cost function.

(ii) *Selling price is constant per unit:* In order to increase sales volume the selling price might be reduced. Therefore selling price will not be a linear function of volume. A series of linear relationships may provide a reasonable approximation of the true revenue function.

(iii) *The sales mix is known:* It is unlikely that the planned sales mix will be equal to the actual sales mix. To incorporate the possibility that actual sales mix may differ from the planned sales mix a range of total cost and revenue curves should be prepared corresponding to each possible sales mix. This will give a range of break-even points and profit/losses for possible mixes of sales.

Answer to problem 9.18

See 'Cost–Volume–Profit Analysis Assumptions' in Chapter 9 and 'Cost–Volume–Profit Analysis Under Conditions of Uncertainty' in Chapter 12 for the answer to this question.

Measuring costs and benefits for decision-making

Questions 10.1 to 10.4 can be used as an introduction to relevant costs for decision-making. 10.8 to 10.16 are the most difficult questions in this chapter and are more appropriate to a second year course. The questions are summarised as follows:

10.1	Make or buy decision plus acceptance of an order below full cost.
10.2	Make or buy decision.
10.3	Decision on whether a project involving sunk and opportunity costs should be continued.
10.4	Dropping a segment and determining optimal production schedule where a limiting factor applies.
10.5	Dropping a segment in a public transport organisation.
10.6	Evaluation of an incentive scheme using a relevant cost approach.
10.7 to 10.9	Determining an optimal production schedule where a limiting factor applies.
10.10 to 10.12	Calculation of relevant costs for a pricing decision. You may prefer to answer these questions after you have completed Chapter 11.
10.13 to 10.15	Dropping a segment. 10.13 is the least difficult question but part (b) requires a knowledge of learning curves (see Chapter 20). 10.15 also requires the application of CVP analysis.
10.16	Determining the optimum output decision. This question requires the preparation of marginal cost and revenue schedules.
10.17	A discussion question on relevant costs.

Answer to problem 10.1

(a) Direct Wages Percentage Overhead Rate is calculated as follows:

$$\frac{\text{£64,000 (variable)} + \text{£96,000 (fixed)}}{\text{Direct labour costs (£80,000)}} = 200\% \text{ of direct wages}$$

$$\text{Variable overhead rate} = \frac{\text{£64,000 Variable}}{\text{£80,000 Direct labour costs}} = 80\% \text{ of direct wages}$$

Problem 1	£	*per unit*	*2,000 units*
Additional revenue		16.00	32,000
Additional costs:			
Raw materials	8.00		
Direct labour	4.00		
Variable overhead (80% × £4)	3.20	15.20	30,400
Contribution to fixed costs and profit		£0.80	£1,600

The order should be accepted because it provides a contribution to fixed costs and profits. It is assumed that direct labour is a variable cost.

Problem 2
Relevant manufacturing costs of the component:

	£
Raw material	4.00
Direct labour	8.00
Variable overhead (80% × £8)	6.40
	18.40

The additional costs of manufacturing are lower than the costs of purchasing. Therefore the company should manufacture the component. It is assumed that spare capacity exists.

(b) Relevant cost and revenue principles have been followed. See Chapter 10 for an explanation of relevant cost and revenue principles.

Answer to problem 10.2

	£
(a) Purchase price of component from supplier	50
Additional cost of manufacturing (variable cost only)	34
Saving if component manufactured	16

The component should be manufactured provided the following assumptions are correct:

   (i) Direct labour represents the *additional* labour cost of producing the component.
  (ii) The company will not incur any additional fixed overheads if the component is manufactured.
 (iii) There are no scarce resources. Therefore the manufacture of the component will not restrict the production of other more profitable products.

(b)(i) Additional fixed costs of £56,000 will be incurred but there will be a saving in purchasing costs of £16 per unit produced. The break-even point is 3,500 units (fixed costs of £56,000 ÷ £16 per unit saving). If the quantity of components manufactured per year is less than 3,500 units then it will be cheaper to purchase from the outside supplier.

(ii) The contribution per unit sold from the existing product is £40 and each unit produced uses 8 scarce labour hours. The contribution per labour hour is £5. Therefore if the component is manufactured 4 scarce labour hours will be used resulting in a lost contribution of £20. Hence the relevant cost of manufacturing the components is £54 consisting of £34 incremental cost plus a lost contribution of £20. The component should be purchased from the supplier.

(c) The book value of the equipment is a sunk cost and is not relevant to the decision whether the company should purchase or continue to manufacture the components. If we cease production now the written-down value will be written off in a lump sum, whereas if we continue production, the written-down value will be written off over a period of years. Future cash outflows on the equipment will not be affected by the decision to purchase or continue to manufacture the components. For an illustration of the irrelevance of the written-down value of assets for decision-making purposes see 'Replacement of Equipment' in Chapter 10.

Answer to problem 10.6

(a) *Preliminary calculation*

Weekly labour hours available=4,200 hours (105 operatives at 40 hours per week)
Maximum production=7,000 units (4,200 hours÷0.6 hours per unit)
Contribution per unit (1)=£3.40
Lost sales from 210 hours idle time (2)=350 units (210 hours÷0.6 hours per unit)

Note
(1) Direct labour is a fixed cost (see below). The contribution per unit is calculated by deducting materials and variable overhead from the selling price.
(2) Lost sales only apply when demand is in excess of maximum production from production labour hours.

Comments
The company operates a time rate method of remuneration with a guaranteed weekly wage. Therefore the total wages bill for direct workers will not be affected by the amount of idle time. Consequently the additional labour cost when idle time applies is zero.

In the first week demand of 6,500 units can still be satisfied even with 210 idle hours. Maximum production will be 6,650 units (7,000 units less 350 units) with 210 hours idle time. This is in excess of 6,500 units demand. Because the company incurs no additional labour costs and does not lose any profits from lost production then the relevant cost of idle time is zero.

In the second week demand is in excess of maximum production. Hence the 210 hours idle time will result in lost sales of 350 units at a contribution of £3.40 per unit. That is a total of £1,190. The cost of the idle time is the lost profits of £1,190.

(b)(i) Maximum capacity at present is 7,000 units (see calculation in (a)).
The profit at 7,000 units is as follows:

		£
Contribution (7,000 units at £3.40)		23,800
Less fixed costs:		
Labour (4,200 hours at £3)	12,600	
Fixed overhead (7,000 units at £0.90)	6,300	18,900
Profit		4,900

With the incentive scheme direct labour is a variable cost. The number of units sold to obtain a profit of £4,900 is calculated as follows:

$$\frac{\text{Fixed costs (£6,300)} + \text{Required profit (£4,900)}}{\text{Contribution per unit (£1.40)}} = 8,000 \text{ units}$$

Contribution per unit now includes a variable labour cost of £2 per unit.

(ii) The maximum production if the incentive scheme is introduced will be 8,400 units (4,200 hours ÷ 0.5 hours per unit). Comparing both alternatives the profits at this output level will be as follows:

Incentive scheme

Contribution (8,400 units at £1.40)	£11,760
Fixed costs	£6,300
Profit	£5,460

Existing scheme plus purchases from a supplier

	£
Profit from maximum manufacturing output of 7,000 units	4,900
(See (bi) for calculation)	
Contribution from 1,400 units purchased from supplier (1)	1,400
Profit	6,300

Note
(1) Contribution = Selling price of £5 less variable cost of £4.

From the above figures it appears that it is more profitable to purchase shortbuns when required rather than introducing the incentive scheme. However, it should be noted that the fixed labour cost is £12,600 when the incentive scheme is not introduced. If output in the future is going to be less than 6,300 units (£12,600 ÷ £2 incentive scheme unit labour cost) then profits will be higher with the incentive scheme. This is because the labour cost will be less than £12,600 when output is lower than 6,300 units.

Answer to problem 10.7

Preliminary calculations
Variable costs are quoted per acre but selling prices are quoted per tonne. Therefore it is necessary to calculate the planned sales revenue per acre. The calculation of the selling price and contribution per acre is as follows:

	Potatoes	Turnips	Parsnips	Carrots
(a) Yield per acre in tonnes	10	8	9	12
(b) Selling price per tonne	£100	£125	£150	£135
(c) Sales revenue per acre				
(a × b)	£1,000	£1,000	£1,350	£1,620
(d) Variable cost per acre	£470	£510	£595	£660
(e) Contribution per acre	£530	£490	£755	£960

Profit statement for current year

(a)(i)

	Potatoes	Turnips	Parsnips	Carrots	Total
(a) Acres	25	20	30	25	
(b) Contribution per acre	£530	£490	£755	£960	
(c) Total contribution					
(a × b)	£13,250	£9,800	£22,650	£24,000	£69,700
				Less fixed costs	£54,000
				Profit	£15,700

Profit statement for recommended mix

(ii)

	Area A (45 acres)		Area B (55 acres)		
	Potatoes	*Turnips*	*Parsnips*	*Carrots*	*Total*
(a) Contribution per acre	£530	£490	£755	£960	
(b) Ranking	1	2	2	1	
(c) Minimum sales requirements in acres (1)		5	4		
(d) Acres allocated (2)	40			51	
(e) Recommended mix (acres)	40	5	4	51	
(f) Total contribution (a × e)	£21,200	£2,450	£3,020	£48,960	£75,630
				Less fixed costs	£54,000
				Profit	£21,630

Notes

(1) The minimum sales requirement for turnips is 40 tonnes and this will require the allocation of 5 acres (40 tonnes ÷ 8 tones yield per acre). The minimum sales requirement for parsnips is 36 tonnes requiring the allocation of 4 acres (36 tonnes ÷ 9 tonnes yield per acre).

(2) Allocation of available acres to products on basis of a ranking which assumes that acres are the key factor.

(b)(i) Production should be concentrated on carrots which have the highest contribution per acre (£960).

£

(ii) Contribution from 100 acres of carrots (100 × £960)   96,000
Fixed overhead   54,000
Profit from carrots   42,000

(iii) Break-even point in acres for carrots $= \dfrac{\text{Fixed costs (£54,000)}}{\text{Contribution per acre (£960)}}$

$= 56.25$ acres

Contribution in sales value for carrots = £91,125 (£56.25 acres at £1,620 sales revenue per acre).

Answer to problem 10.10

(a)   *Cost Estimate*

£

Direct Materials and Components
   2,000 units of A at £20 per unit (1)   40,000
   200 units of B at £20 per unit (2)   4,000
   Other material components   12,500
                                              56,500
Direct Labour (3)   —
Overhead:
   Department P (200 hours at £30) (4)   6,000
   Department Q (400 hours at £8) (5)   3,200
Estimating Department (6)   —
Planning Department (6)   —
                                              65,700

Notes

(1) It is assumed that using material A on the contract will result in the materials being replaced. Therefore additional (opportunity) costs to the company will be the replacement costs of the materials.

(2) The alternative uses of the materials are to sell them or to use them as substitute materials. The savings are greater, when the materials are used as a substitute. Therefore, the company will be worse off by £20 per unit of materials used on the contract. Hence the opportunity cost of material B is £20 per unit.

(3) The company appears to have a temporary excess supply of the labour. The total labour cost will be the same whether or not the contract is undertaken. Therefore the opportunity cost is zero.

(4) Acceptance of the contract will result in the department losing the opportunity of charging out 200 hours at £30 per hour.

(5) The company will incur £3,200 additional costs if the contract is undertaken.

(6) It is assumed that the company will not incur additional costs in the Estimating and Planning Departments if the contract is undertaken. The costs already incurred by the Estimating Department on the contract are sunk costs. Therefore the opportunity cost is zero for both departments.

(b) The opportunity cost approach is a suitable approach for short-term decision-making. This approach ensures that alternative actions are only charged with the additional costs resulting from the action. Whenever the additional revenues are in excess of the relevant or opportunity costs for a particular course of action then a company will increase it's total profits or reduce it's total loss. However, in the long-term a company must cover all it's costs, not just the opportunity costs, if it is to be profitable. In the situation described in the question the opportunity cost approach is appropriate because the company has spare capacity. The opportunity cost of the contract is £65,700 whereas the cost as per the conventional pricing procedure used in the question is £85,500. If the latter cost is used as a basis of a price quotation then there is a danger that the company will lose the contract. As long as the contract price is in excess of the opportunity cost of £65,700 the company will increase it's total profits.

The following problems are likely to be encountered:

   (i) Fixed costs may be ignored and insufficient contribution may not be generated to cover fixed costs (see section on 'Emphasis on the Short-term' in Chapter 10 for an explanation of this).
   (ii) Lack of understanding of opportunity costs and the difficulty in determining opportunity costs. This requires a knowledge of alternative uses of resources and this information might be difficult to obtain in practice.

(c) When a course of action requires the use of scarce resources it is necessary to incorporate the lost profits which will be foregone from using scarce resources. Only by adopting such an approach can we ensure an optimal allocation of scarce resources. For a more detailed discussion and an illustration of this point see sections 'Decision-Making and the Influence of Limiting Factors' and 'Make-or-Buy Decisions' in Chapter 10.

Answer to problem 10.13

(a) The question indicates that a choice should be made between the following three alternatives:
   (i) Close department K immediately.
   (ii) Operate department K for a further year at 10,000 units
   (iii) Operate department K for a further year at 20,000 units
The *relevant* information is presented in the following schedule:

	Immediate closure £	10,000 units £	20,000 units £
Relevant cost savings and revenues			
Sale of production	—	90,000	160,000
Material B—Saving (2)	18,000	9,000	—
Sale (2)	5,000	—	—
Sale of machine (5)	43,000	35,000	30,000
Total revenue/savings	66,000	134,000	190,000
Relevant costs			
Labour—Training	—	20,000	20,000
Variable costs	—	30,000	60,000
Material A—Disposal fixed cost (1)	2,000	2,000	2,000
Disposal variable cost (1)	15,000	10,000	5,000
Material B—Purchase cost (2)	—	—	10,000
Variable overhead (3)	—	13,000	26,000
Salary of Foreman (4)	2,000	6,000	6,000
Advertising	—	—	15,000
Total relevant costs	19,000	81,000	144,000
Excess of savings and revenues over costs	47,000	53,000	46,000

Notes

(1) Fixed costs of disposing of the materials are common to all alternatives. An alternative presentation is to exclude these fixed costs from the analysis. The disposal variable cost consists of the unused litres of material A for each alternative multiplied £0.50 per litre.

(2) Immediate closure enables 10,000 units to be used as a substitute material thus saving £18,000. The remaining 5,000 units are sold to yield net revenue of £1 per unit.

Production of 10,000 units will result in 5,000 unused units of material B. This results in a saving of substitute materials of £9,000 (5,000 × £1.80). Production of 20,000 units results in the stock of material B being used. It is also necessary to purchase 5,000 additional units at £2 per unit.

(3) Units produced × variable overhead rate of £1.30 per unit.

(4) Immediate closure requires that £2,000 be paid to the foreman compared with £6,000 if the department is not closed.

(5) Sales value now = £43,000.

Sales value in one year = £40,000 − (£0.50 × production level).

On the basis of the above information Hilton Ltd should operate the department at a level of 10,000 units for the coming year.

(b)(i) The excess of savings and revenues over costs for the immediate closure will be increased by £8,000 to £55,000 (£47,000 + £8,000). The immediate closure will now be the best action in terms of maximising short-term profits.

(ii) A 90% learning curve means that each time production doubles the average time taken to produce each unit falls to 90% of the previous average figure (see Chapter 20).

Average time per unit for 5,000 units = 1 hour
Average time per unit for 10,000 units = 0.9 hours
Average time per unit for 20,000 units = 0.81 hours
Revised labour cost for 10,000 units = £27,000 (10,000 × 0.9 hours × £3)
Revised labour cost for 20,000 units = £48,600 (20,000 × 0.81 hours × £3)

The analysis in part (A) will be altered as follows:

	10,000 units £	20,000 units £
Labour costs without learning effect	30,000	60,000
Labour costs with learning effect	27,000	48,600
Reduction in labour costs	3,000	11,400
Revised net savings/revenue	56,000 (53,000 + 3,000)	57,400 (46,000 + 11,400)

Hilton Ltd should now operate department K at 20,000 units activity during the coming year.

Answer to problem 10.17

See Chapter 10 for the answer to this question.

Accounting information for pricing decisions

All the questions in this chapter are applicable to a second year course. Details are as follows:

11.1 to 11.3   Various discussion questions.
11.4 to 11.6   Questions based on a relevant cost approach requiring the use of demand schedules for pricing decisions.
11.7 to 11.10   Establishing optimal selling prices from economic cost and revenue functions.

For additional relevant cost questions requiring the setting of minimum selling prices see 10.10 to 10.12 in Chapter 10. For pricing decisions under conditions of uncertainty see 12.7 to 12.10 in Chapter 12.

Answer to problem 11.1

Several factors should be considered in the determination of pricing policy. The most important factor is price elasticity of demand but if price is to be set in order to maximise profits knowledge of cost structures and cost behaviour will also be of great importance. Knowledge of price demand relationships and costs at different output levels is necessary to determine the optimum price. This is the price which results in marginal revenue being equal to marginal cost. The emphasis should be placed on providing information on the effect of changes in output on total cost rather than providing average unit cost information.

When cost information is presented using absorption costing then the resulting selling price calculation will be a function of the overhead apportionments and recovery methods used and the assumed volume of production. At best the calculated selling price will only be appropriate for one level of production and a different selling price would be produced for different output levels. Single cost figures calculated using absorption costing also fail to supply information on the effect of changes in output on total cost. For other disadvantages which apply when absorption costing is used in the determination of pricing policy see 'Limitations of Cost-Plus Pricing' in Chapter 11.

The advantage claimed from the use of absorption costing in price determination is that all manu-facturing costs are included in the cost per unit calculation so that no major manufacturing cost is over-looked. With variable costing there is a danger that output will be priced to earn a low contribution which is insufficient to cover total fixed costs. Also the use of production facilities entails an opportunity cost from the alternative use of capacity foregone. The fixed cost per unit of capacity used can be regarded as an attempt to approximate the opportunity cost from the use of productive capacity. In spite of these claimed advantages the presentation of relevant costs for pricing decisions (see Chapter 11) is likely to be preferable to information based on absorption cost.

Answer to problem 11.2

(i) Short-run profits are maximised at the output level where marginal revenue equals marginal cost. The optimum selling price is that which corresponds to the optimal output level (see Figure 11.3 in Chapter 11). From Figure 11.3 we can see that with imperfect competition (no pricing decision is necessary with perfect competition) firms are faced with a downward sloping demand curve. The highest selling price will apply to the first unit sold but Figure 11.3 indicates that it is unlikely that this will be at the point where marginal revenue equals marginal cost.

(ii) The objective is to maximise total contribution not unit contribution. Contribution per unit sold is the difference between marginal revenue and marginal cost. It is unlikely that contribution per unit will remain constant over the entire range of output. In Chapter 9 we noted that variable cost per unit and selling price per unit may change in relation to output. With a downward sloping demand curve marginal revenue will decline thus causing contribution per unit to decline as output is increased. From Figure 11.3 in Chapter 11 we can see that profit is maximised where $MR = MC$. This is not at the point where unit contribution (difference between marginal revenue and marginal cost) is the greatest.

(iii) Joint costs are allocated on an arbitrary basis and costs which include arbitrary allocations are inappropriate for product, project or divisional comparisons. Performance should be judged on the basis of comparisons between controllable costs and revenues. With profit centres measures such as controllable residual income should be used whereas contribution should be used for comparing products.

(iv) This statement presumably refers to the use of cost-plus pricing methods. If prices are set completely on a cost-plus basis then accounting information will determine the selling price. Consequently the marketing and production people might feel that they have no influence in determining selling prices with pricing dominated by a concern for recovering full costs. If cost-plus pricing is used in a rigid way then marketing and production people may well consider the statement in the question to be correct. Cost information should be used in a flexible manner and is one of several variables that should be used in determining selling prices. If this approach is adopted then the statement in the question will be incorrect.

(v) Management accounting should not be constrained by the requirements of external reporting. The emphasis should be on assembling financial information so as to help managers make good decisions and to plan and control activities effectively. In Chapter 8 we noted that there are strong arguments for adopting a system of variable costing in preference to absorption costing. If management accounts were consistent with SSAP 9 then the financial information might motivate managers to make wrong decisions.

(vi) All costs must be covered in the long-run if a firm is to be profitable. Therefore the objective should be to recover R and D expenditure in the long-run. R and D expenditure should be regarded as a pool of fixed costs to which products should generate sufficient contribution. Giant Steps Ltd should not rely on a policy of recovering R and D in relation to expenditure on each individual product. Price/demand relationships for some products might mean that the associated R and D cannot be recovered while other products might be able to recover more than their fair share. Once a product is launched only the incremental costs are relevant to the pricing decision. The objective should be to obtain a selling price in excess of relevant short-run costs and to provide a contribution to fixed costs and profit. R and D should be regarded as part of the pool of fixed costs to be recovered.

Answer to problem 11.3

(a) See Chapters 10 and 11 for the answer to this question. In particular the answer should indicate:

(i) Information presented to the product manager should be *future* costs not past costs;

(ii) *Incremental* cost and revenue information should be presented and the excess of incremental revenues over incremental costs compared for different selling price and sales quantity levels. Costs which are common to all alternatives are not relevant for decision-making purposes;

(iii) Decisions involve a choice between alternatives and this implies that a choice leads to foregoing *opportunities*. Therefore relevant cost information for a pricing decision should include future cash costs and imputed (opportunity) costs;

(iv) *Sunk costs* are past costs and not relevant to the pricing decision;

(v) Pricing decisions should be based on estimates of demand schedules and a comparison of marginal revenues and costs.

(b) See 'Reasons for Using Cost-Based Pricing Formulas' in Chapter 11 for the answer to this question. Note that overhead allocation is an attempt to provide an estimate of the long-run costs of producing a product.

(c) There is no specific answer to this question. The author's views on this question are expressed in Chapter 11.

Answer to problem 11.4

(a) Exhibit 1 presents the likely effects on the financial implications of the proposal. Exhibit 1 should be considered in the light of the following comments:

(i) It is assumed that once the printing run has been carried out the total production level cannot be altered. It is also assumed once the selling price has been set it cannot be altered.

(ii) The company's practice of apportioning fixed costs will not affect future costs and revenues. Therefore such costs are not included in Exhibit 1.

(iii) It is assumed that the marketing and editorial costs would be incurred only if the annual is published. Therefore an additional £10,000 should be deducted from each of the outcomes in Exhibit 1. However, the pricing and output decision will not be affected by inclusion of editorial and marketing costs.

(iv) The cost of the inspection copies is not included in Exhibit 1 because the cost does not change significantly with changes in selling price. Therefore inspection costs are not critical to the pricing decision.

Comments on Exhibit 1
The ranking for each selling price in terms of contribution for expected, minimum and maximum sales is as follows:

		Ranking	
Selling price £	Expected sales	Minimum sales	Maximum sales
5	9	8	9
10	7	5	7
11	5	6	5
12	6	7	1
13	4	4	2
14	2	2	4
15	1	1	6
16	3	3	3
20	8	9	8

An analysis of the above rankings suggests that the selling price should be set between £12 and £16 with the final choice depending on management's attitude towards risk. If the decision is based on expected or minimum sales then a selling price of £15 is recommended. As no information is given on the likelihood of demand being above or below expected sales it is not possible to state whether or not the print run should be set at minimum, expected or maximum sales. Assuming a print run based on expected sales then the print run should be set at 6,500 copies for a £15 selling price.

It should be noted that the annual is expected to provide a contribution towards general fixed costs at selling prices ranging between £12 and £16. (This contribution should be after a further deduction of £10,000 for specific fixed costs for marketing and editorial costs, plus approximately £200 for inspection copies.)

(b)(i) On the assumption that the acceptance of the American publisher's offer would not affect decisions already taken with respect to the U.K. market, the change in the financial position would be as follows:

	£
Increase in sales revenue (6,000 × £1.50)	9,000
Increase in production costs:	
(£18,900 for an output of 9,000 copies	
less £15,000 for an output of 3,000 copies)	3,900
Additional profits	5,100

(ii) $\text{Break-even point} = \dfrac{\text{Incremental cost}}{6,000 \text{ units}} = \dfrac{£3,900}{6,000} = £0.65 \text{ per copy}$

Exhibit 1

Expected sales									
Proposed selling price (£)	5	10	11	12	13	14	15	16	20
Sales (000's copies)	15	10	9	8	7.5	7	6.5	6	3
Sales (£000's)	75	100	99	96	97.5	98	97.5	96	60
Variable costs (£000's) (53⅓% of sales)	40	53.33	52.77	51.17	51.97	52.23	51.97	51.17	31.98
Net revenues	35	46.67	46.23	44.83	45.53	45.77	45.53	44.83	28.02
Total production costs	22.5	20.00	18.9	17.6	17.25	16.80	16.25	15.9	15.0
Contribution to editorial and marketing costs (£000's)	12.5	26.67	27.33	27.23	28.28	28.97	29.28	28.93	13.02
Ranking	9	7	5	6	4	2	1	3	8
Minimum sales									
Selling price (£)	5	10	11	12	13	14	15	16	20
Sales (000's copies)	10	8	7	6	6	6	6	5	1
Sales (£000's)	50	80	77	72	78	84	90	80	20
Variable costs (£000's) (53⅓% of sales)	26.65	42.64	41.04	38.38	41.58	44.77	47.97	42.64	10.66
Net revenues	23.35	37.36	35.96	33.62	36.42	39.23	42.03	37.36	9.34
Total production costs	20	17.6	16.8	15.9	15.9	15.9	15.9	15.9(1)	15.0(1)
Contribution to editorial and marketing costs (£000's)	3.35	19.76	19.16	17.72	20.52	23.33	26.13	21.46	(5.66)

Exhibit 1

Ranking	8	5	6	7	4	2	1	3	9
Maximum sales									
Selling price	5	10	11	12	13	14	15	16	20
Sales (000's copies)	20	12	11	10	9	8	7	7	5
Sales (£000's)	100	120	121	120	117	112	105	112	100
Variable costs (£000's)									
($53\frac{1}{3}\%$ of sales)	53.33	63.96	64.49	63.96	62.36	59.7	55.97	59.7	53.33
Net revenues	46.67	56.04	56.51	56.04	54.64	52.3	49.03	52.3	46.67
Total production costs	30.0(1)	24.0(1)	22.0(1)	20.0	18.9	17.6	16.8	16.8	15.9(1)
Contribution to editorial and marketing costs (£000's)	16.67	32.04	34.51	36.04	35.74	34.7	32.23	35.5	30.77
Ranking	9	7	5	1	2	4	6	3	8

Note

(1) The production cost for these items is estimated since no information is given in the question regarding the costs at these output levels.

Answer to problem 11.7

(a) Fixed overhead per unit allocated to Exco (£60,000 ÷ 15,000 units) = £4
    Fixed overhead per unit allocated to Wyeco (£300,000 ÷ 30,000 units) = £10
    ∴ Variable cost per unit of Exco = £8 (£12 − £4)
       Variable cost per unit of Wyeco = £14 (£24 − £10)

	Exco	Wyeco
Contribution per unit	£8	£18
Finishing time per unit	1 hour	$\frac{1}{2}$ hour
Contribution per hour of finishing time	£8	£36
Ranking	2	1

The finishing time available is calculated as follows:

15,000 units planned output of Exco at 1 hour per unit = 15,000 hours
30,000 units planned output of Wyeco at $\frac{1}{2}$ hour per unit = 15,000 hours
                                                                      30,000 hours

The policy should be to sell the maximum of 40,000 units of Wyeco which will require 20,000 hours of finishing time. The remaining 10,000 hours of finishing time should be used to produce 10,000 units of Exco.

(b) The price/sales relationship for each product is presented in the following graphs:

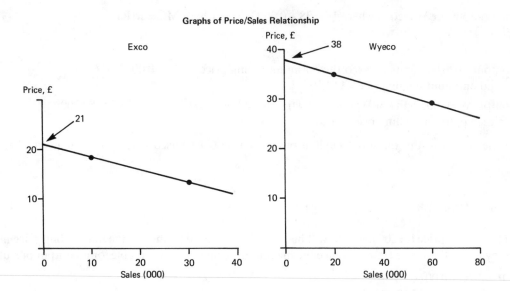

Graphs of Price/Sales Relationship

From the above graphs it can be seen that if the selling price is £21 for Exco and £38 for Wyeco the demand will be zero. In order to increase demand of Exco from 10,000 to 30,000 units the selling price must be reduced by £5. Therefore to increase demand by one unit selling price must be reduced by £5/20,000 units or £0.00025. Hence the maximum selling price attainable for an output of x units is:

$P = £21 - 0.00025x$ (Exco)

Applying the same approach the maximum selling price for an output of x units of Wyeco is:

$P = £38 - 0.00015x$ (Wyeco)

Profit is maximised where $MC = MR$

Exco $MC = £8$ per unit variable cost
Wyeco $MC = £14$ per unit variable cost

$$MR = \frac{dTR}{dx}$$

Exco Total Revenue $(R) = x(21 - 0.00025x)$
$\qquad = 21x - 0.00025x^2$
Wyeco Total Revenue $(TR) = x(38 - 0.00015x)$
$\qquad = 38x - 0.00015x^2$

Exco $\dfrac{dTR}{dx} \qquad = 21 - 0.0005x$

Wyeco $\dfrac{dTR}{dx} \qquad = 38 - 0.0003x$

∴ Optimum output for Exco is where $8 = 21 - 0.0005x$ (i.e. where $MC = MR$)
∴ $0.0005x = 13$
∴ $x = 26,000$ units

Optimum output for Wyeco is where $14 = 38 - 0.0003x$ (i.e. where $MC = MR$)
   $\therefore 0.0003x = 24$
      $\therefore x = 80,000$ units

At an output of 26,000 units of Exco the optimum selling price $= £21 - 0.00025 \, (26,000)$
   $\therefore$ Exco optimum selling price $= £14.50$

At an output of 80,000 units of Wyeco the optimum selling price $= £38 - 0.00015 \, (80,000)$
   $\therefore$ Wyeco optimum selling price $= £26$

(c) For the answer to this question see 'Reasons for Using Cost-Based Pricing Formulas' in Chapter 11.

Answer to problem 11.8

(a)(i) If the selling price is £200 demand will be zero. To increase demand by one unit, selling price must be reduced by £1/1000 units or £0.001. Hence the maximum selling price attainable for an output of x units is:

   $P = £200 - 0.001x$
   At an output level of 100,000 units
      $P = £200 - 0.001 \, (100,000)$
        $= £100$ per unit

	£
Total contribution at an output level of 100,000 units $(100,000 \times (£100 - £50))$	5,000,000
Less fixed costs $(100,000 \times £25)$	2,500,000
Profit	2,500,000

(ii) Profit is maximised where $MC = MR$
                  $MC = £50$ per unit variable cost (given)

$$MR = \frac{dTR}{dx}$$

$$TR = x(200 - 0.001x)$$
$$= 200x - 0.001x^2$$

$$\frac{dTR}{dx} = 200 - 0.002x$$

   $\therefore$ Optimum output is where $50 = 200 - 0.002x$ (i.e. where $MC = MR$)
                  $\therefore 150 = 0.002x$
                  $\therefore x = 75,000$ units
   At an output level of 75,000 units the selling price $= 200 - 0.001 \, (75,000)$
                           $= £125$
   $\therefore$ Profit at 75,000 units: Contribution $(75,000 \times £75) = £5,625,000$
                           Less fixed costs $= £2,500,000$
                           $£3,125,000$

(b)(i) Revised fixed costs $= £3,000,000$.
       The optimal output level will not be affected by a change in fixed costs. Therefore the selling price should not be changed. Profit will decline by £500,000.
   (ii) Revised marginal cost $= £60$.

The new optimum is where $60 = 200 - 0.002x$
$$\therefore 0.002x = 140$$
$$\therefore x = 70,000 \text{ units}$$
At this output level $P = 200 - 0.001 \ (70,000)$
$$\therefore P = £130$$

(c) Profit before advertising expenditure:

		£
Total contribution $(70,000 \times (£130 - £60))$		4,900,000
Less fixed costs		3,000,000
	Profit	1,900,000

After the introduction of the advertising expenditure $P = 210 - 0.001x$
$$TR = x(210 - 0.001x)$$
$$= 210x - 0.001x^2$$
$$\therefore MR = 210 - 0.002x$$
The revised optimum output is where $60 = 210 - 0.002x$
$$0.002x = 150$$
$$\therefore x = 75,000$$
The optimum price at this output level is where $P = 210 - 0.001 \ (75,000)$
$$\therefore P = 135$$
Total contribution $(75,000 \times (£135 - £60) = £5,625,000$
Revised fixed costs $= £4,000,000$
Profit $= £1,625,000$

Therefore profits will decline by £275,000 if the advertising campaign is undertaken.

(d) The original budgeted output of 100,000 units was higher than the optimum output level. The solution to (a)(ii) indicates that the optimum output level is achieved by reducing production to 75,000 units and increasing the selling price to £125. Beyond an output level of 75,000 units marginal cost per unit is in excess of marginal revenue. This is because selling price is reduced in order to expand output. Consequently marginal revenue declines and is less than marginal cost. This means that profits decline when output is in excess of 75,000 units. This analysis is based on the following assumptions:

(1) The demand schedule can be predicted accurately;
(2) Marginal cost per unit is constant at all output levels;
(3) Fixed costs are constant throughout the entire output range.

The analysis also showed that the change in fixed costs had no effect on the MR and MC function so that the optimum output level and price did not change. When MC increases the effect is to decrease output level and increase price.

The effect of the advertising campaign is to shift the demand curve to the right thus causing sales demand to be higher at each selling price or the selling price to be higher at each demand level. However, the increased advertising costs are in excess of the additional revenue thus resulting in a reduction in profits.

Decision-making under conditions of uncertainty

.

The questions in this chapter are appropriate for a second year course. 12.1 to 12.5 are the easiest questions. The following is a description of each question:

12.1	Part a consists of the use of probabilities for competitive bidding. Part b is concerned with sub-contracting under conditions of uncertainty.
12.2	Analysis of the effect on profits of a competitor's response to various courses of action.
12.3	The calculation of expected values to determine whether a charity organisation should hold a dinner dance.
12.4	Acceptance of a contract at a given price when demand is uncertain.
12.5	Selection of the most profitable product when demand is uncertain.
12.6	Output decision requiring commitment to an output level given that demand is uncertain.
12.7 to 12.10	Pricing decisions under conditions of uncertainty. 12.8 requires the preparation of a decision tree.
12.11 and 12.12	Both problems are concerned with selecting which machine should be hired given that each machine is capable of producing different output levels. 12.11 requires the construction of a decision tree and the application of the maximin criterion.
12.13	Calculation of the expected value of perfect and imperfect information. The calculation of the expected value of information is also required in sections of questions 12.3, 12.5, 12.6, 12.9 and 12.12.

Answer to problem 12.1

(a) It is assumed that if XY Ltd and one or more of the other firms bid the lowest price, XY Ltd will be awarded the contract. The expected contribution for each bid price is as follows.

Price bid £	Total contribution at this bid £	Probability that XY Ltd will obtain contract at each bid price	Expected contribution £
45	130,000	1.00	130,000
50	180,000	0.95	171,000
55	230,000	0.85	195,500

Price bid £	Total contribution at this bid £	Probability that XY Ltd will obtain contract at each bid price	Expected contribution £
60	280,000	0.65	182,000
65	330,000	0.40	132,000
70	380,000	0.15	57,000
75	430,000	0.05	21,500

Expected profits will be maximised at a bid price of £55. However, expected value is a long-run decision criterion and may not be appropriate for 'one-off' decisions. Management might prefer to compare the contributions and the associated probabilities for each bid price and make a decision on the basis of their risk/return preference.

(b) *North area*
No alternative to AB Ltd exists. Therefore servicing in the north will be subcontracted to AB Ltd at £18,000. This cost will be offset by the contribution of £1,500 from the sale of necessary spares to AB Ltd.

South area
There are two alternatives—buy from AB or CD Ltd. Both firms will buy the necessary spares from AB Ltd. Therefore this factor is not relevant to the decision. The relevant information is as follows:

	£
AB Ltd	
Fixed charge of	20,000
CD Ltd	£
Fixed charge of	18,000

Expected additional charge:

£	Probability	£
0	0.40	—
900	0.30	270
2,200	0.20	440
3,500	0.10	350
		1,060
		19,060

Applying the expected value approach the work should be subcontracted to CD Ltd. However, an examination of the probability distribution indicates that the charge from CD Ltd could be as high as £21,500 with a probability of 0.10. The probability that the charge will be in excess of £20,200 is 0.3 and the probability that it will be below £20,200 is 0.7. The decision depends on management's attitude towards risk.

Midlands area
There are two alternatives—AB Ltd, or XY Ltd can use its own organisation. The relevant information is as follows:

AB Ltd	£
Fixed charge of	11,500

Own Organisation
Expected cost of extra staff

£	Probability	£
4,500	0.20	900
7,000	0.35	2,450
11,000	0.45	4,950
		8,300

Contribution lost from
sale of spares:
2,500 units × £0.50   1,250
                           9,550

If the decision is based on an expected value approach then XY Ltd should use it's own organisation. However, it should be noted that there is a 0.45 probability that the cost will be £12,250.

Summary of the decisions using the expected value approach

North   AB Ltd
South   CD Ltd
Midlands   Own Organisation

Answer to problem 12.3

(a) Based on past experience the probability of ticket sales is as follows:

No. of tickets sold	Probability
250–349	0.2 (4 out of 20)
350–449	0.3 (6 out of 20)
450–549	0.4 (8 out of 20)
550–649	0.1 (2 out of 20)
	1.0

The average revenue per person from the dinner and dance is £26 (£20 + £5 + £1) and the fixed costs are £4,500 (£700 + £2,800 + £800 + £200). The expected profit from the dinner and dance is calculated as follows:

(1) Ticket sales (mid-point) taken	(2) Probability	(3) Income £	(4) Food £	(5) Fixed costs £	(6) Profit (Loss) £	(7) Expected value (2 × 6) £
300	0.2	7,800	4,800	4,500	(1,500)	(300)
400	0.3	10,400	4,800	4,500	1,100	330
500	0.4	13,000	6,000	4,500	2,500	1,000
600	0.1	15,600	7,200	4,500	3,900	390
					Expected profit	1,420

Based on past experience the probability of the number of programme pages sold is:

Programme pages sold	Probability
24	0.2 (4 out of 20)
32	0.4 (8 out of 20)
40	0.3 (6 out of 20)
48	0.1 (2 out of 20)
	1.0

The expected profit on programme advertising is calculated as follows:

Programme pages sold	Probability	Income £	Costs £	Profit/(Loss) £	Expected value £
24	0.2	1,680	2,120	(440)	(88)
32	0.4	2,240	2,160	80	32
40	0.3	2,800	2,200	600	180
48	0.1	3,360	2,240	1,120	112
				Expected profit	236

Total expected profit is £1,656 (£1,420 + £236).

(b) It is assumed that the policy is not to hold a dinner and dance each year and to accept losses in some years and profits in other years. If this is the policy then there is no point in spending £500 on the market research enquiry.

Spending £500 on market research is justifiable only if it affects action taken. For example, if the expenditure indicated that a loss would be incurred then the function will be cancelled and benefits would be obtained. However, if the expenditure indicated that a profit will be made then no benefits will be obtained. From part (A) it can be seen that a loss will occur only if 300 tickets are sold (if 400 or more tickets are sold a total profit is obtained even if a loss is incurred on programme sales). The expected loss that will be incurred if 300 tickets are sold is calculated as follows:

Loss from sale of 300 tickets £	Profit/(Loss) on programmes £	Total loss £	Joint probability	Expected value £
(1,500)	(440)	1,940	0.2 × 0.2 = 0.04	(77.6)
(1,500)	80	1,420	0.2 × 0.4 = 0.08	(113.6)
(1,500)	600	900	0.2 × 0.3 = 0.06	(54.0)
(1,500)	1,120	380	0.2 × 0.1 = 0.02	(7.6)
			Expected loss	(252.8)

The expected value of the benefits of market research is £252.8 and the cost of the research is £500. Therefore the expenditure is not justified on an expected value criterion.

Answer to problem 12.5

(a) The fixed costs are as follows:

	A ($£000$'s)	B ($£000$'s)	C ($£000$'s)
Rights	130	190	200
Manufacturing cost	120	20	20
Advertising	50	30	20
Total	300	240	240
Contribution per unit	200	80	60

Statement of expected money value of each product

Product A	Sales volume	Total contribution ($£000$'s)	Fixed cost ($£000$'s)	Profit ($£000$'s)	Probability	Expected value 000's
	0	0	−300	−300	0.1	−30
	2,500	500	−300	200	0.4	80
	4,000	800	−300	500	0.5	250
						£300

Product B	Sales volume	Total contribution	Fixed cost	Profit	Probability	Expected value
	3,000	240	−240	0	0.1	0
	4,000	320	−240	80	0.3	24
	6,000	480	−240	240	0.3	72
	8,000	640	−240	400	0.3	120
						£216

Product C	Sales volume	Total contribution	Fixed cost	Profit	Probability	Expected value
	7,000	420	−240	180	0.8	144
	8,000	480	−240	240	0.1	24
	9,000	540	−240	300	0.1	30
						£198

Product A has the highest expected value and should be selected if the objective is to maximise expected value.

(b) The following points should be included:
   (i) *Management's attitude to risk:* C may be preferable because it always produces a profit. Only

product A makes a loss and management may therefore find this the least attractive product.

(ii) *Portfolio approach:* A venture may be negatively or not highly correlated with the firm's existing activities. Therefore the contribution of a venture to overall risk might be small or may even reduce risk. For a discussion of the impact of a decision on a firm's overall risk see 'Portfolio Analysis' in Chapter 12.

(iii) *Accuracy of cost and revenue estimates and associated probabilities:* Only if the cost and revenue estimates and subjective probabilities are accurate will the final calculation of expected value be accurate.

(c) If the market research indicates that sales demand will be zero then the venture should not be undertaken. The fixed costs are avoidable. Therefore the only costs incurred will be the cost of the market research of £20,000. Consequently the loss will be £20,000. If the research indicates sales levels will be 2,500 or 4,000 units than A's profits will be reduced by the cost of the market research. The revised outcomes are as follows:

Sales (units)	Total profit (£000's)	Probability	Expected value (£000's)
0	− 20	0.1	−2
2,500	180	0.4	72
4,000	480	0.5	240
			310

The increase in expected money value is £10,000 (£310,000 revised expected value less £300,000 expected value on the basis of the initial estimates in (A)). Therefore it is worthwhile undertaking the market research. This is due to the change in the worst outcome from a loss of £300,000 to a loss of only £20,000. However, this is gained at the expense of reducing other profitable outcomes by £20,000.

Answer to problem 12.7

(a)

	£70	£80	£90
Selling price	£70	£80	£90
Max. demand	75,000	60,000	40,000
Max. revenue	£5,250,000	£4,800,000	£3,600,000
Total variable cost	£3,750,000	£3,000,000	£2,000,000
Fixed cost	800,000	800,000	800,000
R & D costs	250,000	250,000	250,000
	£4,800,000	£4,050,000	£3,050,000
Estimated profit	£450,000	£750,000	£550,000

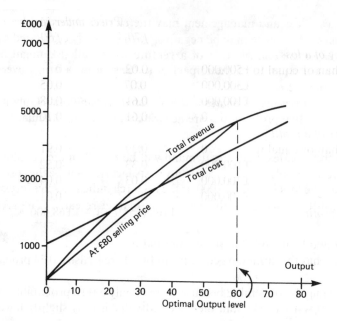

The above analysis is based on the maximum sales demand. On this basis the analysis indicates that profits are maximised at an output level of 60,000 units when the selling price is £80. It is preferable to use the 'most likely' demand level and to incorporate uncertainty around the 'most likely' demand into the analysis.

(b) For a selling price of £90 there are three different demand levels and for each demand level there are three different outcomes for actual unit variable cost. Therefore there are nine possible outcomes. The contribution and probability of each outcome is presented in the following schedule:

(1)	(2)	(3)	(4)	(5)	(6)	(7)	(8)
		Unit			Total	Joint	Weighted outcome
Demand 000's	Probability	variable cost (£)	Probability	Unit (£) contribution	contribution £000's	probability (2 × 4)	(6 × 7) £000's
20	0.2	60	0.2	30	600	0.04	24.00
20	0.2	55	0.7	35	700	0.14	98.00
20	0.2	50	0.1	40	800	0.02	16.00
35	0.7	60	0.2	30	1,050	0.14	147.00
35	0.7	55	0.7	35	1,225	0.49	600.25
35	0.7	50	0.1	40	1,400	0.07	98.00
40	0.1	60	0.2	30	1,200	0.02	24.00
40	0.1	55	0.7	35	1,400	0.07	98.00
40	0.1	50	0.1	40	1,600	0.01	16.00
						1.00	1,121.25

	£
Expected total contribution	1,121,250
Fixed costs	1,050,000
Expected profit	71,250

(c) To compare the three selling prices it is necessary to summarise the information in part B for a £90 selling price in the same way as part (C) of the question. Note that fixed costs are deducted from the total contribution column in the schedule presented in (B) to produce the following statement:

	Prices under review		
	£70	£80	£90
Probability of a loss			
Greater than or equal to £500,000	0.02	0	0
£300,000	0.07	0.05	0.18
£100,000	0.61	0.08	0.20
0	0.61	0.10	0.34
Probability of a profit			
Greater than or equal to 0	0.39	0.91	0.80
£100,000	0.33	0.52	0.66
£300,000	0.03	0.04	0.15
£500,000	0	0.01	0.01
Expected profit	Loss (£55,750)	£68,500	£71,250

The following items should be included in the memorandum:
 (i) The £90 selling price has the largest expected profit but there is also a 0.34 probability of not making a profit.
 (ii) Selling price of £80 may be preferable because there is only a 0.10 probability of not making a profit. A selling price of £80 is least risky and the expected value is only slightly lower than the £90 selling price.
(iii) Subjective probability distributions provide details of the uncertainty surrounding the estimates and enable the decision-maker to select the course of action which is related to his personal risk/profit trade-off (see Chapter 12 for an explanation of this).
(iv) Subjective probabilities are subject to all the disadvantages of any subjective estimate (e.g. Bias).
 (v) Calculations are based on discrete probabilities. For example this implies that there is a 0.7 probability that demand will be exactly 35,000. A more realistic interpretation is that 35,000 represents the mid-point of demand falling within a certain range. See article by Flower for a discussion of this point. Details of this article can be found in the references at the end of Chapter 12.

(d) If the increase in fixed costs represents an additional cost resulting from an increase in volume then this incremental cost is relevant to the pricing decision. If the fixed costs represent an apportionment then it is not relevant. Nevertheless we noted in Chapter 11 that selling prices should be sufficient to cover the common and unavoidable long-run fixed costs.

The research and development expenditure is a sunk cost and is not a relevant cost as far as the pricing decision is concerned. However, the pricing policy of the company may be to recover the research and development expenditure in the selling price. The amount recovered per unit sold should be a policy decision. Note that the decision to write off research and development in one year instead of three years will affect the reported profits.

Answer to problem 12.8

The variable cost per litre is as follows:

	£
Direct materials	0.12
Direct wages	0.24
Indirect wages etc. ($16\frac{2}{3}\% \times$ £0.24)	0.04
	0.40

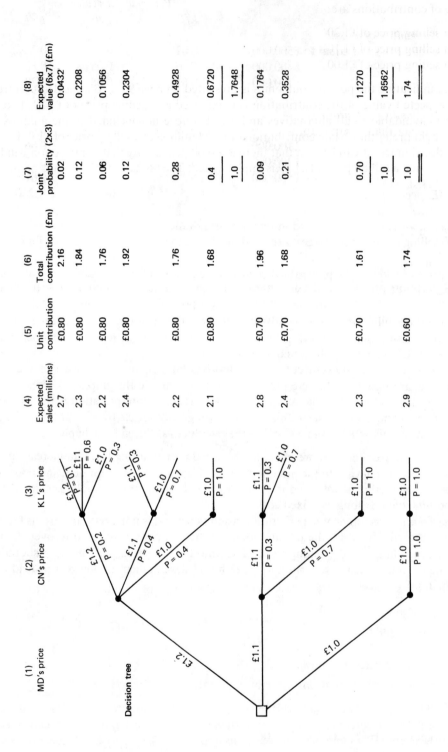

(1) MD's price	(2) CN's price	(3) KL's price	(4) Expected sales (millions)	(5) Unit contribution	(6) Total contribution (£m)	(7) Joint probability (2x3)	(8) Expected value (6x7) (£m)
			2.7	£0.80	2.16	0.02	0.0432
			2.3	£0.80	1.84	0.12	0.2208
			2.2	£0.80	1.76	0.06	0.1056
			2.4	£0.80	1.92	0.12	0.2304
			2.2	£0.80	1.76	0.28	0.4928
			2.1	£0.80	1.68	0.4	0.6720
						1.0	1.7648
			2.8	£0.70	1.96	0.09	0.1764
			2.4	£0.70	1.68	0.21	0.3528
			2.3	£0.70	1.61	0.70	1.1270
						1.0	1.6562
			2.9	£0.60	1.74	1.0	1.74

Decision tree

and the range of contributions are:

£0.80 for a selling price of £1.20
£0.70 for a selling price of £1.10
£0.60 for a selling price of £1.00

A decision tree indicating the possible outcomes is presented on page 90. From the decision tree it can be seen that the expected value of the contribution is maximised at a selling price of £1.20. Fixed costs are common and unavoidable to all alternatives and are therefore not included in the analysis. However, management might prefer the certain contribution of £1.74 million at a selling price of £1.0. From columns 6 and 7 of the decision tree it can be seen that there is a 0.60 probability that contribution will be in excess of £1.74 million when a selling price of £1.20 is implemented. The final decision depends on management's attitude towards risk.

Answer to problem 12.11

(a)(i) See decision tree.

(ii)(1) The assumption underlying the maximin technique is that the worst outcome will occur. The decision-maker should select the outcome with the largest possible payoff. From the decision tree we can see that the payoffs for the worst possible outcomes are as follows:

	Payoff (£000's)
Hire machine 200	55
Hire machine 300	45
Hire machine 600	38.5
Do not franchise	90

The decision is not to franchise using the maximin criterion.
(2) The expected values for each alternative (see decision tree) are as follows:

	(£000's)
Hire of machine 200	87.0
Hire of machine 300	101.0
Hire of machine 600	99.0
Do not franchise	90.0

The company will maximise expected value of the contributions if it hires the 300 batch machine
(3) The probability of a contribution of less than £100,000 for each alternative can be found by adding the joint probabilities from payoffs of less than £100,000. The probabilities are as follows:

Hire of machine 200=0.85
Hire of machine 300=0.55
Hire of machine 600=0.65
Do not franchise   =1.00

The company should hire the 300 machine adopting this decision criterion.

(b) The approaches in part (A) enable uncertainty to be incorporated into the analysis and for decisions to be based on a range of outcomes rather than a single outcome. This approach should produce better decisions in the long-run. The main problem with this approach is that only a few selected outcomes with related probabilities are chosen as being representative of the entire distribution of possible outcomes.

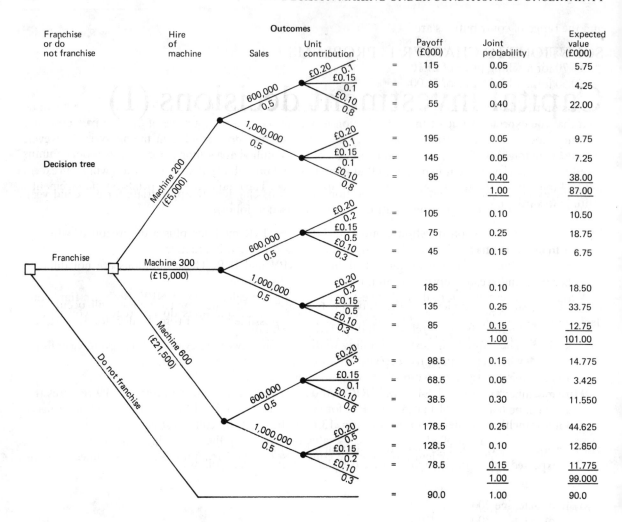

Franchise or do not franchise	Hire of machine	Sales	Outcomes Unit contribution		Payoff (£000)	Joint probability	Expected value (£000)
			£0.20 0.1	=	115	0.05	5.75
			£0.15 0.1	=	85	0.05	4.25
		600,000 0.5	£0.10 0.8	=	55	0.40	22.00
		1,000,000 0.5	£0.20 0.1	=	195	0.05	9.75
			£0.15 0.1	=	145	0.05	7.25
	Machine 200 (£5,000)		£0.10 0.8	=	95	0.40 1.00	38.00 87.00
Franchise	Machine 300 (£15,000)	600,000 0.5	£0.20 0.2	=	105	0.10	10.50
			£0.15 0.5	=	75	0.25	18.75
			£0.10 0.3	=	45	0.15	6.75
		1,000,000 0.5	£0.20 0.2	=	185	0.10	18.50
			£0.15 0.5	=	135	0.25	33.75
			£0.10 0.3	=	85	0.15 1.00	12.75 101.00
	Machine 600 (£21,500)	600,000 0.5	£0.20 0.3	=	98.5	0.15	14.775
			£0.15 0.1	=	68.5	0.05	3.425
			£0.10 0.6	=	38.5	0.30	11.550
		1,000,000 0.5	£0.20 0.5	=	178.5	0.25	44.625
			£0.15 0.2	=	128.5	0.10	12.850
			£0.10 0.3	=	78.5	0.15 1.00	11.775 99.000
Do not franchise				=	90.0	1.00	90.0

Decision tree

(See Flower (1971) listed in References and Further Reading in Chapter 12 for a detailed discussion of this topic.) The approach also gives the impression of accuracy which is not justified. Comments on the specific methods used in (A) are as follows:

Maximin: Enables an approach to be adopted which minimises risk. The main disadvantage is that such a risk averse approach will not result in decisions which will maximise long-run profits.

Expected value: For the advantages of this approach see 'Expected Value' in Chapter 12. The weaknesses of expected value are as follows:

(1) It ignores risk. Decisions should not be made on expected value alone. It should be used in conjunction with measures of dispersion.

(2) It is a long-run average payoff. Therefore it is best suited to repetitive decisions.

(3) Because it is an average it is unlikely that the expected value will occur.

Probability of earning an annual contribution of less than £100,000: This method enables decision-makers to specify their attitude towards risk and return and choose the alternative which meets the decision-makers risk-return preference. It is unlikely that this approach will be profit-maximising or result in expected value being maximised.

Capital investment decisions (1)

With the exception of 13.2 and 13.3 the questions set in this chapter are appropriate for a second year course. The questions (all ignoring taxation) are summarised as follows:

13.1   A discussion question comparing NPV and IRR methods plus a discussion of why the NPV method is not the most frequently used method in practice.

13.2 and 13.3   Questions requiring the calculation of NPV and IRR. These questions are not difficult and are appropriate as an introduction to discounting.

13.4 and 13.5   These are more difficult questions requiring the calculation of NPV. Both are time consuming requiring approximately one hour. These questions do not require you to distinguish between relevant and irrelevant cash flows.

13.6 and 13.7   These questions test your ability to distinguish between relevant and irrelevant cash flows when calculating the present values of alternative courses of action.

13.8   Comparison of two projects with unequal lives.

13.9 to 13.12   Comparison of NPV and IRR methods for mutually exclusive projects. 13.9 requires the construction of a graph of NPVs for various discount rates. 13.11 and 13.12 contain projects with two internal rates of return. 13.12 is the most difficult question.

13.13   Calculation of a break-even sales value incorporating the time value of money.

13.14   A difficult problem requiring the comparison of incremental costs and revenues so as to determine whether or not the sale of a press is justified.

Answer to problem 13.2

(a) The IRR is where:

$$\text{Annual cash inflows} \times \text{Discount factor} = \text{Investment cost}$$
$$\text{£4,000} \times \text{Discount factor} = \text{£14,000}$$
$$\therefore \text{Discount factor} = \frac{\text{£14,000}}{\text{£4,000}}$$
$$= 3.5$$

We now work along the five row table of the cumulative discount tables to find the discount rate with a discount factor closest to 3.5. This is 13%. Therefore the IRR is 13%.

(b) The annual savings necessary to achieve a 12% internal rate of return is where:

$$\text{Annual savings} \times 12\% \text{ Discount factor} = \text{Investment cost}$$
$$\text{i.e. Annual savings} \times 3.605 = \text{£14,000}$$
$$\therefore \text{Annual savings} = \frac{\text{£14,000}}{3.605}$$
$$= \text{£3,883}$$

(c) NPV is calculated as follows:

£4,000 received annually from years 1–5:

	£
£4,000 × 3.791 discount factor	15,164
Less investment cost	14,000
NPV	1,164

Answer to problem 13.5

(a) *Re-location option (88 employees)*

Costs	£
Interest free loan	88,000
Relocation grant (88 × £750)	66,000
Personnel costs (£15,000 × 0.89)	13,350
	167,350
Loan repayment:	
Leavers (say 9) 9,000 × 0.89	(8,010)
Others (say 79) 79,000 × 0.57	(45,030)
PV of costs	114,310

Benefits (based on 79 employees)

	£	
Saving in recruiting costs (79 × £50)		3,950
Increased production (79 × 12 × £120)	113,760	
Reduced rejects (79 × 6 × £80)	37,920	
	151,680 × 0.89	134,995
PV of benefits		138,945
NPV from relocation		24,635

Note

It is assumed that the cash flows for the loan, grant and recruiting costs occur at year 0. It is also assumed that the benefits from increased production and reduced rejects occur 1 year later. This assumption is incorrect but avoids the need to use mid-year discount tables. Using mid-year discount tables will not significantly alter the above NPV calculation.

Retraining (334 employees)

Costs	£
Cost of training course (334 × £180)	60,120
Administration costs	5,000
Salary (334 × £350 × 2)	233,800
	298,920

Benefits	
Recruitment cost: 70% × 334 × £50 (treated as an immediate saving)	11,690
Saving from loss of production	
(70% × 334 × £100 × 6 months discounted at 0.89)	124,849
	136,539
Net cost of retraining	162,381

The saving from loss of production is assumed to be received at the end of year 1 for discounting purposes.

Early retirement (40 employees)

40 × 2,500 × 3.60 discount factor (5 years)	£360,000

Redundancy (138 employees)

	£
Category P (70 employees × 15 weeks due × £90 per week)	94,500
Category Q (68 employees × 4 weeks due × £80 per week)	21,760
	116,260
Government refund (assumed immediate): 41% × 116,260	47,667
Net cost to the company	68,593

Summary of the total cost of the scheme

	£
Relocation	(24,635)
Retraining	162,381
Retirement	360,000
Redundancy	68,593
	566,339

Average cost per scheme employee (£566,339 ÷ 600)	£944

Redundancy cost of all employees

	£
Category P (396 employees × 15 weeks due × £90 per week)	534,600
Category Q (204 employees × 4 weeks due × £80 per week)	65,280
	599,880
Government refund of 41% (assumed immediate)	245,951
Net cost to the company	353,929
Average cost per employee	£590

Therefore the average cost per employee of the proposed scheme of £944 is less than twice the average redundancy cost (£590 × 2). Hence the proposed scheme is acceptable.

(b)(i) The non-financial benefits to the present employees are:
   A. They are given some element of personal choice.
   B. Employees with strong links with the company can maintain those links by accepting schemes 1 or 2.
   C. Employees can avoid the psychological effects of unemployment.
   D. Employees are given the opportunity to acquire different skills through retraining.

   (ii) The non-financial benefits to the company are:
   A. Industrial relations are not likely to deteriorate as much as the alternative of making all employees redundant.
   B. Less adverse publicity in terms of social responsibility.
   C. Maintaining employees who have strong links with the company.
   D. The morale of other employees might not suffer if they perceive the company to be a caring employer.

Answer to question 13.6

(a) The relevant cash flows and their assumed timing are shown below:

	Dec. 31 1983 Delivery Ship 1	Dec. 31 1984 Delivery Ship 2	Dec. 31 1985 Delivery Ship 3
Sales value	250	250	250
Labour costs	(132)	(145)	(160)
Redundancy cost saved (see part B)	132	—	—
Materials	(108)	(117)	—
Variable overhead	(11)	(12)	(13)
	131	(24)	77

The investment cost at time zero is £145,000 consisting of the foregone sales value of the shipyard (£120,000) and materials (£25,000). The present value calculations for each discount rate are as follows:

Cost of capital	12%	16%	20%
Present value of cash flows (000's)			
Year 1	117 (131×0.893)	113 (131×0.862)	109 (131×0.833)
Year 2	(19) (24×0.797)	(18) (24×0.743)	(17) (24×0.694)
Year 3	55 (77×0.712)	49 (77×0.641)	45 (77×0.579)
	153	144	137
Less investment cost	145	145	145
Net present value	8	(1)	(8)

At a cost of capital of 12% the shipyard should be kept open, but at 16% or 20% it should be closed.

(b)(i) The book value of the equipment is not relevant to the decision but the £120,000 selling price is relevant as the company will be deprived of this sales revenue if it continues to build ships.

(ii) The question states that redundancy payments are equal to one year's labour cost. It is assumed that the labour cost will be equal to the 1983 labour cost. For the purpose of discounting it is assumed that all labour costs are paid at the end of the year.

(iii) The relevant cost for the first ship is the foregone income from the sale of the stock materials. The relevant material costs for the second and third ships is the replacement price of the materials not in stock, suitably inflated for price rises.

(iv) Depreciation is not a relevant cost and head office costs will presumably be allocated to other ship-yards if this shipyard is closed down.

(v) The cost of capital is assumed to include a premium for inflation. Therefore the cash flows are also adjusted for inflation.

(c) The expected cost of capital is:

$(12\% \times 0.5) + (16\% \times 0.4) + (20\% \times 0.1) = 14.4\%$

and the revised NPV calculation is:

$$\frac{131}{1.144} + \frac{(24)}{(1.144)^2} + \frac{77}{(1.144)^3} - 145 = 2.7$$

Therefore the shipyard should be kept open.

An alternative approach is to construct a probability distribution using the calculations in (A):

NPV	Probability	Expected value
8	0.5	4
(1)	0.4	(0.4)
(8)	0.1	(0.8)
		2.8

Applying the expected value approach the project should be undertaken but management might prefer to examine the probability distribution. The decision will then depend on management's attitude to risk.

Answer to problem 13.8

The NPV calculations are as follows:

Purchase new automatic testing equipment (production director's suggestion)

Years 1 and 2 £12,000 × 1.7355 discount factor	= 20,826
Less investment cost	= 20,000
NPV	= 826

Terminate agency agreement (marketing director's suggestion

	£
Years 1 and 2 £1,300 × 1.7355 discount factor	= 2,256
Less investment cost	= 2,000
NPV	= 256

Purchasing the new automatic equipment yields an additional NPV of £570 and involves an additional investment of £18,000. The above comparisons are not comparable as they entail different investments. This can be overcome by considering how the unused funds of £18,000 will be invested assuming that the agency is terminated. If the funds can be invested to yield a NPV in excess of £570 then the agency agreement should be selected. Otherwise the new automatic equipment should be purchased. The indication in the question is that the surplus funds will be invested at the cost of capital of 10%. This will yield a zero NPV and the financial director is correct when he states that the funds invested should yield a return in excess of the target of 10%. A positive NPV will accrue only if the funds are invested in excess of 10%.

The production director is correct in stating that risk should be taken into account. The riskier the investment the greater the return demanded by investors. In other words the greater the risk the greater the discount rate. Therefore it is incorrect to use the average cost of capital as the discount rate if the projects in the question are not typical of the average risk of all the firm's investment projects. It appears that the purchase of the new automatic equipment is below average risk and that a discount rate of less than 10% should be used. This will increase the differential NPVs between the purchase of automatic equipment and the termination of the agency. Assuming that the firm does not foresee any alternative use of the unused funds of £18,000 in the future other than investing at 10% then the new automatic equipment should be purchased. It is assumed that no serious liquidity problems are likely to exist in the next two years.

Note that NPV has been used in the analysis. Because of the reasons described in Chapter 13 the NPV method is preferred to the IRR method.

Answer to problem 13.9

(a) The NPVs at various discount rates are as follows:

	10% £	20% £	30% £	35% £
Project X				
Year 1	727,200	666,400	615,200	592,800
Year 2	413,000	347,000	296,000	274,500
Year 3	225,300	173,700	136,500	121,800
	1,365,500	1,187,100	1,047,700	989,100
Investment cost	1,000,000	1,000,000	1,000,000	1,000,000
NPV	365,500	187,100	47,700	(10,900)
Project Y				
Year 1	90,900	83,300	76,900	
Year 2	247,800	208,200	177,600	
Year 3	1,126,500	868,500	682,500	
	1,465,200	1,160,000	937,000	
Investment cost	1,000,000	1,000,000	1,000,000	
NPV	465,200	160,000	(63,000)	

The above NPVs are plotted on the following graph:

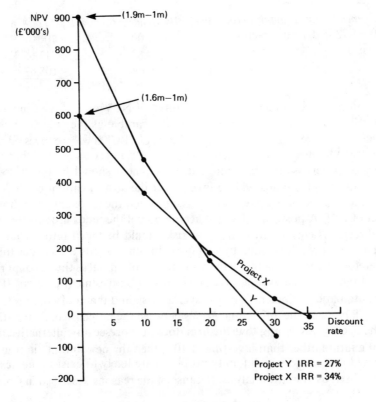

(b) The IRR of project X is 34% and the IRR of project Y is 27%.

(c) The graph indicates that the NPVs intersect at a discount rate of 18%. At a discount rate of less than 18% project Y yields the higher NPV but at a discount rate in excess of 18% project X yields the higher NPV.

(d) The following additional information would be useful in choosing between the two projects:
   (i) A probability distribution of the possible cash flows of each project.
   (ii) A consideration of whether either project will affect the firm's overall risk position. In other words the investment must be viewed within the context of the firm's overall portfolio of investments.
   (iii) An investigation as to whether or not the projects are mutually exclusive as both projects yield positive NPVs at a discount rate of 10% and 20%.
   (iv) A more accurate estimate of the cost of capital and consideration of whether the choice between projects will affect this.

(e) For a discussion of the relative merits of the NPV and IRR methods see 'Comparison of NPV and IRR' in Chapter 13.

Answer to problem 13.11

(a) *Alternative 1*
NPV:

Year	Cash flow (£000's)	Discount factor	PV (£000's)
0	−100	1.00	−100
1	+255	0.83	+211.65
2	−157.5	0.69	−108.675
		NPV =	2.975

IRR: The cash flow sign changes after year 1 which implies that the project will have two IRRs. Using the interpolation method the NPV will be zero at a cost of capital of 5% and 50%. Therefore the IRRs are 5% and 50%.

Alternative 2
NPV:

Year	Cash flow (£000's)	Discount factor	PV (£000's)
0	−50	1.00	−50
1	0	0.83	0
2	+42	0.69	+28.98
3	+42	0.58	+24.36
		NPV =	+ 3.34

IRR: At a 25% discount rate the project has a NPV of −1.616.
Using the interpolation formula:

$$IRR = 20 + \frac{3,340}{3,340 - (-1,616)} \times (25 - 20)$$

$$= 23.4\%$$

Summary

	NPV	IRR
Alternative 1	£2,975	5% or 50%
Alternative 2	£3,340	23.4%

(b) The projects are mutually exclusive and capital rationing does not apply. In these circumstances the NPV decision rule should be applied and Alternative 2 should be selected. Because of the reasons described in Chapter 13 the IRR method should not be used for evaluating mutually exclusive projects. Also note that Alternative 1 has two IRRs. Therefore the IRR method cannot be used to rank the alternatives.

Before a final decision is made the risk attached to each alternative should be examined. For example novelty products are generally high risk investments with short lives. Therefore Alternative 1 with a shorter life might be less risky. Other considerations include the possibility of whether the promotion of this novelty product will adversely affect the sales of the other products sold by the company. Also will the large expenditure on advertising for Alternative 1 have a beneficial effect on the sales of the company's other products?

(c) The answer should include a discussion of the payback method particularly the limitations which are discussed in Chapter 13. It should be stressed that payback can be a useful method of investment appraisal when liquidity is a problem and the speed of a project's return is particularly important. It is also claimed that payback allows for uncertainty in that it leads to the acceptance of projects with fast paybacks. This approach can be appropriate for companies whose products are subject to uncertain short lives. Therefore there might be an argument for using payback in Khan Ltd.

The second comment by Mr. Court concerns the relationship between reported profits and the NPV calculations. Projects ranked by the NPV method can give different rankings to projects which are ranked by their impact on the reported profits of the company. The NPV method results in the maximisation of the present value of future cash flows and is the correct decision rule. If investors give priority to reported profits in valuing shares (even if reported profits do not give an indication of the true economic performance of the company) then Mr. Court's comments on the importance of a project's impact on reported profits might lead to the acceptance of Alternative 1. However, if investors are aware of the deficiencies of published reported profits and are aware of the company's future plans and cash flows then share values will be based on PV of future cash flows. This is consistent with the NPV rule.

Capital investment decisions (2)

These questions are more difficult than those set in Chapter 13. Details are as follows:

14.1 to 14.3	These questions focus on the impact of taxation when calculating NPVs. 14.1 and 14.3 involve a lease or buy decision.
14.4	Single period capital rationing problem. See 22.10 to 22.12 in Chapter 22 for additional questions on single and multi-period capital rationing.
14.5	Impact of inflation on capital investment decisions. This question involves adjusting cash flows when differential rates of inflation occur.
14.6	Calculation of a minimum contract price using inflation adjustments and discounting.
14.7	Determining optimal replacement policy for a fleet of motor vehicles. This question also involves discounting and the adjustment of cash flows for inflation.
14.8	NPV calculation and sensitivity analysis. A good question for testing your understanding of sensitivity analysis.
14.9	NPV and IRR calculation plus the calculation of NPV using the simulation method of incorporating risk into the analysis.
14.10	A discussion of the risk adjusted required rate of return based on the principles of the capital asset pricing model.
14.11 to 14.14	Construction of a probability distribution of NPVs and the calculation of expected NPV. 14.11 is not a difficult question and is therefore an appropriate introduction to problems in this area. 14.14 requires the construction of a decision tree and is the most difficult question.
14.15	Calculation of expected NPV requiring the adjustment of cash flows for taxation payments.
14.16	An appraisal of an investment in a foreign country requiring the use of discounting and currency conversions.

Answer to problem 14.3

(a) The annual variable operating cost savings if the company manufactures material Kay are as follows:

Year	Savings per unit	No. of units (000's)	Total Savings (£000's)
1	5 (£20 − £15)	20	100
2	9 (£24 − £15)	20	180
3	10 (£25 − £15)	20	200
4	13 (£30 − £17)	10	130
5	18 (£35 − £17)	10	180

The cash inflows and outflows are shown in the following schedule.

	Year 0	Year 1	Year 2	Year 3	Year 4	Year 5	Year 6
		Cash inflows and outflows (£000's)					
Variable operating cost savings		100	180	200	130	180	
Handling costs saved		40	40	40	40	40	
Additional rates		(20)	(20)	(20)	(20)	(20)	
Total annual savings		120	200	220	150	200	
Tax on annual savings			(60)	(100)	(110)	(75)	(100)
Purchase of land	(120)					160	
Existing machine and tax	(80)	40				10	(5)
New machine and tax	(400)	200					
Net cash flow	(600	360	140	120	40	295	(105)
Discount factor at 15%	1.000	0.870	0.756	0.658	0.572	0.497	0.432
Present value	(600)	313.2	105.84	78.96	22.88	146.615	(45.36)

$$NPV = £22.135$$

Therefore the project is worthwhile.

(b) The relevant pre-tax discount rates for both methods of financing are 10%. Leasing reduces a firm's debt capacity and therefore the opportunity cost of capital is considered to be 10% pre tax. The after-tax cost of capital for both methods of financing is 5%. The present value for each method of financing is calculated as follows:

Purchase

	Year	(£000's)	Discount factor at 5%	PV (£000's)
Purchase of machine	0	400	1.000	400.00
Tax saving	1	(200)	0.952	(190.40)
			PV of cost	£209.60

Leasing

Year	Rentals (£000's)	Tax (£000's)	Net cash flow (£000's)	Discount factor at 5%	PV (£000's)
0	60		60	1.000	60.00
1	100	(30)	70	0.952	66.64
2	100	(50)	50	0.907	45.35
3	100	(50)	50	0.864	43.20
4	100	(50)	50	0.823	41.15
5		(50)	(50)	0.784	(39.20)
				PV of cost	£217.14

Therefore purchase is less expensive than leasing.

(c) Here the tax benefits will not affect cash flows until year 3. Using the same discount rates as before the PV of leasing and purchase are as follows:

Purchase

	Year	(£000's)	PVF at 5%	PV (£000's)
Purchase of machine	0	400	1.000	400.00
Tax saving	3	(200)	0.864	(172.80)
			PV of costs	£227.20

Leasing

Year	Rentals (£000's)	Tax (£000's)	Net cash flow (£000's)	PVF at 5%	PV (£000's)
0	60		60	1.000	60.00
1	100		100	0.952	95.20
2	100		100	0.907	90.70
3	100	(130)	(30)	0.864	(25.92)
4	100	(50)	50	0.823	41.15
5		(50)	(50)	0.784	(39.20)
				PV of costs	£221.93

Because of the impact of the tax delay, leasing proves to be the less expensive alternative *at the discount rates used.*

(d)(i) The merit of Turnbull's policy is that it has established a formal policy for evaluating capital investment decisions. The main danger of it's policy is that all projects are appraised initially as if they are to be purchased. If a project fails this test then it is not considered for leasing. However, it is possible that a project which is not worthwhile if purchased will be worthwhile if leased but with Turnbull's system this will never be determined.

(ii) The tax delay differs between the circumstances between (b) and (c) in the early years of the analysis. In (b) the delay is one year throughout whereas in (c) the delay varies but after year 2 reverts to one year. The greater the tax delay the less is the impact of the tax deductability of debt interest and therefore the higher will be the effective after-tax rate of the debt interest. Therefore different after-tax discount rates should be used for circumstances (b) and (c).

One solution to the problem is to use the pre-tax rates of 10% and then include the discounted value of cash savings caused by the tax savings from the debt interest. This method is called the 'Adjusted Present Value Approach'. For a discussion of this approach see Brearley, R. and Myers, S. 'Principles of Corporate Finance' Chapter 19, McGraw-Hill (1981).

Answer to problem 14.4

(a) It is assumed that investment funds are restricted to one period only. Applying the procedure suggested in Chapter 14, the projects are ranked according to the profitability index. The profitability index is calculated by dividing the present value of the projects' cash flows by the investment cost. The present values of the projects are calculated as follows:

	£
Project A: PV of returns for 6 years (£72,500 × 3.685)	= 267,163
Project B: PV of returns for 5 years with one year's delay £30,000 × (3.685 − 0.862)	= 84,690
Project C: PV of returns for 3 years (£45,000 × 2.246)	= 101,070
Project D: PV of returns for 8 years (£57,000 × 4.344)	= 247,608
Project E: PV of returns for 4 years (£70,000 × 2.798)	= 195,860
Project F: PV of returns for 7 years (£36,000 × 4.039)	= 145,404

The profitability index for each project is:

$$\text{Project A} \quad \frac{£267,613}{£250,000} = 1.07$$

$$\text{Project B} \quad \frac{£84,690}{£70,000} = 1.21$$

$$\text{Project C} \quad \frac{£101,070}{£110,000} = 0.92$$

$$\text{Project D} \quad \frac{£247,608}{£210,000} = 1.18$$

$$\text{Project E} \quad \frac{£195,860}{£170,000} = 1.15$$

$$\text{Project F} \quad \frac{£145,404}{£135,000} = 1.08$$

The projects are ranked as follows: B, D, E, F and A which cost respectively £70,000, £210,000, £170,000, £135,000 and £250,000. Project C should be rejected as the profitability index is less than 1. Accepting the first four projects will entail an investment of £585,000. Because the full amount of the £600,000 funds available for investment is not used up it is possible to experiment by introducing project A and dropping two other projects. However, total present value is not increased by adopting this substitution process. Therefore the optimal solution is to undertake projects B, D, E and F.

(b) Other factors which should be taken into account include:
 (i) Risk: Are the cash flows from each project equally risky?
 (ii) Inflation: Will all the projects be affected equally by inflation?
(iii) Interdependence: Do all the projects show the same relative movements with changes in the economy? A portfolio approach should be considered. One does not want all the projects to do equally badly in a slump and equally as well in a boom. Risk is reduced if some projects do well when others do badly and vice versa. Therefore the correct balance of projects should be selected.
(iv) Qualitative factors: How much weighting should be given to qualitative factors? Project C involves expenditure on safety equipment. Management might consider that the qualitative factors outweigh the negative NPV.
 (v) Do all the projects have to be undertaken now? Is it possible to undertake A in later years? If not can other projects be delayed to enable A to be undertaken now?
(vi) Future constraints: Will capital rationing apply to other periods? Projects with high cash flows in early years might enable additional projects to be undertaken later.

Answer to problem 14.5

(a) All cash flows are assumed to arise on the last day of the year to which they relate. Therefore a cash flow for the year in which production begins is assumed to be received at the end of year 2. (Note that production begins one year from now). Consequently cash flows at the end of year 2 are subject to two years compound inflation rate as the receipts and payments in the question are expressed at current prices at the start of year 1. The calculations are as follows:

(1) *Contribution from sales before labour cost*
Labour costs are excluded from this calculation as they are subject to a different rate of inflation. At current prices the contribution per unit is:

	£
Selling price	35
Materials	(8)
Variable cost	(4)
Contribution (before labour)	23

Production will start in one years time and the first cash flow will be received at the end of year 1 (Year 2 for discounting purposes). The cash flows are as follows:

$$£$$
$$\text{Year 2: } 5,000 \times £23 \ (1.10)^2 = 139,150$$
$$3: 5,000 \times £23 \ (1.10)^3 = 153,065$$
$$4: 5,000 \times £23 \ (1.10)^4 = 168,371$$
$$5: 2,500 \times £23 \ (1.10)^5 = \ \ 92,604$$
$$6: 2,500 \times £23 \ (1.10)^6 = 101,865$$

(2) *Calculation of labour costs*
This is a relevant cost as the six employees would not be paid if the Oakman were not produced.

$$£$$
$$\text{Year 2: } 5,000 \times 2 \text{ hrs} \times £3 \ (1.15)^2 = 39,675$$
$$3: 5,000 \times 2 \text{ hrs} \times £3 \ (1.15)^3 = 45,626$$
$$4: 5,000 \times 2 \text{ hrs} \times £3 \ (1.15)^4 = 52,470$$
$$5: 2,500 \times 2 \text{ hrs} \times £3 \ (1.15)^5 = 30,171$$
$$6: 2,500 \times 2 \text{ hrs} \times £3 \ (1.15)^6 = 34,696$$

(3) *Redundancy payments*
If the Oakman is produced the company will avoid redundancy payments of £20,700 (6 men × 1,000 hrs × £3 (1.15)) at the end of year 1 but three employees will be made redundant at the end of the third year of the project's life (i.e. four years from now). The redundancy payment will be £15,741 (3 men × 1,000 hrs × £3 $(1.15)^4$).

(4) *Purchase and maintenance of machine*
The purchase price of the machine in one year's time will be £209,000 (£190,000 × 1.10). The overhaul in respect of the machine at the end of the second year of it's life (three years from now) will be £79,860 (60,000 $(1.10)^3$).

Statement of cash flows

Year	1	2	3	4	5	6	7
Contribution from sales before labour cost		139,150	153,065	168,371	92,604	101,865	
Labour cost		−39,675	−45,626	−52,470	−30,171	−34,696	
Redundancy payments				−15,741			
Redundancy payments avoided	20,700						
Purchase of special machine	−209,000						
Machine overhaul			−79,860				
	−188,300	99,475	27,579	100,160	62,433	67,169	0
Taxation at 52% (see note 1)		97,916	−51,727	−14,341	−52,083	−32,465	−34,928
Net money cash flow	−188,300	197,391	−24,148	85,819	10,350	34,704	−34,928
Discount factors at 20%	0.83	.69	0.58	0.48	0.40	0.33	0.28
Present value of annual cash flows	−156,289	136,200	−14,006	41,193	4,140	11,452	−9,780

NPV = £12,910

Bailey Ltd should undertake production of the Oakman as it yields a positive NPV of £12,910.

Notes

(1) In this question taxation is payable on net *cash* income. Therefore incremental tax is 52% of the incremental cash flows in the above schedule. The payment is lagged by one year and the first year allowance is assumed to be used in the year following capital expenditure.

(2) Head office apportioned fixed overheads are not a relevant cost. The apportionment of the machine cost and overhaul are already included in the cash flows. Consequently the apportionments are not included in the analysis.

(3) The discount rate includes a premium for inflation. Therefore the cash flows are adjusted for inflation.

(b) The investment appraisal problems caused by the existence of high rates of inflation are as follows:
  (i) Inflation adds to the uncertainty of the cash flows and the discount rate calculation.
 (ii) With different inflation rates applying to different items (e.g. labour and materials) the cash flows will be highly sensitive to changes in inflation.
(iii) Inflation expectations are unlikely to remain constant over a project's life. Consequently the discount rate is unlikely to be constant over the project's life.
(iv) The introduction of government controls at high rates of inflation will restrict the ability to pass on the price increases of the inputs by increasing selling prices.

Answer to problem 14.8

(a) *Preliminary calculations*   £

Contribution per unit:	Selling price	22.00
	Materials and labour	(9.50)
	Variable overheads	(2.50)
		10.00

Annual contribution: 10,000 units at £10 per unit = £100,000.

Feasibility study: This is a sunk cost and not relevant to the decision.

Factory rental: This cost (£8,000) is avoidable if Azams are not produced. Therefore it is a relevant cost.

Managers salary: This is an avoidable cost of £7,000 p.a. less a cost saving of £2,000 p.a. Therefore the relevant cost is £5,000 p.a.

NPV calculation

Annual net cash inflows are £87,000 (£100,000 − £13,000)

PV of £87,000 for five years = £376,710 (£87,000 × 4.33)

Less investment cost =	£250,000
NPV	£126,710

On the basis of the NPV decision rule the project should be undertaken.

(b) *Product life*

Let x = product's life.

NPV is zero where £87,000x = £250,000

$$\therefore x = \frac{£250,000}{£87,000}$$

$$= 2.874$$

At a 5% discount rate we find the number of years which will have a discount factor of 2.874. From the cumulative tables:

5% for 3 years = 2.723
5% for 4 years = 3.546

$$\therefore \text{Number of years} = 3 + \frac{2.874 - 2.723}{3.546 - 2.723} (4 - 3 \text{ years})$$

$$= 3.18 \text{ years}$$

Therefore the product's life can fall by approximately 1.82 years before the project will yield a negative NPV. This represents a decline of approximately 36%.

Annual sales volume

Contribution per unit = £10

Annual rental = £8,000

Annual salary = £5,000

Let x = annual sales volume

NPV will be zero where:

£10x (4.33) − £8,000 (4.33) − £5,000 (4.33) − £250,000 = 0

$$\therefore\ 43.3x - 34,640 - 21,650 - 250,000 = 0$$
$$\therefore\ 43.3x = 306,290$$
$$\therefore\ x = \frac{306,290}{43.3}$$
$$= 7,074\ \text{units}$$

Note that 4.33 in the above calculations represents the discount factor for five years.

Therefore annual sales volume can fall by approximately 2,926 units or 29% before the project will produce a negative NPV.

Material cost per Azam

The material cost per unit used in the above calculation is £4.50. Therefore the unit contribution without material costs is £14.50. The annual total contribution without material costs is £145,000.

Let x = Total annual material costs
∴ NPV will be zero where
$$£145,000\ (4.33) - £13,000\ (4.33) - £250,000 - x(4.33) = 0$$
$$\therefore\ £627,850 - £56,290 - £250,000 - £4.33x = 0$$
$$\therefore\ 321,560 = 4.33x$$
$$\therefore\ x = \frac{321,560}{4.33}$$
$$= £74,263$$

This represents a material cost per unit of £7.43 (£74,263 ÷ 10,000 units). Therefore the material cost per unit can increase by £2.93 (£7.43 − £4.50) or 65% before the project will yield a negative NPV.

(c) The analysis in (a) ignores long-term marketing implications. For example will the product open up new markets with prospects for further expansion. Also will it result in a reduction or expansion of the sales of existing products? The analysis ignores taxation which can have an important effect on cash flows. In addition the analysis fails to incorporate uncertainty. For example estimates of the future sales volume, product life, material and labour costs and the rate of inflation are included in the calculations in (a). The actual values of each of these variables may be different from the estimated values. In order to overcome such problems sensitivity analysis has been used in (b). However, this approach has a number of limitations. For a discussion of these limitations see 'Sensitivity Analysis' in Chapter 14.

It would be helpful if probability distributions could be produced for the various cash flow outcomes and an indication from a risk point of view of how total company risk will be affected when this project is combined with the company's existing projects. In other words a portfolio theory approach is required indicating whether or not the risk of the project is low, medium or high when it is combined with the company's existing projects.

Answer to problem 14.9

(a) The NPV calculations for discount rates of 10%, 30% and 40% are as follows:

Year	Cash flow (£000's)	10% Discount factor (£000's)		30% Discount factor (£000's)		40% Discount factor (£000's)	
1984	(500)	0.91	(455)	0.77	(385)	0.71	(355)
1985	(500)	0.83	(415)	0.59	(295)	0.51	(255)
1986	600	0.75	450	0.46	276	0.36	216
1987	600	0.68	408	0.35	210	0.26	156
1988	600	0.62	372	0.27	162	0.19	114
1989	600	0.56	336	0.21	126	0.13	78
		NPV	696	NPV	94	NPV	(46)

Applying the interpolation method:

$$A + \frac{C}{C-D} \times (B-A)$$

where A = Discount rate of the low trial
   B = Discount rate of the high trial
   C = NPV of cash inflow of low trial
   D = NPV of cash inflow of high trial

Hence $30\% + \dfrac{94}{94-(-46)} \times (40-30) = 36.7\%$

 (i) IRR = 36.7%
(ii) NPV = £696,000
Note that the cash flows are expressed in 1983 pounds and the discount rate does not include a premium for inflation.

(b) The following items could be tested for sensitivity:
   (i) Effect of variations in capital investment cost.
   (ii) Amount of cash flows (inflows and outflows).
   (iii) Effect of delays in bringing the project into production.
   (iv) Effect of the variations in the life of the project.
   (v) Timing of cash flows.

(c)(i) Random no.	Investment cost (£000's)	Random no.	Income (£000's)	Random no.	Costs (£000's)
0–09	450	0–09	650	0–09	170
10–59	500	10–24	700	10–29	185
60–89	550	25–49	750	30–69	200
90–96	600	50–84	800	70–89	215
97–99	650	85–99	850	90–99	230

Random number 35 for plant = £500,000 investment cost
Random number 06 for income = £650,000 for income
Random number 93 for costs = £230,000 for costs

The net present value of the above cash flows is calculated as follows:

Year	Cash flow	Discount factor	PV
	(£000's)		(£000's)
1984	(500)	0.91	(455)
1985	(500)	0.83	(415)
1986	420 (650 – 230)	0.75	315
1987	420	0.68	286
1988	420	0.62	260
1989	420	0.56	235
		NPV	226

The above calculation would represent one run from a large number of computer runs.
(ii) For the advantages of the simulation method see 'Simulation' in Chapter 14.

Answer to problem 14.10

(a) The answer should stress that there is a relationship between risk and the required rate of return (discount rate). The capital asset pricing model specifies that there is a linear relationship between risk and the discount rate. The relationship is shown in the following diagram:

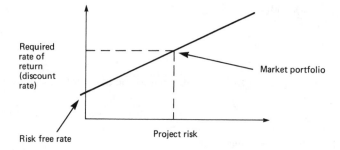

According to the capital asset pricing model the benchmark investment for determining the required rate of return for an investment is the market portfolio consisting of an investment in the equivalent of all UK risky securities. The FT 500 index can be used as a proxy for investing in the market portfolio. Based on a knowledge of the required rate of return and risk (measured in terms of the standard deviation of the returns) of the market portfolio, all other investments are related to this risk and return. This process can be illustrated from the information given in the question:

> The risk premium over the risk free rate for investing in the market portfolio $= 5\%$
> The required rate of return for a risk free investment $\qquad = 10\%$

An investment twice as risky as the market portfolio will attract a risk premium of 10% ($2 \times 5\%$) and the overall required rate of return is equal to the risk free rate (10%) plus a risk premium (10%). Therefore the required rate of return is 20%. Alternatively if an investment is half as risky as the market portfolio the risk premium will be $2\frac{1}{2}\%$ ($\frac{1}{2} \times 5\%$) and the overall required rate of return will be $12\frac{1}{2}\%$.

The implication of the capital asset pricing model for the project quoted in the question is that the projects returns are 1.6 times more variable than the average project for the economy as a whole (see note (iii) in the question). In other words the project is 1.6 times more risky than the market portfolio. Therefore the risk premium required for this project is 8% (1.6 × 5% market portfolio risk premium) and when this is added to the risk free required rate of return, the required rate of return will be 18%. This discount rate of 18% should be applied to the expected value of the cash flows and if the NPV is positive then the project should be accepted.

The use of a single overall discount rate of 16% (the weighted average cost of capital) for all projects does not allow for the differing risks of each project. Such an approach is appropriate only when a project's risk is equal to the average risk of all the firm's investment projects.

(b) For a discussion of alternative methods of allowing for risk in project appraisal see 'Risk and Uncertainty' in Chapter 14.

Answer to problem 14.14

(a) If the survey is not undertaken then the following decisions should be made:
   (i) Should the drilling rights be purchased? [Decision point 1 in the Decision Tree]
   (ii) Should oil be extracted? [Decision points 2, 3 and 4 in the Decision Tree]
Decision (ii) must be made before decision (i) can be considered. The sequence of decisions, possible outcomes and resulting cash flows is shown in the following decision tree:

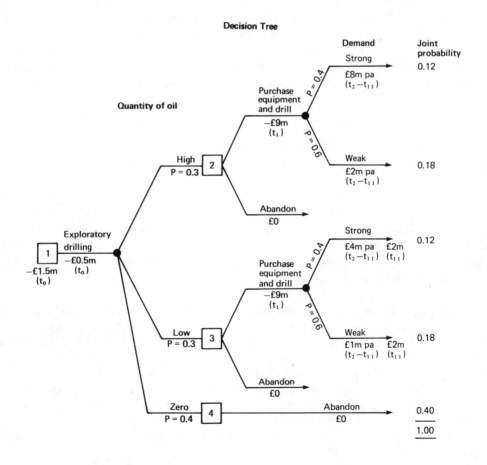

Decision Tree

The NPVs for each of decision points 2, 3 and 4 *at time 1* are as follows:

Decision point 2: High oil quantity

(£8m p.a. × 4.19 discount factor × 0.4) + (£2m p.a. × 4.19 × 0.6) − £9m

NPV = £9.44m

Decision point 3: Low oil quantity

(£4m p.a. × 4.19 × 0.4) + (£1m p.a. × 4.19 × 0.6) + (£2m × 0.16) − £9m

NPV = £0.54m

Decision point 4: Zero oil

NPV = 0

On the basis of the above information drilling and oil extraction should be undertaken if the exploratory drilling indicates that oil is present. Clearly the drilling will not be undertaken if no oil is present. Note that each of the above decisions are taken at t_1 (∴ t_0 for discounting purposes). Therefore expenditure at t_0 will be a sunk cost at t_1.

We can now calculate the expected value PV of decision 1 *at t_0*. The calculation is as follows:

$$(£9.44m × 0.83 × 0.3) + (£0.54m × 0.83 × 0.3) − £1.5m − £0.5m$$
$$∴ \text{ Expected NPV} = £0.48m$$

Note that 0.83 is the discount factor for 20% for 1 year. On the basis of the expected NPV decision rule the drilling rights should be purchased. Note that the above calculations convert the t_1 NPVs calculated earlier to t_0 NPVs and that the probabilities of each outcome if the drilling is undertaken are 0.3.

(b) The maximum value the company should place on the survey is equal to the difference between the expected NPV with the survey and the expected NPV without the survey.

At t_0 the purchase of the drilling rights are a relevant cost. Therefore with perfect information drilling will not be undertaken if the survey indicates that the quantity of oil present is low as the costs (with the purchase of the rights) will be in excess of the expected PV of the cash inflows. Therefore the expected NPV with the survey will be as follows:

$$(£9.44m × 0.83 × 0.30) − (0.3 × £1.5m) = £1.9m$$

Note that exploratory drilling will not be necessary if the survey is undertaken.

∴ Value of survey = (expected NPV with survey) − (expected NPV without survey)

= (£1.9m) − (£0.48m)

= £1.42m

(c) The limitations of expected present values as a criterion for making investment decisions are as follows:

(i) The assigning of probabilities to individual outcomes is subjective and different probabilities will yield different expected values. Ideally probabilities should be derived from observations of a large number of trials of similar projects. It is unlikely that similar projects have been repeated in the past.

(ii) Expected values are average outcomes and do not indicate the risk associated with the decision. There is a need to consider the dispersion of the distribution so that the range of possible outcomes can be identified. The actual range of possible outcomes is not indicated in the expected value calculation.

(iii) The interpretation of expected values is based on the principle that if the project was undertaken many times then the average result will tend towards the expected value. It is unlikely that capital projects will be undertaken more than once and therefore there is a strong chance that the actual result will not tend towards the expected value.

(iv) Because expected value does not measure risk it is not possible for the company to assess the risk-return trade-off.

SOLUTIONS TO CHAPTER 15 PROBLEMS

The budgeting process

15.1 to 15.8 are appropriate questions for a first year course and 15.9 to 15.18 for a second year course. Details of the questions are:

15.1 to 15.5	Preparation of functional budgets.
15.6 to 15.9	Preparation of cash budgets.
15.10	Construction of a model in the form of equations for the preparation of a cash budget.
15.11	Preparation of a budgeted profit statement for the trustees of a public hall. Approximately two hours are needed to complete this question.
15.12	Preparation of a manpower budget and evaluation of alternative budget proposals.
15.13 to 15.18	Various discussion questions relevant to the topics covered in Chapter 15.

Answer to problem 15.2

The calculation of the standard cost and selling price for each product is as follows:

	Aye £	Bee £
Direct material cost	128	160
Direct wages	60	40
Production overhead (see note 1):		
16 hours at £12	192	
10 hours at £12		120
Production cost	380	320
Other overheads	76	64
Total cost	456	384
Profit margin $\left(\dfrac{20}{100-20}\times \text{total cost}\right)$	114	96
Selling price	570	480

Note

(1) Production overhead absorption rate $=\dfrac{£900,000}{75,000 \text{ hours}}=£12$ per hour

(a) *Production budget* (*units*)

	Aye	Bee
Sales	2,400 (£1,368,000 ÷ £570)	3,200 (£1,536,000 ÷ £480)
plus:		
Closing stocks	$\frac{500}{2,900}$ £190,000 ÷ £380)	$\frac{1,100}{4,300}$ (£352,000 ÷ £320)
less:		
Opening stocks	(400) (£152,000 ÷ £380)	(800) (£256,000 ÷ £320)
Production required	2,500	3,500

(b) *Purchases budget*

	X kilos	Y kilos	Z kilos
Materials			
Production:			
Aye—2,500 units	60,000	25,000	12,500
Bee—3,500 units	105,000	28,000	35,000
	165,000	53,000	47,500
plus:			
Closing stocks	35,000	27,000	12,500
	200,000	80,000	60,000
less:			
Opening stocks	(30,000)	(25,000)	(12,000)
Purchases required (kilos)	170,000	55,000	48,000
Cost per kilo	£2	£5	£6
Purchase cost	£340,000	275,000	£288,000

Total purchases = £903,000

(c) *Production cost budget*

	Aye	Bee	Total
Production (units)	2,500	3,500	—
	£	£	£
Direct materials:			
X at £2 per kilo	120,000	210,000	330,000
Y at £5 per kilo	125,000	140,000	265,000
Z at £6 per kilo	75,000	210,000	285,000
	320,000	560,000	880,000
Direct wages:			
Unskilled at £3 per hour	75,000	52,500	127,500
Skilled at £5 per hour	75,000	87,500	162,500
	150,000	140,000	290,000
Production overhead:			
Direct labour hour rate (£12 per hour)	480,000	420,000	900,000
Production cost	950,000	1,120,000	2,070,000

Answer to problem 15.4

(a) *Production budget (units) and material purchases budget*

	K	B	Total
Budgeted sales	3,000	4,500	
Add closing stock (1)	750	1,500	
	3,750	6,000	
Less anticipated opening stock	1,050	1,200	
Production requirements	2,700	4,800	
Material consumption	6 kilos	2 kilos	
Material requirements (production budget)	16,200 kilos	9,600 kilos	25,800
Add closing stock (2)			4,300
			30,100
Less opening stock			3,700
Total materials to be purchased (kilos)			26,400
Budgeted material cost per kilo			£3
Total materials to be purchased (£)			£79,200

Notes

(1) There are 60 days in an accounting period. The budged sales quantities per day are 50 units for K ($3,000 \div 60$) and 75 ($4,500 \div 60$) units for B. Therefore the budged closing stocks are as follows:

K = 15 days at 50 units per day = 750 units
B = 20 days at 75 units per day = 1,500 units

(2) 10 days consumption at 430 kilos ($25,800 \div 60$) per day

Direct wages budget

	K	B	Total
Budgeted production (see production budget)	2,700 units	4,800 units	
Standard hours per unit	5	3	
Budgeted production in standard hours	13,500	14,400	27,900
Budgeted production *input* hours worked			31,000

$$\left(\frac{100}{90} \times 27,900\right)$$

Add budgeted downtime ($20\% \times 31,000$)	6,200
Total attendance hours required	37,200

Budgeted wages paid:	£
Normal time (65 workers $\times$ 40 hrs $\times$ 12 weeks = 31,200 hours) at £4	124,800
Overtime ($37,200 - 31,200 = 6,000$ hours) at £6	36,000
Total budgeted wages paid	160,800

(b) The following additional information is required:
 (i) Payment terms offered by each supplier.
(ii) Intervals when wages are paid.
(iii) Timing of payments deducted from employees to be paid to relevant authorities.

(iv) Analysis of wages paid each week during the period if production, overtime etc. are not constant each week.

(v) Analysis of total purchases on a weekly basis.

Answer to problem 15.7

(a)(i) Cash budget for weeks 1–6

Week	1	2	3	4	5	6
	£	£	£	£	£	£
Receipts from debtors (see note 1)	24,000	24,000	28,200	25,800	19,800	5,400
Payments:						
To material suppliers (see note 3)	8,000	12,500	6,000	0	0	0
To direct workers (see note 4)	3,200	4,200	2,800	0	0	0
For variable overheads (see note 5)	4,800	3,200	0	0	0	0
For fixed overheads (see note 6)	8,300	8,300	6,800	6,800	6,800	6,800
Total payments	24,300	28,200	15,600	6,800	6,800	6,800
Net movement	(300)	(4,200)	12,600	19,000	13,000	(1,400)
Opening balance (week 1 given)	1,000	700	(3,500)	9,100	28,100	41,100
Closing balance	700	(3,500)	9,100	28,100	41,100	39,700

Notes

(1) Debtors

Weeks	1	2	3	4	5	6
Units sold (note 2)	400	500	400	300	—	—
Sales (£)	24,000	30,000	24,000	18,000	—	—
Cash received (70%)		16,800	21,000	16,800	12,600	—
(30%)			7,200	9,000	7,200	5,400
Given	24,000	7,200				
Total receipts (£)	24,000	24,000	28,200	25,800	19,800	5,400

(2) Sales in week 4 = Opening stock (600 units) + Production in weeks 1 and 2(1,000 units) less sales in weeks 1–3 (1,300 units) = 300 units

(3) Creditors

Week	1	2	3	4	5	6
	£	£	£			
Materials consumed at £15	9,000	6,000	—	—	—	—
Increase in stocks	3,500	—				
Materials purchased	12,500	6,000				
Payment to suppliers	8,000	12,500	6,000	0	0	0
	(given)					

(4) Wages	1	2	3	4	5	6
	£	£	£			
Wages consumed at £7	4,200	2,800	0	0	0	0
Wages paid	3,200	4,200	2,800	—	—	—
	(given)					

(5) Variable overhead payment = budgeted production × budgeted cost per unit

(6) Fixed overhead payments for weeks 1–2 = fixed overhead per week (£9,000) less weekly depreciation (£700).

Fixed overhead payments for weeks 3–6 = £8,300 normal payment less £1,500 per week

(ii) *Comments*

(a) Finance will be required to meet the cash deficit in week 2 but a lowering of the budgeted material stocks at the end of week 1 would reduce the amount of cash to be borrowed at the end of week 2.

(b) The surplus cash after the end of week 2 should be invested on a short-term basis.

(c) After week 6 there will be no cash receipts but cash outflows will be £6,800 per week. The closing balance of £39,700 at the end of week 6 will be sufficient to finance outflows for a further 5/6 weeks (£39,700 ÷ £6,800 per week).

(b) The answer should include a discussion of the matching concept emphasising that revenues and expenses may not be attributed to the period when the associated cash inflows and outflows occur. Also some items of expense do not affect cash outflow (e.g. depreciation).

Answer to problem 15.10

(a) Let t equal month for which forecast is required so that:

$$t_0 = \text{Current month}$$
$$t_1 = \text{Next month}$$
$$t_{-1} = \text{Previous month}$$

Let S equal the sales for the current month.

The equations for use in the cash budgeting model are as follows:

$$\text{Sales} = S(1.01)^t$$

Cost of sales = 0.75 S (gross profit margin is $33\frac{1}{3}\%$ on cost of sales. Therefore cost of sales is 75% of sales)

Cash collections t month from now:

$$0.2S\,(1.01)^t + 0.8\,(0.2S\,(1.01)^{t-1}) + 0.8\,(0.6S\,(1.01)^{t-2}) + 0.8(0.2S(1.01)^{t-3})$$

Purchases t months from now:

$$0.75S\,(1.01)^{t+2}$$

Payments for purchases t months from now:

$$0.75S\,(1.01)^{t+1}$$

Payment for expenses t months from now:

$$0.05S\,(1.01)^{t-1} + 3,000 + 10,000$$

(b) S for June = £100,000

$$t = 3 \text{ (month of September is } t+3 \text{ months from June)}$$

Collections during September:

$$0.2S\,(1.01)^t + 0.8\,(0.2S\,(1.01)^{t-1}) + 0.8\,(0.6S\,(1.01)^{t-2}) + 0.8\,(0.2S\,(1.01)^{t-3})$$
$$= 0.2\,(100,000)(1.01)^3 + 0.8\,(0.2)(100,000)(1.01)^2 + 0.8\,(0.6)(100,000)(1.01) + 0.8\,(0.2)(100,000)$$
$$= £20,606 + £16,322 + £48,480 + £16,000$$
$$= £101,408$$

Payments for purchases during September:

$$0.75S\,(1.01)^{t+1}$$
$$=0.75\,(100,000)(1.01)^4$$
$$=\pounds78,045$$

Payment for expenses during September:

$$=0.05S\,(1.01)^2+3,000+10,000$$
$$=\pounds5,100+\pounds3,000+\pounds10,000=\pounds18,100$$

The cash flow statement for September is as follows:

	£	£
Receipts from sales		101,408
Payments: Purchases	78,045	
Payroll	5,100	
Utilities	3,000	
Other costs	10,000	96,145
Increase in cash		5,263

(c) The following procedures can be applied to incorporate uncertainty:
 (i) Sensitivity analysis
(ii) Expected values
(iii) Simulation
For an explanation of each of the above items see Chapter 14. The most simple approach for cash budgeting is to apply sensitivity analysis. By asking 'what if' questions such as changes in percentages for cash received each month from debtors, or changes in sales growth, the variability of possible outcomes can be ascertained.

Answer to problem 15.13

See 'Incremental and Zero-Base Budgeting' in Chapter 15 for a description of zero-base budgeting and an explanation of how it differs from other more traditional forms of budgeting. In profit orientated organisations those costs which are of a discretionary nature such as service and support activities are appropriate candidates for zero-base budgeting. Examples of departments which fall into this category include personnel, research and development, accounts, data processing etc.

Answer to problem 15.14

(a/b) See 'Incremental and Zero-Base Budgeting' in Chapter 15 for the answer to this question.

(c) It is preferable to introduce zero-base budgeting selectively rather than introducing it 'across the board'. The approach should initially be applied to those activities where immediate benefits are likely. This might lead to a greater acceptance by its users. Care should be taken in selecting the activities to which zero-base budgeting is to be applied. In Chapter 15 you will have noted that it is best suited to non-manufacturing activities and non-profit making organisations. When the system is introduced, meetings and seminars should be arranged explaining the principles of zero-base budgeting. Because zero-base budgeting is costly and time-consuming there are strong arguments for selective ad hoc applications which are likely to yield benefits. It is unlikely that a universal application of zero-base budgeting in an organisation can be justified.

Answer to problem 15.15

(a/b) See 'Incremental and Zero-Base Budgeting' in Chapter 15 for the answer to this question.

(c) The problems that might be met in introducing zero-base budgeting include:
  (i) The implementation of zero-base budgeting might be resisted by staff. Traditional incremental budgeting tends to protect the empire that a manager has built. Zero-base budgeting challenges this empire and so there is a strong possibility that managers might resist the introduction of such a system.
 (ii) There is a need to combat a feeling that current operations are efficient.
(iii) The introduction of zero-base budgeting is time-consuming.
 (iv) Lack of top-management support.

(d) See 'Incremental and Zero-Base Budgeting' in Chapter 15 for the answer to this question.

Answer to problem 15.16

(a) Corporate planning can be defined as 'The systematic study of *long-term* objectives and the strategies required to achieve them. Budgeting is the preparation of detailed financial and/or quantitative statements which are drawn up and approved prior to a defined period of time (normally one year). For a comparison of the aims and main features of corporate planning and budgeting systems see 'Stages in the Planning Process' and 'Purposes of Budgeting' in Chapter 15.

(b) See 'Incremental and Zero-Base Budgeting' in Chapter 15 for the main items which should be included in answering this question.

Answer to problem 15.17

For the steps in the preparation of master budgets see 'Stages in the Budgeting Process' in Chapter 15.
    The main budgets that should normally be prepared are:
  (i) Sales budget.
 (ii) Production budget.
(iii) Direct material usage budget.
 (iv) Direct materials purchase budget.
  (v) Direct labour budget.
 (vi) Factory overhead budget.
(vii) Selling expenses budget.
(viii) Administration budget.
 (ix) Cash budget.
  (x) Budgeted balance sheet and profit and loss account.
For comments and illustrations of the above budgets see the detailed illustration presented in Chapter 15.

Answer to problem 15.18

(i)(a) A three-level budget involves preparing budgets based on the following assumptions about uncertain future events:
  (i) The most likely outcome occurs.
 (ii) The optimistic outcome occurs.

(iii) The pessimistic outcome occurs.

In it's most simplest form a three-level budget might be prepared for sales volume only but three-level budgets can also be prepared for uncertain cost items such as changes in wage rates or material prices.

(b) Probabilistic budgets can be prepared using joint probabilities ascertained from decision tree analysis. When more than one variable is uncertain and the value of one variable is dependent on the value of other variables then a decision tree is a useful analytical tool for clarifying the range of alternative courses of action and their possible outcomes. For an illustration of the process see 'Decision Tree Analysis' and 'Use of Cost Information for Pricing Decisions Under Conditions of Uncertainty' in Chapter 12. In the budgeting process a decision tree is a useful tool for calculating the expected values of sales revenues and costs when interdependencies exist. A decision tree is also a useful tool for assisting in constructing probability distributions. Such probability distributions can be used to aid decision-making at the planning stage and assessing the significance of actual deviations from the budget. For example, a probability distribution might indicate that the probability for spending in excess of £100,000 of the expected value is 0.05. If a difference of £100,000 actually occurs then the probability distribution provides a useful indication of the significance of the variance.

(c) For a description of how the simulation approach can be applied to the budgeting process see 'Simulation' in Chapter 14.

(ii)(a) The three-level budget approach recognises that more than one outcome is possible and indicates the range of possible outcomes. Such an approach enables managers to qualify their predictions and provides more useful information than a single value estimate.

(b) The probability approach using the decision tree technique is an improvement on method A because it enables uncertainty of the range of possible outcomes to be quantified in the form of an expected value calculation. This is preferable to a three-level budget which merely identifies uncertainty but does not quantify it. When probability distributions are constructed then the budget indicates the probabilities of possible outcomes occurring. It was noted in (i)(b) that this approach is useful for selecting alternative courses of action at the planning stage and enabling actual outcomes to be interpreted more meaningfully.

Hence from a decision-making and control point of view the probability approach is superior to adopting a three-level budget.

(c) Simulation enables complex inter-relationships to be expressed in terms of probability distributions and expected values. For a description of the advantages of simulation over the decision tree approach see 'Simulation' in Chapter 14. In addition simulation enables one to test the sensitivity of the outcomes by asking 'What if?' questions for a wide range of eventualities and environmental changes.

SOLUTIONS TO CHAPTER 16 PROBLEMS

Control in the organisation

Questions 16.1 and 16.2 are appropriate for a first year course but 16.3 to 16.5 are more suitable for a second year course. Details of the questions are as follows:

16.1 Comments on a budgetary control system.

16.2 and 16.3 Preparation of flexible budgets. 16.2 is similar to Example 16.3 in Chapter 16. 16.3 is not an easy question.

16.4 Construction of performance measures for a company's sales force.

16.5 Design of a management control system. This question is also relevant to Chapter 23.

16.6 to 16.9 Various discussion questions relevant to Chapter 16. 16.9 requires some knowledge of standard costing and cost estimation.

Answer to problem 16.1

(a)(i) Activity varies from month to month but quarterly budgets are set by dividing total annual expenditure by 4.

(ii) The budget ought to be analysed by shorter intervals (e.g. monthly) and costs estimated in relation to monthly activity.

(iii) For control purposes monthly comparisons and cumulative monthly comparisons of planned and actual expenditure to date should be made.

(iv) The budget holder does not participate in the setting of budgets.

(v) An incremental budget approach is adopted. A zero-base approach would be more appropriate

(vi) The budget should distinguish between controllable and uncontrollable expenditure.

(b) The information which should flow from a comparison of the actual and budgeted expenditure would consist of the variances for the month and year to date analysed into the following categories:

(i) Controllable and uncontrollable items.

(ii) Price and quantity variances with price variance analysed by inflationary and non-inflationary effects.

(c)(i) Flexible budgets should be prepared on a monthly basis. Possible measures of activity are number of patient days or expected laundry weight.

(ii) The laundry manager should participate in the budgetary process.

(iii) Costs should be classified into controllable and non-controllable items.

(iv) Variances should be reported and analysed by price and quantity on a monthly and cumulative basis.

(v) Comments should be added explaining possible reasons for the variances.

Answer to problem 16.2

Departmental flexible budget

Budgeted production: 20,000 standard hours
Actual production: 17,000 standard hours

Item of expense	Budget formula	(1) Flexible budget based on 17,000 standard hours £	(2) Actual costs £	(3) Budget based on 19,000 input hours £	(4) Total variance (1–2) £	(5) Price variance (3–2) £	(6) Effic'y variance (1–3) £
Direct labour	£2 per DLH	34,000	39,000	38,000	5,000A	1,000A	4,000A
Variable overhead	£1 per DLH	17,000	24,000	19,000	7,000A	5,000A	2,000A

Answer to problem 16.6

See 'Responsibility Accounting' in Chapter 16 for the answer to this question.

Answer to problem 16.7

For the answer to both parts of this question see 'Control of Non-Manufacturing Costs' in Chapter 16.

Answer to problem 16.8

(a) The answer should include the following points:
  (i) The system should lead to improved performance measures and cost control.
  (ii) Service departments are motivated to provide services efficiently because any excess spending might lead to an investigation as to why it is cheaper to buy from outside the local authority.
  (iii) The user departments will have greater independence as they will be charged the economic price (or lower) for the services they use. The user department is likely to view this as a fairer method than the alternative of a charge based on the costs of the service department only.

(b) Problems which might be encountered include:
  (i) How should cost be determined? Should it include the direct cost of the service department only or should it include indirect costs of the service departments such as apportionments of central administrative charges?
  (ii) How should the market price be determined if there are several different market prices or the services offered are not identical?
  (iii) Difficulty in monitoring the scheme. The costs might exceed the benefits if the services departments provide a wide variety of services resulting in many cost and market value comparisons.
  (iv) Acceptance by the service departments. The new system might be seen as a method of imposing punitive controls.
  (v) If the user department charges for its services and its costs include transferred in costs which are below the market price then it may be underpricing its services.

(c) The above problems might be overcome by:
  (i) Market prices could be established by inviting tenders from suppliers and basing the market price on the lowest tender. This is the market price which the user department would have paid if the department were free to obtain the services from outside the organisation. However, the minimum market price should represent a long run price and not a temporary distress price.
  (ii) The scheme should be clearly explained to all interested parties emphasising that the aim is to encourage increased efficiency and to help managers control their activities more effectively. It should be emphasised that the objective is not to use the new system as a basis for undertaking punitive post mortems.
  (iii) Comparisons of market and cost based charges should be on a random basis rather than comparing each transaction.
  (iv) The user department should ensure that margins are added to the service department transferred costs so as to ensure that its services are charged out at a fair market price.

Answer to problem 16.9

(a) The desirable attributes of a suitable measure of activity for flexing the budget are as follows:
  (i) The measure selected should exert a major influence on the costs of the activity. The objective is to flex the budget to ascertain the costs that should be incurred for the actual level of activity. Therefore the costs of the activity and the measure selected should be highly correlated.
  (ii) The measure selected should not be affected by factors other than volume. For example if direct labour cost is selected as the activity measure then an increase in wage rates will cause labour cost to increase even when activity remains constant.
  (iii) The measure should be easily understood. Complicated indexes are unlikely to be satisfactory.
  (iv) The measure should be easily obtainable without too much cost.
  (v) The measure should be based on output rather than input in order to ensure that managers do not obtain larger budget allowances for being inefficient. For an illustration of this point see Example 16.2 in Chapter 16. Standard hours of output should be used rather than actual hours of input.

(b) Because the activities of a service or overhead department tend not to be repetitive it is unlikely that a system of standard costing can be justified. Output will be fairly diverse and it may not be possible to find a single output measure that is highly correlated with costs. It might be necessary to flex the budget on inputs rather than outputs. Also several variables are likely to cause changes in cost rather than a single measure of output and an accurate flexible budget may require the use of multiple regression techniques. However, because multiple regression measures might not be easily obtainable and understood a single input measure may be preferable.

It may be necessary to use several measures of activity within a cost centre for the different costs. For example machine maintenance costs might be flexed according to machine hours and lighting and heating costs might be flexed according to labour hours of input.

(c) Suitable measures include the following:
  (i) *Standard hours of output:* This measure is suitable when output is sufficiently standardised to enable standard labour times to be established for each activity. This measure is unsatisfactory where labour efficiency is unlikely to be constant or output is too diverse to enable standard times to be established.

  (ii) *Direct labour hours of input:* This measure is suitable where costs are highly correlated with labour hours of input, output cannot be measured in standard hours and labour efficiency is fairly constant. This measure is unsatisfactory if these conditions do not hold because labour hours will be an unsatisfactory guide to output.

(iii) *Direct labour costs:* This measure is suitable where the same conditions apply as those specified in (ii) and the wage rates are not consistently changing. If these conditions do not apply then this measure will be unsatisfactory.

Standard costing and variance analysis (1)

The most difficult questions set in this chapter are 17.10, 17.13 and 17.15 to 17.17. Details of the questions are:

17.1 and 17.2	These questions require the calculation of labour and material variances and are appropriate as an introduction to variance analysis.
17.3	Calculation of labour, material and overhead variances.
17.4	Calculation of overhead variances and an analysis of the overhead expenditure variance.
17.5	Calculation of sales margin variances.
17.6 and 17.7	Preparation of statements analysing the reasons for changes in profits.
17.8 to 17.10	Calculation of prices and quantities when the variances are given in the question. Question 17.10 is not easy.
17.11 to 17.13	Calculation of production ratios. Question 17.13 is appropriate for a second year course.
17.14 to 17.17	Reconciliation of budgeted and actual profit incorporating materials, labour, overhead and sales variances. Questions 17.15 to 17.17 are appropriate for a second year course.

Answer to problem 17.2

(a) The calculation of the standard purchase price for each item of materials is as follows:

Powder: £1.50 per tube. Each tube requires 2 lbs of powder
$\therefore$ price per lb = £0.75
Chemicals: £0.60 per tube. Each tube requires $\frac{1}{4}$ litre of chemical
$\therefore$ price per litre = £2.40
Tube: £0.30 per tube

The standard wage rate is £4.50 per hour and the standard cost of producing one tube is £1.80. Therefore the standard time is 0.4 hours $\left(\dfrac{£1.80}{£4.50}\right)$.

Material price variances = (standard price − Actual price) × actual purchases

$$
\begin{array}{lll}
 & \text{\pounds} & \text{\pounds} \\
\text{Powder} = (\text{\pounds}0.75 - \text{\pounds}0.70) \times 10,000 = & 500\text{F} & \\
\text{Chemicals} = (\text{\pounds}2.40 - \text{\pounds}2.30) \times \quad 600 = \text{\pounds}60\text{F} & & \\
\qquad\qquad (\text{\pounds}2.40 - \text{\pounds}2.50) \times \quad 600 = \text{\pounds}60\text{A} & \text{Nil} & \\
\text{Tubes} = (\text{\pounds}0.30 - \text{\pounds}0.40) \times \quad 200 = \text{\pounds}20\text{A} & & \\
\qquad\quad (\text{\pounds}0.30 - \text{\pounds}0.30) \times 5,000 = \underline{\text{Nil}} & \underline{20\text{A}} & \text{\pounds}480\text{F}
\end{array}
$$

Material usage variances = (standard quantity – actual issues) × standard price

$$
\begin{array}{ll}
\text{Powder} = (4,500 \times 2 = 9,000 - 9,800) \times \text{\pounds}0.75 = 600\text{A} & \\
\text{Chemicals} = (4,500 \times \tfrac{1}{4} = 1,125 - 1,050) \times \text{\pounds}2.40 = 180\text{F} & \\
\text{Tubes} = (4,500 \times 1 = 4,500 - 4,520) \times \text{\pounds}0.30 = \underline{\quad 6\text{A}} & \text{\pounds}426\text{A}
\end{array}
$$

Wage rate = (standard rate – actual rate) × actual hours

$$
= \left(\text{\pounds}4.50 - \frac{\text{\pounds}8,910}{2,050} \right) \times 2,050 = \text{\pounds}315\text{F}
$$

Labour efficiency = (standard hours – actual hours) × standard rate
   $(4,500 \times 0.4 \text{ hrs} = 1,800 \text{ hrs} - 2,050) \times \text{\pounds}4.50 = \text{\pounds}1,125\text{A}$

(b) See Chapter 17 for a discussion of the possible causes of material and labour variances. Causes which might be specifically related to this question include:

   (i) Favourable price variance and adverse usage variance for powder. This may be due to the purchase of inferior quality materials resulting in excessive usage and an adverse labour efficiency variance.

   (ii) The adverse usage variance for powder may also be due to inefficient handling or split bags.

Answer to problem 17.4

(a) Fixed overhead rate = $\dfrac{\text{Budgeted fixed overheads}}{\text{Budgeted production (standard hours)}} = \dfrac{\text{\pounds}10,000}{8,000} = \text{\pounds}1.25$ per standard hour

Variable overhead rate = $\dfrac{\text{Budgeted variable overheads}}{\text{Budgeted production (standard hours)}} = \dfrac{\text{\pounds}28,000}{8,000} = \text{\pounds}3.50$ per standard hour

Fixed overhead volume variance =
   (Budgeted production – actual production) × fixed overhead rate
   (8,000   – 8,400) × £1.25   = £500F
Fixed overhead expenditure variance =
   (Budgeted fixed overhead – actual fixed overhead)
   (£10,000   – £9,715)   = £285F
Variable overhead expenditure variance (1) =
   (Flexed variable overheads – actual variable overheads)
   (8,400 × £3.50 = £29,400 – £30,580)   = £1,180A

Note
(1) Variable overhead expenditure is flexed on output and not input since the question specifies that variable overheads vary with standard hours produced.

(b) Department operating statement

	Month *Flexed budget* *(note 1)* £	*Actual* £	*Variance* £
Fixed overheads:			
Salaries	6,750	6,400	350F
Maintenance	3,250	3,315	65A
Variable overheads:			
Power	18,480	20,140	1,660A
Consumable materials	6,300	5,960	340F
Indirect labour	4,620	4,480	140F
	39,400	40,295	895A

Notes

(1) Fixed overheads are not flexed. Variable overheads are flexed on the basis of actual production in standard hours:

		£
Power	$17,600 \times 8,400/8,000 =$	18,480
Consumable materials	$6,000 \times 8,400/8,000 =$	6,300
Indirect labour	$4,400 \times 8,400/8,000 =$	4,620

(c) The volume variance represents the under/over recovery of overhead due to actual production being different from budgeted production. The volume variance is written off back to the profit and loss account as a period cost. Profits will change to the extent that part of the fixed overheads as represented by the volume variance will not be capitalised in stocks. To the extent that any production in excess of budget has been sold then profits will increase by the amount of profits on the increased sales.

Answer to problem 17.5

(a) Sales margin variances are more informative than sales revenue variances because they help evaluate the selling function's share in the organisation's *profit* and it's responsibility for any deviation from budgeted *profit*. For a comparison of sales revenue and sales margin variances see 'Sales Variances' in Chapter 17.

(b)(i) Total sales margin variance = actual profit − budgeted profit.

Actual profit is defined as actual sales volume × (actual selling price − standard cost) and budget profit is defined as budgeted sales volume × (budgeted selling price − standard cost).

The calculation of actual selling price for each product is as follows:

A £31 (£34,100 ÷ 1,100)
B £10 (£52,000 ÷ 5,200)
C £22 (£24,200 ÷ 1,100)

Actual profit − Budgeted profit

A = (1,100 × (£31 − £16) = £16,500) − (1,500 × (£30 − £16) = 21,000) = £4,500A
B = (5,200 × (£10 − £9) = £5,200) − (3,500 × (£10 − £9) = 3,500) = £1,700F
C = (1,100 × (£22 − £18) = £4,400) − (1,000 × (£20 − £18) = 2,000) = £2,400F

£400A

(ii) Sales margin price variance = (actual margin − standard margin) × actual sales volume
$$A = (£15 − £14) × 1,100 = £1,100F$$
$$B = (£1 − £1) × 5,200 = Nil$$
$$C = (£4 − £2) × 1,100 \quad = £2,200F$$
$$\underline{3,300F}$$

(iii) Sales margin volume variance = (actual sales volume − budgeted sales volume) × standard margin
$$A = (1,100 − 1,500) × £14 = £5,600A$$
$$B = (5,200 − 3,500) × £1 \quad = £1,700F$$
$$C = (1,100 − 1,000) × £2 \quad = \quad £200F$$
$$\underline{£3,700A}$$

Answer to problem 17.6

(a) *Preliminary calculations*

	£
1980 sales at 1981 budgeted price increase (1.1 × £6,000)	6,600

$$∴ \text{% increase in volume from 1980 to 1981} = 16\tfrac{2}{3}\% \left(\frac{£7,700 − £6,600}{£6,600} \right)$$

The effect of the 10% selling price increase is calculated as follows:

	£
1981 sales volume at 1980 prices ($116\tfrac{2}{3}\% × £6,000$) =	7,000
1981 sales volume at 1981 prices (actual sales) =	7,700
Difference due to selling price increase =	£700

The contribution for 1980 was £1,200 (£6,000 − £4,800).
   The effect of the sales volume increase (with price and efficiency changes kept constant) is to increase contribution by £200 ($16\tfrac{2}{3}\% × £1,200$).

Direct materials

	1980	1981
Price per unit	£125 $\left(\dfrac{£3,000}{24} \right)$	£120 $\left(\dfrac{£3,240}{27} \right)$

Effect of reduction in material price of £5 per unit:

27 (in 000's units) × £5 = £135 increase in profits (in £000's)
Material usage for 1981 based on 1980 usage [24,000 + ($16\tfrac{2}{3}\% × 24,000$)] = 28,000 units
Actual material usage for 1981   = 27,000 units
Saving due to reduction in material usage   1,000 units

The monetary saving due to a reduction in material usage (with the price changes effect removed) is 1,000 units at £125 = £125 (in £000's).

Direct wages and variable overhead

	1980	1981
Rate per hour	£5 $\left(\dfrac{£1,800}{360}\right)$	£5.15 $\left(\dfrac{£2,060}{400}\right)$

Effect of increase in direct wages and variable overhead of £0.15 per hour:
   400 (in 000's hours) × £0.15 = £60 decrease in profits (in £000's)

Labour hours for 1981 based on 1980 efficiency $[360,000+(16\frac{2}{3}\% \times 360,000)]=420,000$ hrs
Actual labour hours used for 1981 $=400,000$ hrs
Saving   20,000 hrs

The monetary saving due to an increase in labour efficiency (with the price changes effect removed) is 20,000 hours at £5 per hour = £100 (in £000's).

Statement analysing the reasons for the change in profits

	£000's	£000's
Profit 1979/80		400
Add: Profit increases due to:		
Increase in selling price	700	
Increase in sales volume	200	
Reduction in material prices	135	
Improved usage of materials	125	
Increase in labour efficiency	100	1,260
		1,660
Less: Profit reductions due to:		
Increase in wage rate	60	
Increase in expenditure on fixed		
overheads (£1,500 − £800)	700	760
Profit 1980/81		900

(b) Profit–volume ratio $=20\% \left(\dfrac{£1,200}{£6,000} \times 100\right)$

Let x = break-even sales
   ∴ Break-even sales is where 0.20x = £800,000 (fixed overhead)
         ∴ Break-even sales = £4,000,000

$$\text{Margin of safety} = \frac{1980 \text{ sales} - \text{break-even sales}}{1980 \text{ sales}}$$

$$= \frac{£6,000,000 - £4,000,000}{£6,000,000}$$

$$= 33\tfrac{1}{3}\% \text{ or } £2,000,000 \text{ sales}$$

Answer to problem 17.9

(a) *Calculation of product standard cost and selling price*

	£
Direct materials (5 Kg at £4)	20
Direct wages (2 hours at £3)	6
Fixed overhead $\left(\dfrac{£240,000}{120,000 \text{ hours}} \times 2 \text{ hours}\right)$	4
Total cost	30
Profit margin (25% of sales price)	10
Selling price	40

Budgeted monthly production and sales:

$$= 5,000 \text{ units} \left[\frac{£50,000 \text{ (budgeted monthly profit)}}{£10 \text{ (budgeted profit per unit)}}\right]$$

Profit and loss account—October

	£	£
Sales (4,800 units at £41—see note 1)		196,800
Less direct materials (24,800 Kgs at £4.20—see note 2)	104,160	
Direct labour (9,000 hours at £3.40—see note 3)	30,600	
Fixed overheads (see note 4)	18,600	153,360
Net profit		43,440

Notes

(1) Sales margin volume variance:

    (actual sales volume − budgeted sales volume) × standard margin

    $(? - 5,000) \times £10$ = £2,000A

    ∴ actual sales volume = 4,800 units

Sales margin price variance:

    (actual margin − standard margin) × actual sales volume

    $(? - £10) \times 4,800$ = £4,800F

    ∴ actual margin $= \dfrac{£52,800}{4,800} = £11$

    ∴ actual selling price = £30 standard cost + actual margin (£11)

                 = £41

(2) Material usage variance:

    (standard quantity − actual quantity) × standard rate

    $(4,800 \times 5 = 24,000 - ?) \times £4$ = £3,200A

    ∴ actual quantity $= \dfrac{(24,000 \times £4) + £3,200}{£4}$

                 = 24,800 Kg

Material price variance:

    (Standard price − actual price) × actual quantity

    $(£4 - ?) \times 24,800$ = £4,960A

    ∴ actual price $= \dfrac{(24,800 \times £4) + £4,960}{£24,800}$

                 = £4.20 per Kg

(3) Labour efficiency variance:
   (standard hours − actual hours) × standard rate
   $(4,800 \times 2 = 9,600 - ?) \times £3$ $= £1,800F$

   $\therefore$ actual hours $= \dfrac{(9,600 \times £3) - £1,800}{£3}$

   $= 9,000$ hours

Wage rate variance:
   (standard rate − actual rate) × actual hours
   $(£3 − ?) \times 9,000$ $= £3,600A$

   $\therefore$ actual rate $= \dfrac{(9,000 \times £3) + £3,600}{9,000}$

   $= £3.40$

(4) Fixed overhead expenditure variance:
   Budgeted fixed overheads − actual fixed overheads

   $\left(\dfrac{£240,000}{12} − ?\right)$ $= £1,400F$

   $\therefore$ actual fixed overheads $= £18,600$

(b) For the answer to this question see 'Types of Cost Standards' in Chapter 17.

Answer to problem 17.11

(a) A standard hour is a hypothetical hour which represents the amount of work which should be performed in one hour under standard conditions.

(b)(i) The productivity of direct operatives can be measured by the following ratio:

$$\frac{\text{Standard hour equivalent for actual production}}{\text{Actual direct hours worked}} = \frac{460 \text{ hrs (1)}}{400 \text{ hrs}}$$

$$= 115\%$$

(ii) $\dfrac{\text{Standard hour equivalent of actual production}}{\text{Standard hour equivalent of budgeted production}} = \dfrac{460 \text{ hrs}}{500 \text{ hrs (2)}}$

$$= 92\%$$

(iii) The capacity utilisation ratio measures the actual utilisation of labour hours against budgeted labour hours. The ratio is as follows:

$$\frac{\text{Actual direct labour hours worked}}{\text{Budgeted labour hours}} = \frac{400}{500} \text{(3)}$$

$$= 80\%$$

Notes
(1) The standard hour equivalent of actual production is calculated as follows:

Actual production ÷ expected output per hour
Cups   4,260 ÷ 30 = 142 standard hours
Saucers 6,400 ÷ 40 = 160 standard hours
Plates   3,950 ÷ 25 = 158 standard hours
460 standard hours

(2) Standard hour equivalent of budgeted production:

Budgeted production ÷ expected output per hour
Cups   4,500 ÷ 30 = 150 standard hours
Saucers 4,000 ÷ 40 = 100 standard hours
Plates   6,250 ÷ 25 = 250 standard hours
500 standard hours

(3) At the planning stage the budgeted labour hours will be equal to budgeted production of standard hours. See 'Overhead Variances' in Chapter 17 for an explanation of this. Therefore budgeted hours of input are 500 hours.

(c) If all other factors remain unchanged then one would expect an increase in productivity to increase profits assuming that the increased output can be sold. However, increased output might result in a step increase in fixed costs thus reducing overall profits. In addition other variable costs (such as increased material consumption caused by more waste) might increase disproportionately with output. Also if the increase in productivity is due to the purchase of extra capital equipment then total profits may increase but capital employed will also increase. The end result might be that return on capital employed declines.

Answer to problem 17.15

(a) The following variances can be calculated.

	£
(1) Wage rate: (standard wage rate – actual wage rate) × actual hours	
(£2 – £14,000/6,500) × 6,500	= 1,000A
(2) Labour efficiency: (standard hours – actual hours) × standard rate	
(500 × 14 = 7,000 – 6,500) × £2	= 1,000F
(3) Price variance: (standard price – actual price) × actual quantity	
(Output of dept. A) (£9 – £21,000/1,400) × 1,400	= 8,400A
(4) Usage variance: (standard quantity – actual quantity) × standard rate	
(Output of dept. A) (500 × 3 = 1,500 – 1,400) × £9	= 900F
(5) Price variance: (standard price – actual price) × actual quantity	
(Material X) (£5 – £11,500/1,900) × 1,900	= 2,000A
(6) Usage variance: (standard quantity – actual quantity) × standard rate	
(Material X) (500 × 4 = 2,000 – 1,900) × £5	= 500F
(7) Variable overhead: (flexed budget – actual variable overheads)	
Expenditure (6,500 × £1 = £6,500 – £8,000)	= 1,500A
(8) Variable overhead: (standard hours – actual hours) × variable overhead rate	
Efficiency (7,000 – 6,500) × £1	= 500F
(9) Fixed overhead expenditure:	
(Budgeted fixed overheads – actual fixed overheads)	
Department B (400 × £3 = £1,200 – £1,600)	= 400A
Allocated (400 × £8 = £3,200 – £2,900)	= 300F

(10) Volume variance: (actual production – budgeted production) × fixed overhead rate

Department B (500 – 400) × £3	= 300F
Allocated (500 – 400) × £8	= 800F

Department standard cost for actual production (500 × £100)	= 50,000
Actual cost	= 59,000
Total departmental variance	9,000A

Variances (1)–(10) add to £9,000 adverse. However, not all of the variances are within the control of department B. From the information given in the question it is not possible to specify which variances are controllable and non-controllable by department B. The following are assumed to be non-controllable.

Wage rate:	Assumed wage rates are set by personnel department and that the correct grade of labour has been used.
Material price:	Assumed that a central purchasing department exists and that the purchasing officer is responsible for the price variance of material X. The manager of department A is responsible for the price variance for the output of department A.
Allocated fixed overhead expenditure variance:	This expenditure is controllable at the point where it is incurred. The actual spending on allocated fixed overheads is not determined by department B.

The following variances might be controllable by the manager of department B:

Labour efficiency
Material usage
Variable overhead efficiency
Fixed overhead volume
Fixed overhead expenditure

Fixed overhead volume might be due to a failure to achieve budgeted sales or machine breakdowns may have occurred which are beyond the control of department B. Any meaningful analysis of the overhead expenditure variance requires a comparison of actual and budgeted expenditure for each individual item. Only by comparing individual items of expenditure and ascertaining the reasons for the variance can one determine whether the variances are controllable or non-controllable. The foregoing analysis assumes the volume variance and overhead expenditure variances to be controllable by the manager of department B. In the performance report variances should be analysed into their controllable and non-controllable elements as follows:

Department B performance report—month 7

	£	£	£
Standard cost for actual production			50,000
Controllable variances			
Labour efficiency		1,000F	
Material usage: Department A	900F		
Material X	500F	1,400F	
Overhead expenditure: Fixed	400A		
Variable	1,500A	1,900A	
Variable overhead efficiency		500F	
Volume variance: Department B	300F		
Allocated	800F	1,100F	2,100F

Non-controllable variances

Wage rate		1,000A	
Material price: Department A	8,400A		
Material X	2,000A	10,400A	
Fixed overhead expenditure (allocated)		300F	11,100A
Actual cost			59,000

(b) The standard costing system is not being operated effectively at present. The variances attributed to department B are not analysed into their controllable and non-controllable elements. In addition the production manager appears to be using the system in an incorrect manner. He appears to be using the system in a punitive manner which might lead to some of the behavioural problems discussed in Chapter 19. Performance reports should be used to help managers control their activities and not as a recriminatory device.

Standard costing (2): further aspects

Questions 18.6 to 18.21 are appropriate for a second year course. Details of the questions are as follows:

18.1 to 18.4	Accounting entries for a standard costing system.
18.5	Calculation of material mix and yield variances.
18.6 to 18.9	Calculation of sales, labour, material and overhead variances. These questions are similar to the questions set in Chapter 17 but they also include the calculation of sales mix, materials mix and yield variances. They are generally more difficult than the questions set in Chapter 17.
18.10	Accounting disposition of variances.
18.11 to 18.14	Ex-post variance analysis segregating planning and operating variances.
18.15 and 18.16	A relevant cost approach to variance analysis.
18.17 and 18.18	Investigation of variances.
18.19 to 18.21	Various discussion questions relevant to Chapter 18.

Answer to problem 18.1

(a) See 'Material Price Variances' in Chapter 17 for an explanation of why it is preferable to calculate material price variances at the time of receipt rather than at the time of issue.

(b) The price per unit of each component is £4.30 (£1,720 ÷ 400).
Material price variance (calculated at the time of receipt):
(standard price – actual price) × quantity purchased
(£4 – £4.30) × 400   = £120A

Material price variance (calculated at the time of issue):
(standard price – actual price) × quantity issued
(£4 – £4.30) × 150   = £45A

Method 1 (variances calculated at time of receipt
Stores ledger control account

Creditors (AQ × SP) (400 × £4)	1,600	WIP (AQ × SP) (150 × £4)	600
		Balance (250 × £4)	1,000
	1,600		1,600

Price variance account

Creditors A/c	120	P. & L. A/c	120

Creditors control account

		Stores ledger control A/c	1,600
		Price variance A/c	120
			1,720

Work in progress account

Stores ledger control A/c	600	Cost of sales A/c	600

Method 2 (variances calculated at time of issue)
Stores ledger control account

Creditors (AQ × AP)	1,720	WIP (AQ × AP) (150 × £4.30)	645
		Balance (250 × £4.30)	1,075
	1,720		1,720

Price variance account

WIP A/c	45	P. & L. A/c	45

Creditors control account

		Stores ledger control A/c	1,720

Work in progress account

Stores ledger control A/c (AQ × AP)	645	Price variance A/c	45
		Cost of sales A/c	600

With method 1 the stores ledger account is maintained at standard prices whereas with method 2 this account is maintained at actual prices. With method 1 the total price variance of £120 is transferred to profit and loss account in the period when the materials are *purchased* whereas with method 2 the price variance is transferred to profit and loss account at the time of issue.

(c) Closing raw material stock valuation:
    Method 1 = £1,000
    Method 2 = £1,075

(d)(i) A forecast is a prediction of future events which, unlike a budget, ignores management's ability to influence the outcome of future events.
  (ii)–(v) See text for an explanation of these items.

Answer to problem 18.2

The calculation of the product standard cost is as follows:

	£
Direct materials (£400 ÷ 50 units)	8
Direct labour (2 units per employee per hour)	2 ($\frac{1}{2}$ hour at £4 per hour)
Production overhead ($\frac{1}{2}$ hour × £12 per hour—see note 1)	6
	16

Note

(1) The hourly fixed overhead rate is calculated as follows:

$$\frac{£480,000}{50 \text{ weeks} \times 40 \text{ hours} \times 20 \text{ employees}} = £12$$

	£
Material price variance:	
(standard price − actual price) × actual quantity	
(£400 − £390) × 35 tonnes	350F
Material usage variance:	
(standard quantity—actual quantity) × standard price	
(1,660 units × $\frac{1}{50}$ tonne = 33.2 tonne − 35 tonne) × £400	720A
Wage rate variance:	
(standard rate − actual rate) × actual hours	
(£4 − £4.20) × (5 × 40 hours)	40A
Labour efficiency variance:	
(standard hours − actual hours) × standard rate	
[(1,660 × $\frac{1}{2}$ hour = 830 hours) − (20 × 40 hours)] × £4	120F
Fixed overhead expenditure variance:	
(budgeted fixed overheads − actual fixed overheads)	
$\left(\dfrac{£480,000}{50 \text{ weeks}} - £9,700\right)$	100A
Fixed overhead efficiency variance:	
(standard hours − actual hours) × standard fixed overhead rate	
(830 − 800) × £12	360F

Material stores

	£			£
Oct 7 Creditors (AQ × SP)			Oct 7 Work-in-progress (SQ × SP)	
35 tonnes at £400	14,000		33.2 tonnes at £400	13,280
			Material usage variance A/c	
			(1.8 tonnes at £400)	720
	14,000			14,000

Wages control

	£			£
Oct 7 Wages accrued A/c			Oct 7 Work-in-progress (SQ × SR)	
(5 × 40 × £4.20)	3,240		(830 × £4)	3,320
(15 × 40 × £4.0)			Oct 7 Labour rate variance	40
Labour efficiency variance	120			
	3,360			3,360

Production overhead

	£			£
Oct 7 Expense creditors	9,700	Oct 7 Work-in-progress (SQ × SP)		
Volume efficiency variance	360	(830 × £12)		9,960
		Oct 7 Expenditure variance		100
	10,060			10,060

Work-in-progress

	£		£
Oct 7 Material stores (SQ × SP)	13,280	Oct 7 Finished goods	
Oct 7 Wages control (SQ × SR)	3,320	(1,660 × £16)	26,560
Oct 7 Production overhead	9,960		
	26,560		26,560

Creditors

	£		£
Oct 7 Material price variance	350	Oct 7 Raw material stock	14,000

Finished goods

	£		£
Oct 7 Work-in-progress	26,560	Oct 7 Cost of sales	26,560

Cost of sales

	£		£
Oct 7 Finished goods	26,560	Oct 7 Profit and loss	26,560

Variance accounts

	£		£
Material usage variance	720	Material price	350
Labour rate variance	40	Labour efficiency variance	120
Expenditure variance	100	Volume efficiency variance	360
		P. & L. A/c	30
	860		860

Profit and loss account for week ending 7th October 1983

	£	£	£
Sales			33,200
Less: Standard cost of sales			26,560
Standard profit on actual sales			6,640
Production variances:			
Materials			
price	350 (F)		
usage	720 (A)	370 (A)	
Labour			
rate	40 (A)		
efficiency	120 (F)	80 (F)	
Overhead			
expenditure	100 (A)		
efficiency	360 (F)	260 (F)	30 (A)
Actual profit			6,610

Answer to problem 18.5

(i)

Materials	(1) *Standard quantity in standard proportions at standard prices (see note 1)*	(2) *Actual input in standard proportions at standard prices*	(3) *Actual input in actual proportions at standard prices*	(4) *Actual input in actual proportions at actual prices*
A	58 mixes × 40 Kg × £1.50 = £3,480	6,100 × 0.4 × £1.50 = £3,660	2,200 × £1.50 = £3,300	£3,520
B	58 mixes × 30 Kg × £1.20 = £2,088	6,100 × 0.3 × £1.20 = £2,196	2,000 × £1.20 = £2,400	£2,200
C	58 mixes × 10 Kg × £1.40 = £812	6,100 × 0.1 × £1.40 = £854	500 × £1.40 = £700	£750
D	58 mixes × 20 Kg × £0.50 = £580	6,100 × 0.20 × £0.50 = £610	1,400 × £0.50 = £700	£700

Usage variance (col 1–col 3)		Mix variance (col 2–col 3)	
	£		£
A	180F	A	360F
B	312A	B	204A
C	112F	C	154F
D	120A	D	90A
	140A		220F

Price variance (col 3–col 4)		Total variance (col 1–col 4)	
	£		£
A	220A	A	40A
B	200F	B	112A
C	50A	C	62F
D	Nil	D	120A
	70A		210A

Note

(1) 1 tile = $\frac{1}{2}$ m × $\frac{1}{4}$ m = 0.125 m^2

∴ 1 standard mix produces 100 m^2 or 800 tiles (100 m^2 ÷ 0.125 m^2).

For an actual production of 46,400 tiles 58 standard mixes are required (46,400 tiles ÷ 800 tiles).

(ii) Yield variance:

$$\text{actual yield} - \text{standard yield from actual input of material}$$
$$\times$$
$$\text{standard cost per unit of output}$$

Actual yield = 46,400 tiles

Standard yield from actual input of materials:

6,100 Kg of materials are used and each 100 Kg used should yield 800 tiles (see note 1). Therefore standard yield from an input of 6,100 Kg is 48,800 tiles.

$$\text{Standard cost per unit of output} = £0.15 \left(\frac{£120 \text{ standard cost for 1 mix}}{800 \text{ tiles}} \right)$$

∴ yield variance = (46,400 tiles − 48,800 tiles) × £0.15
$$= £360A$$

Check = material mix variance (£220F) + yield variance (£360A) = usage variance (140A)

Answer to problem 18.8

(a) *Workings*

Production for the period:

Sales requirements	1, 000 units
Closing stock	100 units
	1,100 units
Less opening stock	200 units
Production	900 units

Analysis of variances from budgeted performance: months i–iv

Sales function

Sales price variance (1)

(actual margin – budgeted margin) × actual sales volume   £

D (120 – 100) × 600   = 12,000F

R (100 – 90) × 400   = 4,000F   16,000F

Sales mix variance (1)

(actual sales quantity – actual sales quantity in standard proportions) × budgeted margin

D (600 – 500) × 100   = 10,000F

R (400 – 500) × 90   = 9,000A   1,000F

Expenditure variance

(budgeted sales costs—actual sales costs)

(£40,000 – £48,000)   = 8,000A

                                                       9,000F

Purchasing function

Material price variance

(standard price – actual price) × actual quantity

(£2 – £35,000/20,000) × 20,000   = 5,000F

Idle time variance caused by purchasing function (1,000 hrs at £4)   = 4,000A

(see note 2)

Volume variance (3)

(actual production – budgeted production) × fixed overhead rate

(900 – 1,000) × £20   = 2,000A

Purchasing spending variance

(budgeted cost – actual cost)

(£20,000 – £21,000)   = 1,000A

                                                       2,000A

Production function

Wage rate

(standard rate – actual rate) × actual hours

(£3 – £28,000/8,000) × 8,000   = 4,000A

Labour efficiency (4)

(standard hours – actual hours) × standard rate

(900 × 10 = 9,000 – 7,000) × £3   = 6,000F   2,000F

Material usage

(standard quantity – actual quantity) × standard rate

(900 × 20 = 18,000 – 20,000) × £2   = 4,000A

Variable overhead expenditure

(flexed budget – actual variable overheads)

(8,000 × £1 = £8,000 – £10,000)   = 2,000A

Variable overhead efficiency $\qquad$ £

(standard hours – actual hours) × standard rate

$(9,000 – 7,000) × £1$ $\qquad$ = 2,000F

Fixed overhead expenditure

(budgeted fixed overheads – actual fixed overheads)

$(£20,000 – £23,000)$ $\qquad$ = 3,000A

5,000A

Delivery function

Expenditure variance

(flexed budget – actual delivery costs)

$(1,000 × £10 = £10,000 – £12,000)$ $\qquad$ = 2,000A

Summary of variances

Budgeted profit		35,000
Add: Favourable variances: Sales		9,000F
Less: Adverse variances: Purchasing	2,000A	
Production	5,000A	
Delivery	2,000A	9,000A
Actual profit		35,000

Notes

(1) Actual margin = actual selling price – standard cost (not actual cost). See 'sales variances' Chapter 17 for an explanation of why standard cost is deducted from actual selling price. The profit margins are calculated after deducting standard unit costs of £110.

(2) 1,000 hours at £4 (standard wage rate of £3 + variable overhead rate of £1) are charged to purchasing. This is because the purchasing department is responsible for part of the labour efficiency and variable overhead efficiency variance.

(3) It is assumed that the purchasing department is responsible for failing to meet the budgeted production. Therefore the fixed overhead volume variance is charged to the purchasing department.

(4) Actual hours are 7,000 and not 8,000. The 1,000 hours idle time have been charged to the purchasing department.

(b)(i) *Sales function:* The change in sales mix was not significant but increased selling prices were responsible for sales revenue being in excess of budget. The expenditure variance is 20 per cent above target and warrants further investigation.

Purchasing function: Favourable price variance but this may account for the adverse usage variance. £6,000 has been allocated to the department because of the department's inability to provide adequate raw material.

Production function: The efficiency of labour has resulted in a favourable labour and variable overhead efficiency variance. However, the spending variances for labour, fixed and variable overhead are all adverse. These variances may not be controllable by the production function. Also the adverse usage variance might be due to the purchase of inferior quality materials.

Delivery function: There is an overspending of £2,000. Further analysis of this variance is required.

(ii) Major difficulties are:

A. Setting adequate standards.

B. Pinpointing variances to areas of responsibility and analysing into controllable and non-controllable factors.

C. Interrelationships between variances may exist (e.g. material usage and material price).

Answer to problem 18.10

(a)(i) *Actual absorption costing*
Inventory is 20% of the output for the period and there are no opening stocks.
∴ Value of inventory = 20% × £4,080,000 = £816,000.

(ii) *Standard absorption costing with variances written off*
Standard cost of production for period = 50,000 × £75
$$= £3,750,000$$
∴ Closing stock = 20% × £3,750,000
$$= £750,000$$
The variances are written off as a period cost and not included in the stock valuation.

(iii) *Standard absorption costing with variances pro-rated between cost of sales and inventory.*
Variances for the period = £330,000 adverse (4,080,000 − £3,750,000 standard cost).
Variances pro-rated to inventory = £66,000 (£330,000 × 20%).
Inventory valuation = standard cost of inventory (£750,000) + pro-rated variances (£66,000)
$$= £816,000$$

(iv) *Actual direct costing*
Value of inventory = 20% × actual variable costs (£3,700,000)
$$= £740,000$$

(v) *Standard direct costing with variances written off*
Standard variable cost production = £3,250,000 (50,000 × £65 variable standard unit cost)
Inventory valuation = £650,000 (20% × £3,250,000)

(vi) *Standard direct costing with variances pro-rated between cost of sales and inventory.*
Standard variable cost of production = £3,250,000
Actual variable cost of production = £3,700,000
Variance = £450,000 adverse
Inventory valuation = standard variable cost of inventory (£650,000) + pro-rated variances
$$(20\% \times £450,000)$$
$$= £740,000$$

(b) Inventory valuations based on absorption costing treat fixed production overheads as product costs. This will cause the stock valuation to be influenced by the level of activity which is used to determine the fixed overhead rate per unit. In addition profits will be influenced by the production and stockholding policy.

Variable absorption costing methods treat fixed production overheads as period costs resulting in lower stock valuations compared with absorption costing. Profits are a function of sales volume only.

When actual costing methods are used inefficiencies are included in stock valuation. In theory they should be written off in the period when they are incurred. Where a standard costing system is used and variances are pro-rated between cost of sales and inventory the stock valuations are identical to the valuations based on actual cost systems. Therefore the same criticism regarding the inefficiencies being included in the stock valuation apply.

When a standard costing system is used and all variances are written off then inefficiencies are not included in the stock valuation. However, not all variances represent inefficiencies. Some variances may be due to permanent changes in standards (e.g. price variances). Variances which do not reflect inefficiencies should be pro-rated between cost of sales and inventories whereas variances which represent inefficiencies should be written off as a period cost.

(c)(i) *Discussion of the relevance of overhead cost absorption procedures for pricing*
The answer should include the following:

(i) Disadvantages of arbitrary apportionment of joint costs to products;

(ii) Influence of activity level in calculating pre-determined overhead rates. Overhead will only be recovered in sales revenue if demand is equivalent to the activity level that was used to calculate the overhead rate;

(iii) Limitations which apply when common costs are apportioned to products and an example of how this can lead to incorrect decisions;

(iv) Limitations of cost-plus pricing;

(v) Arguments in support of cost-plus pricing;

(vi) A discussion that full costs including overhead apportionments might provide an indication of the long run production cost.

Most of the above points are included in Chapters 10 and 11.

(ii) *Overhead cost absorption cost procedures for control of costs*

The answer should state that costs should be analysed into controllable and non-controllable elements. Apportioned costs should be separately shown in a section headed 'Uncontrollable Costs' in the performance report. The answer should stress accountability and responsibility when costs are attributed to individuals for control purposes. Overhead absorption should be used for product costing purposes but not for cost control purposes.

Answer to problem 18.11

(a) The traditional variance analysis is as follows:

Sales margin volume variance		Nil
(actual sales volume = budgeted sales volume)		
Sales margin price variance		
(actual unit margin − standard unit margin) × actual sales volume		
(£84 − £26) × 1,000		=£58,000F
		£58,000F
Material price		
(standard price − actual price) × actual quantity		
(£5 − £9) × 10,800	= £43,200A	
Material usage		
(standard quantity − actual quantity) × standard price		
(10,000 − 10,800) × £5	= £4,000A	£47,200A
Wage rate		
(standard rate − actual rate) × actual hours		
$\left(£4 - \dfrac{£34,800}{5,800}\right) \times 5,800$	=£11,600A	
Labour efficiency		
(standard hours − actual hours) × standard rate		
(1,000 × 6 = 6,000 − 5,800) × £4	= 800F	£10,800A
Total variances		Nil

Reconciliation:
Budgeted contribution (1,000 × £26)   £26,000
Add favourable sales variances   £58,000
Less adverse cost variances   (£58,000)
                                      Actual contribution   £26,000

(b)

	(a) Original plan	(b) Revised ex post plan	(c) Actual results
Sales	(1,000 × £100)=£100,000	(1,000 × £165) =£165,000	(1,000 × £158)=£158,000
Labour	(6,000 × £4) = £24,000	(6,000 × £6.25)= £37,500	(5,800 × £6) = £34,800
Materials:			
Aye	(10,000 × £5) = £50,000	(10,000 × £8.50)= £85,000	(10,800 × £9) = £97,200
Bee		(10,000 × £7) = £70,000	

Uncontrollable planning variances (A − B)	£	
Sales price	65,000F	
Wage rate	13,500A	
Material price* (50,000 − 70,000)	20,000A	
Substitution of materials variance* (85,000 − 70,000)	15,000A	16,500F

Operational variances		
Sales price (B − C)	7,000A	
Wage rate (5,800 × £0.25)	1,450F	
Labour efficiency (200 hrs at £6.25)	1,250F	
Material price (10,800 × £0.50)	5,400A	
Material usage (800 × £8.50)	6,800A	16,500A
Total variances		Nil

*If the purchasing officer is committed to buying Aye and it is not possible to change to Bee in the short-term then the £15,000 substitution variance is an uncontrollable price variance and the total planning variance will be £35,000 for materials. However, if the purchasing officer can respond to changes in relative prices then the £15,000 should be added to the operational price variance.

Comment on operational variances
The operational variances are calculated on the basis of the revised ex post plan. The ex post plan represents what the target would have been, given the benefit of hindsight. This represents a more realistic target than the original plan. For example, given the conditions for the period the target sales should have been £165,000. Actual sales were £158,000. Therefore the operational sales variance is £7,000 adverse. An explanation of planning and operational variances is presented in the section headed 'Criticisms of Variance Analysis' in Chapter 18.

(c) *Advantages*
(1) Traditional price variance includes unavoidable/uncontrollable elements due to change in environment of £20,000 or £35,000. The revised analysis is more indicative of current purchasing efficiency.
(2) Traditional approach incorrectly values deviations from budgeted efficiency in calculating usage or efficiency variances—A better indication is provided by attributing the current standard cost per unit to the deviations (∴ a variance of £6,800 is a better indication of the excess usage of the materials than the £4,000 under the traditional method).

Disadvantages
(1) Classification into planning (uncontrollable) and avoidable may be difficult (e.g. substitution variance) and arbitrary.
(2) Any error in producing ex post standards will cause a corresponding error in the classification of the variances (for example, we could have used a £9 ex post standard for materials thus affecting both the planning and operational variance).
(3) Excessive costs compared with benefits.
(4) Who sets the ex post standard? If the purchasing officer sets the standard then there is a danger that the standard may be biased to avoid unfavourable operational variances.

Answer to problem 18.15

(a) *Preliminary calculations*
Fixed overhead rate per hour   =£8 (£19,200÷2,400 hours)
Variable overhead rate per hour   =£16 (£38,400÷2,400 hours)
Contribution per unit of sales   =£128 (£268 selling price−£140 variable cost)
Contribution per unit of materials=£8 (£128÷16 units)
Contribution per labour hour   =£32 (£128÷4 hours)

Reconciliation of budgeted and actual profits

	(i) Traditional method £	(ii) Materials scarce £	(iii) Scarce labour hours £	(iv) Sales = Limiting factor £
Budgeted profit	57,600	57,600	57,600	57,600
Direct material usage variance	6,400A(1)	19,200A(2)	6,400A	6,400A
Direct material price variance	0	0	0	0
Wage rate variance	0	0	0	0
Labour efficiency variance	900A(3)	900A	10,500A(4)	900A
Variable overhead efficiency variance	4,800A(5)	4,800A	4,800A	4,800A
Variable overhead expenditure variance	3,600A(6)	3,600A	3,600A	3,600A
Volume efficiency variance	2,400A(7)	0	0	0
Volume capacity variance	800A(8)	0	3,200A(9)	0
Fixed overhead expenditure variance	800A	800A	800A	800A
Sales margin price variance	0	0	0	0
Sales margin volume variance	9,600A(10)	0	0	12,800A(11)
Actual profit	28,300	28,300	28,300	28,300

Notes
(1) 1,600 units at £4 per night.
(2) Acquisition cost of £6,400 plus lost contribution (1,600 units at £8).
(3) 300 hours at £3 per hour.
(4) Acquisition cost of £900 plus lost contribution (300 hours at £32).
(5) 300 hours at £16 per hour.
(6) Flexed budget allowance (2,300 hours at £16) less actual variable overheads (£40,400).
(7) 300 hours at £8 per hour.

(8) 100 unused hours at £8 per hour.
(9) 100 hours at a lost contribution of £32 per hour.
(10) 100 units at a profit margin of £96 per unit.
(11) 100 units at a contribution of £128 per unit.

(b) See 'A Relevant Cost Approach' in Chapter 18 for the answer to this question.

Answer to problem 18.17

(a)(i) Material price variance:
        (standard price – actual price) × actual quantity

$$\left(£0.05 - \frac{£45}{1,000}\right) \times 105,000 \qquad\qquad\qquad\qquad\qquad £525F$$

        Material usage variance:
        (standard quantity – actual quantity) × standard price
        (100,000 – 105,000) × £0.05   £250A

                                                     Total variance   £275F

	Dr.	Cr.
(ii) Dr stores ledger control account (AQ × SP)	5,250	
Cr creditors control account (AQ × AP)		4,725
Cr material price variance account		525
Dr work in progress (SQ × SP)	5,000	
Dr material usage variance account	250	
Cr stores ledger control account (AQ × SP)		5,250

   (iii) On the basis of the above calculations the buyer would receive a bonus of £52.50 (10% × £525) and the production manager would not receive any bonus. It could be argued that the joint price/usage variance should be separated if the variances are to be used as the basis for calculating bonuses (for a discussion of joint price/usage variances see Chapter 17). The revised analysis would be as follows:

Pure price variance:
     (standard price – actual price) × standard quantity
     (£0.05 – £0.045) × 100,000   £500F
Joint price/usage variance:
     (standard price – actual price) × excess usage
     (£0.05 – £0.045) × 5,000   £25F

Buyer's viewpoint
At the purchasing stage the buyer can influence both quality and price. Consequently the buyer can obtain favourable price variances by purchasing inferior quality materials at less than standard price. The adverse effects in terms of excess usage, because of the purchase of inferior quality of materials, are passed on to the production manager and the buyer gains from the price reduction. Indeed, if the joint price/usage is not isolated (see above), the buyer gains if production use materials in excess of standard. Therefore the bonus system might encourage the buyer to purchase inferior quality materials which results in an overall adverse *total* material cost variance and inferior product quality. In summary the bonus system appears to be biased in favour of the buyer at the expense of the production manager.

Production manager's viewpoint
The isolation of the joint price/usage variance might encourage the buyer not to purchase inferior quality materials and this will be to the production manager's advantage. Nevertheless the problem of the control of material quality still exists. The production manager would need to ensure that the quality of material purchased is in line with the quality built into the standard. Therefore some monitoring device is necessary. If variations do occur the quantity standard should be adjusted for the purpose of performance reporting and bonus assessment.

Company's viewpoint
The objective of the bonus system is to encourage goal congruence and increase motivation. Interdependencies exist between the two responsibility centres and it is doubtful that the bonus system encourages goal congruence or improves motivation. If the quality of materials which can be purchased from the various suppliers does not vary then the adverse effects of the bonus system will be reduced. Nevertheless interdependencies will still exist between the responsibility centres. One solution might be to base the bonuses of both managers on the *total* material cost variance. In addition standards should be regularly reviewed and participation by both managers in setting the standards encouraged.

(b)(i) The minimum present value of expected savings that would have to be made in future months in order to justify making an investigation is where

$$IC + P\,(CC) = P\,(x)$$

where IC = Investigation costs
P = Probability process is out of control
CC = Correction cost
x = Present value of expected savings if process is out of control

$$\therefore £50 + 0.5\,(£100) = 0.5x$$
$$\therefore 0.5x = £100$$
$$\therefore x = £200$$

Therefore the minimum present value of expected savings that would have to be made is £200.

(ii) The standard cost will probably represent the mean value and random variations around the mean value can be expected to occur even when the process is under control. Therefore it is unlikely that the £500 variance will be eliminated completely because a proportion of the variance simply reflects the randomness of the variables affecting the standard. If the process is found to be out of control, the corrective action will only confine variances to the normal acceptable range of standard outcomes. If the £500 is an extreme deviation from the standard then it is likely that the potential savings from investigation will be insignificant.

(iii) Applying the notation used in (i) the firm will be indifferent about whether to conduct an investigation when the expected savings resulting from correction are equal to the expected cost of correction,

$$\text{i.e. where } IC + P\,(CC) = P\,(x)$$
$$\text{then if } x = £600$$
$$50 + P\,(100) = P\,(600)$$
$$\therefore 500P = 50$$
$$\therefore P = 10\%$$
$$\text{If } x = £250$$
$$50 + P\,(100) = P\,(250)$$
$$\therefore 150P = 50$$
$$\therefore P = 33\tfrac{1}{3}\%$$

Answer to problem 18.19

(a) See answer to problem 18.20.
(b) See 'Accounting Disposition of Variances' in Chapter 18 for the answer to this question.

Answer to problem 18.20

(a) The management accountant should consider the following factors when deciding whether or not to investigate variances:

(i) *The size of the variances:* This may be expressed in terms of percentage variation from standard or budget. Alternatively statistical techniques can be used to determine the probability of the variance occurring when it is under control. The size of the variance indicates the likelihood that the variance is due to an assignable cause.

(ii) *Costs and benefits of investigation:* The management accountant should assess whether the costs of investigation are less than the benefits that are expected to result from the investigation.

(iii) *Nature of the standard:* Are expected or ideal standards used? If ideal standards are used then investigation of the variances is unlikely to result in the variances being eliminated.

(iv) *Cumulative variances:* A variance showing an increase in size over time may justify an investigation even when the variance for the particular period is not significant. Alternatively a variance which is significant for a particular period but which is decreasing over time may be under control.

(v) *Validity of standard or budget:* The validity of the standard will help the accountant to gauge the significance of the variance. A price variance in times of rapidly rising prices is unlikely to be due to an assignable cause.

(b) The management accountant can take the following action to improve the chances of achieving positive results from investigating variances:

(i) *Speedy identification and reporting of variances:* Significant delays between the occurrence of a variance and its notification to managers will limit the degree of control which managers can achieve. The sooner a variance is identified, the sooner it can be investigated and acted upon.

(ii) *Analysis of variances:* The accountant should provide clues as to the possible reasons for the variances by pinpointing where the variances have arisen. For example, the accountant might identify the reason for a direct material variance as being due to excessive usage of a certain material in a particular process. This should assist the responsibility manager in quickly identifying the cause of the excessive usage.

(iii) *Statistical procedures:* Statistical procedures and quality control charts should be used so as to determine the probability that variances are due to an assignable cause. If managers are required to frequently investigate variances which are due to random variations then it is unlikely that they will give detailed attention to the investigation process. However, if the majority of variances reported are significant then managers will attach greater importance to the investigation process.

(iv) *Develop a team effort approach:* The accountant should be seen by managers as supportive within the control process. If a team effort approach is developed then it is likely that managers will be more actively involved in the investigation process.

Answer to problem 18.21

(a) The following problems might occur during periods of rapid inflation:

(i) The standards will presumably include some assumptions about inflation. If this assumption is not clearly stated then it is difficult to determine how much of a price variance is due to inflation and how much is due to buying efficiency.

(ii) Price indices tend to reflect average price changes. Consequently it is difficult for a company to predict future costs and interpret variances if the specific rate of inflation for its inputs is considerably different from the general rate of inflation.

(iii) Inflation may result in relative changes in the prices of inputs. Therefore standard mixes requiring different inputs may no longer be the most efficient mix.

(iv) If standard prices are not adjusted then the efficiency variances will be understated.

(v) The impact of inflation will have an immediate effect on cash flows but some delay will occur before the full extent of the variances are ascertained. Therefore management may not respond quickly enough to pricing, output and sourcing decisions in order to effectively control cash flows.

(vi) Sharp rises in prices will raise questions as to whether unadjusted standards can be used in the decision-making process (e.g. pricing decisions).

(vii) Administrative work in maintaining up-to-date standards when prices are constantly changing.

(b) (i) When establishing standards the inflation factor that has been assumed should be clearly stated so that variances can be analysed by price and efficiency changes.

(ii) Internal indices of price changes could be maintained for cost items which do not move in line with the general rate of inflation.

(iii) Variances should be analysed by their forecasting and operational elements as indicated in Chapter 18.

(iv) Standard mixes should be established for a range of prices for the material inputs and management should be prepared to implement changes in the mix immediately price changes dictate that a change is necessary.

Behavioural aspects of accounting control systems

The questions set in this chapter consist of a range of discussion questions on various behavioural aspects of accounting control systems. 19.8 to 19.11 are discussion questions which do not require specific answers. They are intended to test independent thought and initiative in relating the behavioural literature to the questions asked. Therefore answers are not provided to these questions.

Answer to problem 19.1

The answer should include a discussion of the following:

 (i) The impact of targets on performance
 (ii) The use of accounting control techniques for performance evaluation
(iii) Participation in the budgeting and standard setting process
(iv) Bias in the budget process
 (v) Management use of budgets and the role of the accountant in the education process.

See Chapter 19 for a discussion of each of the above items.

Answer to problem 19.2

(a) See Chapter 19 for the answer to this question.

(b) See the conclusion to Chapter 19 for the answer to this question.

(c) Figure 16.2 in Chapter 16 illustrates the importance of feedback (information comparing planned and actual outcomes in the control process). Feedback takes the form of control reports issued by the account- ant to the managers responsible for controlling inputs. Effective control requires that corrective action is taken so that actual outputs conform to planned outputs in the future. In order to assist managers in controlling activities the performance reports should highlight those areas which do not conform to plan. The performance reports should also provide clues as to why the actual outputs differ from the planned outputs. Feedback information is necessary to provoke corrective managerial action.

It should be noted that accounting reports of performance also have a direct effect on motivation by giving the department manager knowledge of performance. Knowledge of results has been shown in various psychological experiments to lead to improved performance. This is partly because it conveys information which can be used for acting more effectively on the next trial; but also partly because knowl- edge of results motivates through satisfying the achievement need. Stok investigated the effect of control systems using visual presentation of quality on workers quality performance. He found that visual present-ation of quality had both an information and a motivation effect and both were instrumental in improving performance. It appears that communicating knowledge of results acts as a reward or punishment. It can serve either to reinforce or extinguish previous employee behaviours.

(d) The purpose of goal congruence is to encourage an individual manager's goals to be in agreement with the organisation's goals. For a description of this process see 'The Use of Accounting Control Tech-niques for Performance Evaluation' in Chapter 19.

Reference
Stok, T. L. 'De Arbeider en de Zichbaarmaking van de Kwaliteit' Leiden, Stenfert Kruese, 1959.

Answer to problem 19.3

Managers may be reluctant to participate in setting budgets because of the following reasons:
  (i) Managers may consider that they do not engage in true participation if they cannot influence the budget. They may consider the process to be one of the senior managers securing formal acceptance of previously determined target levels;
 (ii) Personality of budgetees may result in authoritarian managers having authoritarian expectations of their superiors. Consequently authoritarian budgetees may be reluctant to participate in the budget process.
(iii) The degree to which individuals have control over their own destiny (See Brownell's (1981) research in Chapter 19) appears to influence the desire for participation. Managers may believe that they cannot significantly influence results and thus consider participation to be inappropriate;
 (iv) Bad management/superior relationships;
  (v) Lack of understanding of the budget process or a belief by the budgetees that they will be engaging in a process which will be used in a recriminatory manner by their superiors.
The unwanted side effects which might arise from the imposition of budgets by senior management include the following:
  (i) Non-acceptance of budgets;
 (ii) The budgetees might consider the method of performance evaluation to be unjust;
(iii) Creation of anti-management cohesive work groups;
 (iv) Reduced efficiency by work groups so as to protect themselves against what they consider to be increasingly stringent targets;
  (v) The budget system will be undermined. The real problem is the way management use the system rather than inadequacies of the budget system itself;
 (vi) An increase in suspicion and mistrust, so undermining the whole budgeting process;
(vii) Encouraging budgetees to falsify and manipulate information presented to management;
(viii) Organisational atmosphere may become one of competition and conflict rather than one of co-operation and conciliation;
 (ix) Managers might try to achieve the budget at all costs even if this results in actions which are not in the best interests of the organisation.

Answer to problem 19.4

(a) See 'The Use of Budgets as Targets' in Chapter 19 for the answer to this question.

(b) See 'Participation in the Budgeting and Standard Setting Process' in Chapter 19 for the answer to this question.

(c) Management by exception is based on the principle that accounting reports should highlight those activities which do not conform to plans so that managers can devote their scarce time to focusing on these items. Effective control requires that corrective action is taken so that actual outcomes conform to planned outcomes. These principles are based on the following assumptions:

  (i) Valid targets and budgets can be set;
  (ii) Suitable performance measures exist which enable divergencies from plans to be correctly measured;
  (iii) Plans and divergencies from plan are communicated to the individuals who are responsible for implementing the plan;
  (iv) Performance reports correctly distinguish those items which are controllable by a manager from those which are non-controllable;
  (v) Feedback information is translated into corrective action;
  (vi) Management intervention is not required where no adverse variances exist;
  (vii) Divergencies from plan can only be remedied by corrective action.

Management by exception as an effective system of routine reporting will depend on the extent to which the above conditions hold. The system will have to be supplemented by informal controls to the extent that the above conditions do not hold. Management by exception can only be a very effective means of control if behavioural factors are taken into account when interpreting the divergencies from plan. Otherwise there is a danger that other systems of control will have a greater influence on future performance.

(d) The answer should include the following:

  (i) An explanation of why it is considered necessary to distinguish between controllable and uncontrollable costs at the responsibility level;
  (ii) Difficulty in assigning variances to responsibility centres when dual responsibilities apply or interdependencies exist;
  (iii) Possible dysfunctional consequences that might occur when a manager's performance is measured by his success in controlling only those items which have been designated as controllable by him;
  (iv) Arguments for including those uncontrollable items which a manager might be able to influence in a separate section of the performance report.

The above items are discussed in the section headed 'Responsibility Accounting' in Chapter 16.

(e) Budget statements should not be expressed only in monetary terms. This is because all aspects of performance relating to a firm's goals cannot be expressed in monetary terms. Therefore budgetary statements should be supplemented by non-monetary measures. Monetary gains can be made at the expense of items which cannot easily be measured in monetary terms but which may be critical to an organisation's long-term profitability. For example monetary gains can be made by hierarachical pressure to cut costs but such gains might be at the expense of adverse motivational changes, increased labour turnover and reduced product quality. The long-term costs of these items might be far in excess of the cost-cutting benefits.

    A range of non-monetary measures is presented at the end of the 'Responsibility Accounting' section in Chapter 16. However, some qualitative variables (Eg Measurement of attitudes) are difficult to measure but judgements based on interviews can be made. The inclusion of behavioural and qualitative factors in budget statements more accurately reflects the complexity of managerial performance in relation to a number of objectives rather than a single monetary objective. The difficulty with incorporating qualitative variables into budget statements is not sufficient grounds for expressing budget statements only in monetary terms.

Answer to problem 19.5

See 'The Use of Budgets as Targets' in Chapter 19 and 'Establishing Cost Standards' in Chapter 17 for the answer to this question.

Answer to problem 19.6

(a) For the answer to this question see 'The Use of Budgets as Targets' in Chapter 19. In particular the answer should stress that a tight budget is preferable for motivation purposes whereas for planning and control purposes an expected target should be set which management believes will be achieved. Consequently a conflict occurs between the motivational and management reporting objectives.

(b) The levels of efficiency which may be incorporated in the standards used in budgetary control and/or standard costing include the following:

 (i) *Perfection:* Standards based on perfection are termed 'Ideal Standards'. Case 6 illustrated in Figure 19.1 in Chapter 19 is typical of a standard based on perfection. Ideal standards have no motivational advantages and are unsatisfactory for planning and control purposes.
 (ii) *Tight Standards:* These standards represent targets which are set at a level of performance which is difficult, but not impossible, for budgetees to achieve. Cases 3–5 illustrated in Figure 19.1 represent tight standards. It can be seen from Figure 19.1 that tight standards should increase aspiration levels and actual performance. Because tight standards may not be achieved they are unsatisfactory for planning and control purposes.
 (iii) *Expected Performance:* Expected performance standards are based on the level of efficiency expected to be attained (i.e. Case 2 in Figure 19.1). One advantage of expected standards is that variances indicate deviations from management's expectations. A further advantage is that expected standards can be used for planning purposes. Expected standards are likely to be unsatisfactory for motivational purposes as they may not provide sufficient motivation.
 (iv) *Loose Standards:* With loose standards the level of efficiency implied by the standard is less than expected. Case 1 illustrated in Figure 19.1 represents a loose standard. Loose standards are poor motivators and are unsatisfactory for planning and control purposes.

(c) See 'Participation in the Budgeting and Standard Setting Process' in Chapter 19 for the answer to this question.

Answer to problem 19.7

(a)(i) Budgets are used for a variety of purposes, one of which is to evaluate the performance of budgetees. When budgets form the basis for future performance evaluation there is a possibility that budgetees will introduce bias into the process for personal gain and self protection. Factors which are likely to cause managers to submit budget estimates which do not represent their best estimates include:

 (i) *The Reward System:* If managers believe that rewards depend upon budget attainment then they might be encouraged to underestimate sales budgets and overestimate cost budgets.
 (ii) *Past Performance:* If recent performance has been poor managers may submit favourable plans so as to obtain approval from their supervisors. Such an approach represents a trade-off advantage of short-run security and approval against the risk of not being able to meet the more optimistic plans.
 (iii) *Incremental Budgeting:* Incremental budgeting involves adding increments to past budgets to reflect expected future changes. Consequently the current budget will include bias which has been built into previous budgets.

 (iv) *External Influences:* If managers believe that their performance is subject to random external influences then from a self protection point of view they might submit budgets which can easily be attained.

 (v) *Style of Performance Evaluation:* A budget constrained style of evaluation might encourage the budgetee to meet the budget at all costs. Consequently budgetees will be motivated to bias their budget estimates.

(ii) The following procedures should be introduced to minimise the likelihood of biased estimates:

 (i) Encourage managers to adopt a profit conscious style of evaluation.

 (ii) Adopt a system of zero-base budgeting.

(iii) Key figures in the budget process (Eg sales estimates) should be checked by using information from different sources.

(iv) Planning and operating variances (See 'Criticisms of Standard Costing Variance Analysis' in Chapter 18 for a discussion of planning and operating variances) should be segregated. Managers might be motivated to submit more genuine estimates if they are aware that an ex-post budget will be used as a basis for performance appraisal.

 (v) Participation by the budgetees in the budget process should be encouraged so as to secure a greater commitment to the budget process and improve communication between budgetees; their superior and the budget accountants.

Mathematical approaches to cost estimation

Details of the questions are as follows:

20.1 to 20.3   Cost estimation problems using the least squares method. 20.1 and 20.2 are not difficult and can be used as introductory questions. 20.3 requires the adjustment of past costs for price level changes.
20.4 to 20.7   Estimation of costs using the learning curve.
20.8   Estimation of costs according to a formula given in the question.
20.9 to 20.11   Discussion questions related to Chapter 20.

Answer to problem 20.1

(a)(i)

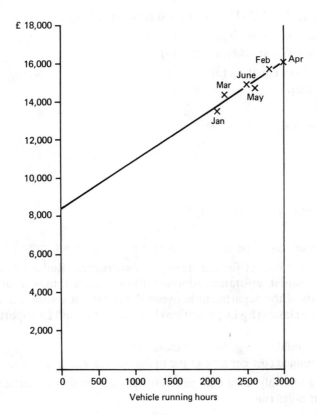

(ii)

Vehicle running hours	Vehicle maintenance cost £		
x	y	x^2	xy
2,100	13,600	4,410,000	28,560,000
2,800	15,800	7,840,000	44,240,000
2,200	14,500	4,840,000	31,900,000
3,000	16,200	9,000,000	48,600,000
2,600	14,900	6,760,000	38,740,000
2,500	15,000	6,250,000	37,500,000
$\sum x = 15,200$	$y = 90,000$	$\sum x^2 = 39,100,000$	$\sum xy = 229,540,000$

The regression equation for a straight line can be found by solving for a and b in the following two equations:

$$\sum y = Na + b\sum x$$
$$\sum xy = \sum xa + b\sum x^2$$

Inserting the figures into the formula we have

$$90,000 = 6a + 15,200b \ldots \ldots (1)$$
$$229,540,000 = 15,200a + 39,100,000b \ldots \ldots (2)$$

Multiply equation (1) by 2,533.3333 (15,200 ÷ 6) and equation (2) by 1

$$228,000,000 = 15,200a + 38,506,666b \ldots \ldots (3)$$
$$229,540,000 = 15,200a + 39,100,000b \ldots \ldots (4)$$

Subtracting equation (4) from equation (3)

$$-1,540,000 = -593,334b$$
$$\therefore b = 2.5955$$

Substituting for b in equation (1)

$$90,000 = 6a + 39,452$$
$$50,548 = 6a$$
$$\therefore a = 8,425$$
$$\therefore y = a + bx$$
$$\therefore y = £8,425 + £2.5955 \, x$$

(b) The following procedure could be used to establish a 'charging out' rate:

 (i) Prepare a departmental budget for the transport department. Budgeted costs will include vehicle running costs, depreciation, insurance, administration, garaging, maintenance costs etc.
 (ii) Apportion total costs of the department between the classes of vehicles. Some costs will be directly attributable to vehicle classes (Eg Depreciation) but other costs will be apportioned on an appropriate basis (Eg Mileage).
 (iii) Estimate budgeted annual mileage for each class of vehicle.
 (iv) Calculate a predetermined cost per mile at the budgeted mileage level for each class of vehicle.

Alternatively a budgeted monthly fixed charge could be made to user departments and only a variable cost per mile charged for miles run.

Answer to problem 20.3

(a) The first stage is to convert all costs to a 1981 basis. The calculations are as follows:

Year	1977 £000's	1978 £000's	1979 £000's	1980 £000's
Raw materials Skilled labour } Unskilled labour	$242(1.2)^4$	$344(1.2)^3$	$461(1.2)^2$	$477(1.2)$
Factory overheads	$168(1.15)^3(1.2)$	$206(1.15)^2(1.2)$	$246(1.15)(1.2)$	$265(1.2)$
Power	$25(1.1)(1.25)^3$	$33(1.25)^3$	$47(1.25)^2$	$44(1.25)$
Raw materials Skilled labour } Unskilled labour	500.94	595.12	663.84	572.4
Factory overheads	306.432	326.304	339.48	318
Power	53.625	64.35	73.32	55
Total (1981 prices)	861,000	986,000	1,077,000	945,000
Output (units)	160,000	190,000	220,000	180,000

The equation $y=a+bx$ is calculated from the above schedule of total production costs (1981 prices) and output. The calculations are as follows:

Output in units (000's) x	Total cost (£000's) y	x^2	xy
160	861	25,600	137,760
190	986	36,100	187,340
220	1,077	48,400	236,940
180	945	32,400	170,100
$\sum x = 750$	$\sum y = 3,869$	$\sum x^2 = 142,500$	$\sum xy = 732,140$

We now solve the following simultaneous equations:

$$\sum y = Na + b\sum x$$
$$\sum xy = \sum xa + b\sum x^2$$
$$\therefore \quad 3,869 = 4a + 750b \ldots \ldots (1)$$
$$732,140 = 750a + 142,500b \ldots \ldots (2)$$

Multiply equation (1) by 190 ($142,500 \div 750$) and equation (2) by 1
$\therefore$ equation 1 becomes $735,110 = 760a + 142,500b \ldots \ldots (3)$
Subtract equation (2) from equation (3)
$$\therefore 2,970 = 10a$$
$$\therefore a = 297$$
Substitute for a in equation (1)
$$\therefore 3,869 = 4(297) + 750b$$
$$2,681 = 750b$$
$$\therefore b = 3.57$$

The relationship between total production costs and volume for 1981 is:

y=£297,000+3.57x
where y=Total production costs (at 1981 price)
and x=Output level

(b) See Chapter 20 for the answer to this question, particularly 'Requirements for Using Mathematical Techniques' and 'Problems when Applying Mathematical Cost Equations'.

(c) General company overheads will still continue whether or not product LT is produced. Therefore the output of LT will not affect general production overheads. Consequently the regression equation should not be calculated from cost data that includes general company overheads. General company overheads will not increase with increments in output of product LT. Hence short-term decisions and cost control should focus on those costs which are relevant to production of LT's. Common and unavoidable general fixed costs are not relevant to the production of LT and should not be included in the regression equation.

Answer to problem 20.4

(a)(i) The cumulative average wages cost per unit for the production of 150 units is £900 (1505.3 × 19.93% × £3). Therefore the variable cost per unit for the production of 150 units is calculated as follows:

	£
Direct materials	1,200
Direct wages	900
Variable production overhead (50% × £900)	450
Variable selling and admin. overhead (10% of selling price)	400
	2,950

Using the above figure the NPV calculation is as follows:

Year	No. of units	Sales at £4000 each (£000's)	Variable costs (1) (£000's)	Fixed overhead (£000's)	Net cash flow (£000's)	12% disc. factor	PV (£000's)
1983	20	80	(59.0)	(12)	9.0	0.893	8.04
1984	40	160	(118.0)	(12)	30.0	0.797	23.91
1985	50	200	(147.5)	(12)	40.5	0.712	28.84
1986	30	120	(88.5)	(12)	19.5	0.636	12.40
1987	10	40	(29.5)	(12)	(1.5)	0.567	(0.85)
	150						72.34
				Less investment cost			70.00
						NPV	2.34

Note
(1) Units produced each year × variable cost per unit of £2950.

(ii) The incremental labour and variable overhead cost for each year is calculated as follows:

Year	Units	Cumulative units	Cumulative labour and variable overhead cost (1) ($£000's$)	Incremental labour and variable overhead cost (2) ($£000's$)	Selling and admin. ($£000's$)	Total variable cost ($£000's$)
1983	20	20	$20 \times 1505.3 \times 0.3813 \times £4.50 = 51.7$	51.7	8	59.7
1984	40	60	$60 \times 1505.3 \times 0.2677 \times £4.50 = 108.4$	56.7	16	72.7
1985	50	110	$110 \times 1505.3 \times 0.2203 \times £4.50 = 164.1$	55.7	20	75.7
1986	30	140	$140 \times 1505.3 \times 0.2038 \times £4.50 = 193.3$	29.2	12	41.2
1987	10	150	$150 \times 1505.3 \times 0.1993 \times £4.50 = 202.5$	9.2	4	13.2

Notes

(1) Cost per unit $= £3$ labour $+$ variable overheads $(50\% \times £3)$

(2) $1984 = £108.4 - £51.7 = 56.7$
$\qquad 1985 = £164.1 - £108.4 = 55.7$

Year	No. of units	Sales ($£000's$)	Direct materials ($£000's$)	Labour and variable overheads ($£000's$)	Variable selling and admin. ($£000's$)	Fixed overhead ($£000's$)	Net cash flow ($£000's$)	Disc. Factor	P.V. ($£000's$)
1983	20	80	(24)	(51.7)	(8)	(12)	(15.7)	0.893	(14.02)
1984	40	160	(48)	(56.7)	(16)	(12)	27.3	0.797	21.76
1985	50	200	(60)	(55.7)	(20)	(12)	52.3	0.712	37.24
1986	30	120	(36)	(29.2)	(12)	(12)	30.8	0.636	19.59
1987	10	40	(12)	(9.2)	(4)	(12)	2.8	0.567	1.59
									66.16
							Less investment cost		70.00
								NPV	(3.84)

(b) Method (i) is incorrect because it incorrectly averages the cummulative labour cost over the five year period. With method (ii) the learning curve benefits are allocated to the years in which the benefits occur. With method (ii) labour costs are higher in the earlier years and lower in the later years whereas method (i) allocates the learning benefits to the earlier years. Method (ii) provides a more accurate estimate of the timing of the cash flows for labour and variable overhead and is therefore recommended.

Answer to problem 20.5

(a) The calculation of the average cost per unit for the initial order of 160 units is as follows:

Direct materials		P	28	
		Q	12	40
Direct labour: dept. 1	5			
2	75			
3	15		95	
Variable overhead $(20\% \times 95)$			19	
Variable cost			154	

Fixed overhead:

Dept. 1	8	
Dept. 2	50	
Dept. 3	12	70
Total cost		224

Profit margin $\left(\begin{array}{l} 2\frac{1}{2}\% \times 40 \\ 12\frac{1}{2}\% \times 184 \end{array}\right)$ 24

Selling price for initial 160 units 248

Costs subject to learning curve:	Depts. 2 and 3 Direct labour	90
	Variable overhead (20% × £90)	18
	Fixed overhead (see note 1)	62
		170
Costs not subject to learning curve:	Direct materials	40
	Dept. 1 Direct labour	5
	Dept. 1 Variable overhead (20% × £5)	1
	Dept. 1 Fixed overhead	8
		54

Note

(1) The total expenditure on fixed overheads will not decrease because of the learning curve but if the mechanical cost-plus pricing procedure suggested in the question is applied then this technique will cause the fixed overheads charged to the order to be related to direct labour hours. Therefore the fixed overhead charged to each order will be related to the learning curve. The learning curve factors applied to the production pattern is as follows:

Order	Order quantity	Cumulative production	x	$y(\%)$
1	160	160	1.0	100
2	80	240	$1.5 \left(\dfrac{240}{160}\right)$	87.6
3	80	320	$2.0 \left(\dfrac{320}{160}\right)$	80.0
4	48	368	$2.3 \left(\dfrac{368}{160}\right)$	76.8
5	48	416	2.6	74.0
6	48	464	2.9	71.5

The incremental cost and unit cost of each order is calculated as follows:

(1)	*(2)*	*(3)*	*(4)*	*(5)*
			Incremental	*Incremental*
Order	*Unit cost*	*Total cost (1)*	*cost of order*	*unit cost (2)*
	£	£	£	£
1	170.00	27,200	27,200	170.00
2	148.92 (87.6% × £170)	35,740	8,540	106.75
3	136.00 (80% × £170)	43,520	7,780	97.25

4	130.56 (76.8% × £170)	48,046	4,526	94.29
5	125.80 (74% × £170)	52,333	4,287	89.30
6	121.55 (71.5% × £170)	56,399	4,066	84.70

Notes
(1) Total cost = unit cost in column 2 × cumulative production
(2) Incremental unit cost = incremental cost of order ÷ order quantity
The selling prices for each order are calculated as follows:

| Order | 1 | 2 | 3 | 4 | 5 | 6 |
	£	£	£	£	£	£
Learning curve unit cost	170.00	106.75	97.25	94.29	89.30	84.70
Non-learning curve unit cost	54.00	54.00	54.00	54.00	54.00	54.00
Unit total cost	224.00	160.75	151.25	148.29	143.30	138.70
Selling price (1)	248.00	176.85	166.15	162.83	157.20	152.00
	A(i)	A(ii)	(A(ii)	A(ii)		

Note
(1) The selling price is calculated by adding $2\frac{1}{2}\%$ of the direct materials and $12\frac{1}{2}\%$ of the conversion cost to the total cost.

The selling price if the whole contract of the six orders is given from the start is calculated as follows:

	£
Average cost per unit subject to learning curve	121.55 (71.5% × £170)
Non-learning curve costs	54.00
	175.55
Profit margin	17.94
	193.49
	(Aiii)

If all six orders are received the total sales revenue will be the same whichever method of pricing the orders is adopted.

	£	
Order 1	39,680	(160 × £248)
Order 2	14,148	(80 × £176.85)
Order 3	13,292	(80 × £166.15)
Order 4	7,816	(48 × £162.83)
Order 5	7,547	(48 × £157.20)
Order 6	7,296	(48 × £152.00)
	89,779	

If a single selling price is charged for all six orders then total sales revenue will be £89,779 (464 × £193.49).
(b) The factors that should be taken into account are:

(i) The extent to which costs are expected to decline as workers become more familiar with the operations. Direct labour and those costs which are related to hours of direct labour input (normally variable overheads) can be expected to decline (per unit) as output increases.

(ii) The extent to which the operations will become repetitive. Standard costing is unsuited to 'one-off' operations.

(iii) The point on the learning curve for the particular operation. If the operation is approaching the steady-state phase then incorporating the learning effects is likely to have little impact on the setting of standard costs.

Answer to problem 20.9

See 'Cost Estimation when the Learning Effect is Present' in Chapter 20 for an explanation of the learning curve. If the learning effect is ignored and standards are set when cumulative output is low then the resulting standards will ignore the cost reductions resulting from the learning curve. Consequently the standards will represent easily attainable standards and favourable variances which are not due to improved efficiency will occur. Alternatively standards might be set at the steady state level and this will result in adverse variances throughout the 'start-up' phase. In order that meaningful targets can be set it is essential that the learning curve principles are applied when setting standards.

Answer to problem 20-10

See 'Requirements for Using Mathematical Techniques' in Chapter 20 for the answer to this question.

Answer to problem 20.11

See Chapter 20 for the answer to this question.

Quantitative models for the planning and control of stocks

Questions 21.1 to 21.4 should be regarded as general introductory questions on the EOQ model. Details of the remaining questions are as follows:

21.5	An evaluation of quantity discounts.
21.6	Make or buy decision incorporating ordering and holding costs.
21.7	Use of probability theory for determining safety stocks.
21.8	Cost of prediction error plus a comparison of the performance evaluation system and the EOQ model.
21.9 and 21.10	Decision-making problems using the EOQ model. These questions are more demanding than 21.1 to 21.8 and are more appropriate to a second year course.
21.11 and 21.12	Discussion questions relevant to Chapter 21.

Answer to problem 21.2

(a) *Item A32—storage and ordering cost schedule*

No. of orders per year	4	5	6	7	8	9	10	11	12
Order size (boxes)	1,250	1,000	833	714	625	556	500	455	417
Average stock (boxes)	625	500	417	357	313	278	250	228	208
	£	£	£	£	£	£	£	£	£
Storage costs (Average stock × 25% at £2)	312.5	250.0	208.5	178.5	156.5	139.0	125.0	114.0	104.0
Ordering costs (£12.5 per order)	50.0	62.5	75.0	87.5	100.0	112.5	125.0	137.5	150.0
Total cost	£362.5	£312.5	£283.5	£266.0	£256.5	£251.5	£250.0	£251.5	£254.0

(b) The number of orders which should be placed in a year to minimise costs is 10.

(c) $EOQ = \sqrt{\dfrac{2DO}{H}}$

   where D = Total demand for period
          O = Ordering cost per order
          H = Holding cost per unit

(d) $EOQ = \sqrt{\dfrac{2 \times 5000 \times 12.5}{0.5}}$

   = 500 units

(e) The maximum saving that could be made if the authority process four orders per year would be

   $\dfrac{£362.50 - £250}{£362.50} = 31\%$

(f) (i) Reducing the number of stock items by eliminating slow moving and obsolete stocks.
    (ii) Standardisation of stock items thus reducing the total number of items in stock.

Answer to problem 21.3

(a) (i) $EOQ = \sqrt{\dfrac{2DO}{H}}$

    where D = Annual demand
           O = Ordering cost per order
           H = Holding cost per unit

    $\therefore EOQ = \sqrt{\dfrac{2 \times 48,000 \times £0.60}{10\% \times £10}}$

    = 240

   (ii) Number of orders required per year are:

    $\dfrac{\text{Annual requirements}}{EOQ} = \dfrac{48,000}{240} = 200$ orders per year

   (iii) Total cost = Holding cost + Ordering cost

    $= \dfrac{240}{2}$ (£1) $+ \dfrac{48,000}{240}$(£0.60)

    = £240

(b) Usage per day = 133.33 (48,000 ÷ 360 days)
    Number of days usage in closing stock = 3 (400 ÷ 133.33)
    Lead time = 3 days
Therefore the next order should be placed immediately.

(c) Some problems when attempting to apply the EOQ formula are:
    (a) Inventory is not always used at a constant rate, and the constant usage assumption is implicit in the
        EOQ formula.

(b) The EOQ formula requires estimates of (a) annual sales, (b) ordering costs, (c) purchase price per unit, and (d) cost of carrying inventories. These items may be extremely difficult to estimate in practice.

Answer to problem 21.5

(a) $EOQ = \sqrt{\dfrac{2DO}{H}}$

$\qquad = \sqrt{\dfrac{2 \times 50,000 \times 100}{0.40}}$

$\qquad = 5,000$

	£
(b) Savings in purchase price (50,000 × £0.02)	1,000

Saving in ordering cost

$$\frac{DO}{Qd} - \frac{DO}{Q} = \frac{50,000\,(100)}{10,000} - \frac{50,000\,(100)}{5,000}$$

	£
	500
Total savings	1,500

(Note Qd represents quantity ordered to obtain discount and Q represents EOQ).
The additional holding cost if the larger quantity is purchased is calculated as follows:

$$\frac{(Qd-Q)H}{2} = \frac{(10,000-5,000)\,0.40}{2} = £1,000$$

As the total savings exceed the total cost increase, the company should take advantage of the quantity discount.

Answer to problem 21.7

(a)

Safety stock	Stockout	Stockout cost at £10 £	Probability	Expected cost £	Total £
500	0	0	0	0	0
400	100	1,000	0.04	40	40
300	200	2,000	0.04	80	
	100	1,000	0.07	70	150
200	300	3,000	0.04	120	
	200	2,000	0.07	140	
	100	1,000	0.10	100	360

Safety stock	Stockout	Stockout cost at £10 £	Probability	Expected cost £	Total £
100	400	4,000	0.04	160	
	300	3,000	0.07	210	
	200	2,000	0.10	200	
	100	1,000	0.13	130	700
0	500	5,000	0.04	200	
	400	4,000	0.07	280	
	300	3,000	0.10	300	
	200	2,000	0.13	260	
	100	1,000	0.16	160	1,200

Safety stock	Stockout cost £	Holding cost £	Total cost £
0	1,200	0	1,200
100	700	100	800
200	360	200	560
300	150	300	450
400	40	400	440
500	0	500	500

The optimal safety stock is 400 units.

(b) The probability of being out of stock at an optimal safety stock of 400 units is 0.04.

Answer to problem 21.8

(a) EOQ $= \sqrt{\dfrac{2DO}{H}}$

$= \sqrt{\dfrac{2 \times 4,000 \times 135}{12}}$

$= 300$

The relevant cost is:
Holding cost + ordering cost

$= \dfrac{300}{2} \text{(£12)} + \dfrac{4,000}{300} \text{(£135)}$

$= £3,600$

(b) Revised EOQ $= \sqrt{\dfrac{2 \times 4,000 \times 80}{12}}$

$= 231$

The relevant cost is:
Holding cost + ordering cost

$$= \frac{231}{2} (£12) + \frac{4,000}{231} (80)$$

$$= £2,772$$

The relevant cost using the original EOQ of 300 units but with an incremental ordering cost of £80 is:

$$\frac{300}{2} (£12) + \frac{4,000}{300} (£80)$$

$$= £2,867$$

Cost of prediction error = £95 (£2,867 − £2,772)

(c) The annual costs of purchasing, ordering and holding the materials consist of:

Holding cost + Ordering cost + Purchase cost

Special offer at £86 $\frac{4,000}{2} (£12) + 0$ $+ 4,000 (£86)$ $= £368,000$

Normal price of £90 $\frac{300}{2} (£12) + \frac{4,000}{300}(£135)$ $+ 4,000 (£90)$ $= £363,600$

Additional cost of special offer   £ 4,400

Therefore the purchase of 4000 units at £86 is not recommended.

(d)

	Budget £	Actual £	Variance £
Material cost	360,000 (4,000 × £90)	344,000 (4,000 × £86)	16,000F
Ordering cost $\left(\frac{D}{Q} \times O\right)$	1,800	0	1,800F
			17,800F

It can be seen that favourable variances would appear on the performance report and goal congruence would not exist. The performance evaluation system conflicts with EOQ decision model. This is because the purchasing officer is not charged for the use of capital but the EOQ model includes a charge for the use of capital. Therefore if an imputed capital charge is not included in the performance report there is a danger that goal congruence will not exist. The revised performance report including a capital charge is shown below:

	Budget £	Actual £	Variance £
Material cost	360,000	344,000	16,000F
Ordering cost	1,800	0	1,800F
Holding cost	1,800	24,000	22,200A
			4,400A

Answer to problem 21.10

(a) The question requires the calculation of the optimum number of units to be manufactured in each production run in order to secure the lowest annual cost. In Chapter 21 we noted that the formula for the optimum number of units to be manufactured (Q) is as follows:

$$Q = \sqrt{\frac{2DS}{H}}$$

where D = Total demand for period
S = Set-up costs
H = Holding cost per unit

The set-up costs and holding cost per unit to be used in the formula are relevant or incremental costs. Those costs that will not change as a result of changes in the number of units manufactured in each batch should not be included in the analysis. These costs include:

 (i) Skilled labour costs (Skilled labour is being paid idle time. Its total cost will not alter as a result of the current decision).
(ii) Fixed overheads (these costs are independent of the batch size).

Therefore the relevant cost of producing product Exe is as follows:

			£
Raw materials—External suppliers			13
Dee standard cost:	Raw materials	8	
	Unskilled labour	4	
	Variable overheads	3	15
Unskilled labour			7
Variable overheads			5
Incremental cost of production			40

The relevant decision variables for the formula are as follows:

  Annual demand of Exe (D) = 4,000 units
  Set-up costs (S)　　　　　　 = £70 (Skilled labour of £66 is not an incremental cost)
  Annual holding costs (H)　 = £14 (cost of storage (£8) plus cost of capital tied up in stocks (£6))
  Storage cost per unit　　　　 (0.40m^2 × £20) = £8
  Incremental interest tied up in each unit of Exe stock
    (15% × £40 incremental cost of Exe) = £6

Applying the above figures to the formula we have:

$$Q = \sqrt{\frac{2 \times 4,000 \times £70}{£14}}$$
$$= 200 \text{ units}$$

Cost of current policy

	£
Set-up costs (4 production runs at £70)	280

Holding cost (Average stocks × unit holding cost)

	£
$\dfrac{1000}{2} \times £14$	7,000
Total cost	7,280

Cost of optimum policy

	£
Set-up costs $\dfrac{4,000}{200}$ production runs at £70	1,400

Holding costs (Average stocks × unit holding cost)

	£
$\dfrac{200}{2} \times £14$	1,400
Total cost	2,800
Annual savings (£7,280 − £2,800)	£4,480

(b) $\qquad Q = \sqrt{\dfrac{2DO}{H}}$

where D = Annual demand
O = Incremental ordering cost per order
H = Holding cost per unit

For producing Wye:

$$Q = \sqrt{\frac{2 \times 10,000 \times £100}{£8}} = 500 \text{ units}$$

Buying in larger quantities in order to take advantage of bulk discounts results in the following savings:

 (i) A saving in purchase price for the period consisting of the total amount of the discount for the period.
(ii) A reduction in total ordering cost because of fewer orders being placed to take advantage of bulk discounts.

The above cost savings must be compared with the increased holding costs resulting from higher stock levels.

We now compare the cost savings with the increased holding costs from increasing the quantity purchased from the EOQ of 500 units to the lowest purchase quantity at which Wye can be purchased at £19.80 per unit (i.e. 1,000 units):

	£
Savings in purchase price (10,000 annual purchases at £0.20)	2,000

Saving in ordering cost

	£
$\dfrac{DO}{Qd} - \dfrac{DO}{Q} = \dfrac{10,000\,(100)}{1,000} - \dfrac{10,000\,(100)}{500}$	1,000

(Note Qd represents quantity ordered to obtain discount and Q represents EOQ)

	£
Total Savings	3,000

The additional holding cost if the larger quantity is purchased is calculated as follows:

$$\frac{(Qd-Q)H}{2} = \frac{(1000-500)\,8}{2} = £2,000$$

Therefore a saving of £1,000 is made if the firm purchases in quantities of 1,000 units at a price of £19.80 per unit.

We now follow the same procedure in order to determine whether it would be better to purchase in quantities of 2,000 units:

	£
Savings in purchase price (10,000 annual purchases at £0.40)	4,000
Saving in ordering cost	
$\dfrac{DO}{Qd} - \dfrac{DO}{Q} = \dfrac{10,000\,(100)}{2000} - \dfrac{10,000\,(100)}{500}$	1,500
Total Savings	5,500

The additional holding cost if we purchase in 2,000 unit quantities instead of 500 unit quantities is as follows:

$$\frac{(Qd-Q)H}{2} = \frac{(2,000-500)\,£8}{2} = £6,000$$

Therefore an additional £500 will be incurred if the firm purchase in 2,000 unit batches compared with purchasing in 500 unit batches.

The above analysis indicates that Pink should purchase in batches of 1,000 units at a price of £19.80 per unit.

(c) Limitations include the following:

   (i) It is very difficult to obtain relevant data. Incremental holding, ordering and set-up costs are very difficult to estimate in practice. In addition many of the fixed costs that were excluded in the analysis may not be fixed over the whole range of output. Some fixed costs may increase in steps as the quantity purchased is increased.

  (ii) Model assumes certainty. A more sophisticated approach is required where demand and the cost structure is uncertain.

 (iii) Model assumes that demand is constant throughout the year. In practice there may be seasonal variations in demand throughout the year.

Answer to problem 21.11

(a) See 'Control of Stocks through Classification' in Chapter 21.

(b) See 'Determining When to Place the Order' and 'Uncertainty and Safety Stocks' in Chapter 21.

(c) See 'Determining the Economic Order Quantity' in Chapter 21.

Answer to problem 21.12

For a discussion of the rationale behind EOQ models see Chapter 21. In particular the answer should stress that some costs will rise with an increase in the order batch size (e.g. Stockholding costs) whilst others will fall (Ordering and stockout costs). The objective is to determine the order level at which total costs are minimised. The operation of the EOQ model depends upon identifying the contributory variables and their relevant costs.

The principles of the EOQ model can be used to determine the delivery service which the company will provide for its finished products. The EOQ model might result in stockouts if the lost profits from the stockout are lower than the costs of maintaining additional stocks. Therefore the model can be used to set optimal stock levels and this has repercussions for the level of delivery service offered to customers for finished goods. Similar principles can be applied for determining the level of repair and follow-up service provided to customers. The principles of the EOQ model can be combined with probability theory for determining the level of service offered to customers, either in terms of delivering products or maintaining a repair service. For an illustration of this approach see 'The Use of Probability Theory for Determining Safety Stocks' in Chapter 21.

SOLUTIONS TO CHAPTER 22 PROBLEMS

The application of linear programming to management accounting

With the exception of 22.1 and 22.2 the questions set in this chapter are appropriate for a second year course. Details of the questions are as follows:

22.1 and 22.2 Calculation of optimum output levels using the graphical LP approach.
22.3 to 22.5 The application of the Simplex method. 22.3 can be used to reinforce your understanding of the final matrix based on the principles outlined in Chapter 22. The model presented in 22.4 is not formulated in the same manner as that described in Chapter 22. The answer to 22.4 includes a reformulation of the matrix based on the principles outlined in Chapter 22.
22.6 to 22.9 Calculation of optimum output levels, shadow prices and marginal rates of substitution using the graphical approach. 22.8 includes the use of probability theory in determining a contribution range. The most difficult question is 22.9.
22.10 to 22.12 Multi-period capital rationing problems.

Answer to problem 22.3

(a) Maximise $C = 3x + 4y + 2z$ subject to:

$$2x + 3y + 4z \leqslant 9,000 \text{ (Materials constraint)}$$
$$4x + y + z \leqslant 9,200 \text{ (Labour constraint)}$$
$$x + 5y + Z \leqslant 8,000 \text{ (Machine hours constraint)}$$
$$x \leqslant 2,100 \text{ (Sales of product x constraint)}$$
$$y \leqslant 1,400 \text{ (Sales of product y constraint)}$$
$$z \leqslant |380 \text{ (Sales of product z constraint)}$$

Let Sm = Unused materials
    Sl   = Unused labour hours
    Smh = Unused machine hours
    Sx   = Unfulfilled sales demand of x
    Sy   = Unfulfilled sales demand of y
    Sz   = Unfulfilled sales demand of z

First Tableau

		x	y	z
Sm	$=9,000$	-2	-3	-4
Sl	$=9,200$	-4	-1	-1
Smh	$=8,000$	-1	-5	-1
Sx	$=2,100$	-1	0	0
Sy	$=1,400$	0	-1	0
Sz	$= 380$	0	0	-1
C	$= 0$	3	4	2

(b) The optimum output is:

	£
1,920 units of x at a contribution of £3 per unit	$=5,760$
1,140 units of y at a contribution of £4 per unit	$=4,560$
380 units of z at a contribution of £2 per unit	$= 760$
Total Contribution	11,080

The slacks on the left side of the final matrix indicate the unused resources which consist of materials (220 units), unfulfilled sales demand of 260 units for product y and 180 units for product x. Labour and machine hours appear as columns in the final matrix. This means that these resources are fully used. The unfulfilled sales demand for product z is also fully used. The opportunity costs of the scarce items are:

Labour $=£11/19$ per labour hour

Machine hours $=£13/19$ per machine hour

Sale of an additional unit of $z=£14/19$ per unit sold

If we can obtain additional labour hours then each labour hour should be used as follows:

Increase x by 5/19 of a unit

Decrease y by 1/19 of a unit

Note that we reverse the signs when additional resources are obtained. The effect of this substitution process on each of the resources and contribution is as follows:

	Labour hours	Materials	Machine hours	Contribution £
Increase x by 5/19	$-1\frac{1}{19}(\frac{5}{19}\times 4)$	$-\frac{10}{19}(\frac{5}{19}\times 2)$	$-\frac{5}{19}(\frac{5}{19}\times 1)$	$+\frac{15}{19}(\frac{5}{19}\times £3)$
Decrease Y by 1/19	$+\frac{1}{19}(\frac{1}{19}\times 1)$	$+\frac{3}{19}(\frac{1}{19}\times 3)$	$+\frac{5}{19}(\frac{1}{19}\times 5)$	$-\frac{4}{19}(\frac{1}{19}\times 4)$
Net effect	-1	$-\frac{7}{19}$	0	$\frac{11}{19}$

The net effect agrees with the labour column of the final matrix. Note that increasing sales of X by 5/19 of a unit reduces the unused sales potential of x (Sx) by 5/19 and decreasing sales of y by 1/19 increases unused sales potential of y (Sy) by 1/19. Similar reasoning can be applied to the remaining columns in the final matrix.

The column headed Sz indicates that if demand for product z can be increased then each additional unit sold will increase contribution by £14/19. To obtain the necessary resources to produce additional units of z it is necessary to reduce production of x by 4/19 and y by 3/19. The opportunity costs and marginal rates of substitution for the scarce resources apply over the following range:

Labour   4,260 hours (9,200−4,940) to 9,797 hours (9,200+597)
Machinery   4,580 hours (8,000−3,420) to 8,418 hours (8,000+418)
Sales demand of z   0 units (380−380) to 451 units (380+71)

(c) See 'Uses of Linear Programming' in Chapter 22 for the answer to this question.

Answer to problem 22.4

	Product 1	Product 2	Product 3	Total
(a) Maximum sales value	£57,500	£96,000	£125,000	
Unit selling price	£23	£32	£25	
Maximum demand (units)	2,500	3,000	5,000	
Hours required on machine (Type A)	2,500(2,500 × 1)	6,000(3,000 × 2)	15,000(5,000 × 3)	23,500
Hours required on machine (Type B)	3,750(2,500 × 1½)	9,000(3,000 × 3)	5,000(5,000 × 1)	17,750

We now compare the machine capacity available with the machine hours required to meet the maximum sales so as to determine whether or not production is a limiting factor.

	Machine Type A	Machine Type B
Hours required (see above)	23,500	17,750
Hours available	9,800	21,000

Because hours required are in excess of hours available for machine type A, but not for machine type B, then it follows that machine type A is the limiting factor. Following the approach illustrated in Example 10.4 in Chapter 10 we calculate the contribution per limiting factor. The calculations are as follows:

	Product 1	Product 2	Product 3
Unit contribution	£5	£7	£8
Contribution per hour of type A machine time	£5 ($£\frac{5}{1}$)	£3.50 ($£\frac{7}{2}$)	£2.67 ($£\frac{8}{3}$)
Ranking	1	2	3

The optimal allocation of type A machine hours based on the above ranking is as follows:

Production	Machine hours used	Balance of machine hours available
2,500 units of product 1	2,500	7,300 (9,800−2,500)
3,000 units of product 2	6,000	1,300 (7,300−6,000)
433 units of product 3	1,300	—

The 433 units of product 3 are obtained by dividing the 1,300 unused machine hours by the 3 machine hours required for each unit of product 3. The proposed production programme results in the following calculation of total profit:

	£
2,500 units of product 1 at £5 per unit contribution	12,500
3,000 units of product 2 at £7 per unit contribution	21,000
433 units of product 3 at £8 per unit contribution	3,464
Total contribution	36,964
Less fixed overheads	21,000
Profit	15,964

(b) There are several ways of formulating the tableaux for a linear programming model. The tableau from the computer package can be reproduced as follows:

	Quantity	S_1	S_4	S_5
S_2	1,150	-0.5	-0.143	0.429
X_2	1,850	0.5	0.143	-0.429
S_3	3,800		0.429	-0.286
X_3	1,200		-0.429	0.286
X_1	2,500	-1	0	0
C	35,050	-1.5	-2.429	-0.714

In Chapter 22 the approach adopted was to formulate the first tableau with positive contribution signs and negative signs for the slack variable equations. The optimal solution occurs when the signs in the contribution row are all negative. The opposite procedure has been applied with the tableau which is presented in the question. Therefore the signs have been reversed in the above tableau to ensure that it is in the same format as that presented in Chapter 22. Note that an entry of 1 in the tableau presented in the question signifies the product or slack variable that is to be entered in each row of the above tableau.

The total contribution is £35,050 consisting of:

2,500 units of product 1 at a contribution of £5 per unit
1,850 units of product 2 at a contribution of £7 per unit
1,200 units of product 3 at a contribution of £8 per unit

The revised fixed overheads are £18,000 resulting in a total profit of £17,050. This is higher than the profit before the fire (£15,964) because the fixed overheads saved by the fire exceed the lost contribution.

The shadow prices (or opportunity costs) for S_4 indicate that if an additional Type A machine hour can be acquired then profits will increase by £2.429 by increasing production of product 3 by 0.429 units and reducing production of product 2 by 0.143 units. Similarly if an additional Type B machine hour can be acquired then profits will increase by £0.714 by increasing production of product 2 by 0.429 units and reducing production of product 3 by 0.286 units. An extra unit of demand for product 1 will yield a contribution of £5 but in order to obtain the resource it is necessary to sacrifice half a unit of product 2. This will result in a loss of contribution of £3.50 ($\frac{1}{2} \times$ £7). Therefore the net gain is £1.50.

The shadow prices indicate the premium over and above the present acquisition costs that the company should be willing to pay in order to obtain extra hours of machine time. The shadow price for product 1 indicates the upper limit to advertising or promotional expenses that should be incurred in order to stimulate demand by one further unit.

(c) In part A there was only one limiting factor. In Chapter 22 we noted that the optimal solution can be derived by using the contribution per key factor approach whenever there is only one production constraint. Where more than one limiting factor exists then it is necessary to use linear programming to determine the optimal production programme.

Answer to problem 22.6

(a) Let M = Number of units of Masso produced and sold
Let R = Number of units of Russo produced and sold
The L.P. model is as follows:
Maximise Z = 40M + 50R (product contributions) subject to:
M + 2R ≤ 700 (Machining capacity)
2.5M + 2R ≤ 1,000 (Assembly capacity)

$M \leqslant 400$ (Maximum output of Masso constraint)
$R \leqslant 400$ (Maximum output of Russo constraint)
$M \geqslant 0$
$R \geqslant 0$

The constraints are plotted on the graph (Figure 1) as follows:

Machining constraint: Line from $M=700$, $R=0$ to $R=350$, $M=0$
Assembly constraint: Line from $M=400$, $R=0$ to $R=500$, $M=0$
Output of/Masso constraint: Line from $M=400$
Output of/Russo constraint: Line from $R=400$

At the optimum point (B in the graph) the output mix is as follows:

	£
200 units of Masso at a contribution of £40 per unit =	8,000
250 units of Russo at a contribution of £50 per unit =	12,500
Total contribution	20,500
Less fixed costs (£7,000 + £10,000)	17,000
Profit	3,500

The optimum output can be determined exactly by solving the simultaneous equations for the constraints that intersect at point B:

$2.5M + 2R = 1,000 \ldots \ldots (1)$
$M + 2R = 700 \ldots \ldots (2)$

Subtract (2) from (1)

$\therefore 1.5M = 300$
$\therefore M = 200$

Substituting in (1): $2.5(200) + 2R = 1,000$
$\therefore R = 250$

(b) *Machining Capacity*

If we obtain additional machine hours, the line $M + 2R = 700$ will shift upwards. Therefore the revised optimum point will fall on the line BD. If one extra machine hour is obtained the constraints $M + 2R = 700$ and $2.5M + 2R$ will still be binding and the new optimal plan can be determined by solving the following equations:

$M + 2R = 701$ (Revised machining constraint)
$2.5M + 2R = 1,000$ (Unchanged assembly constraint)

The values for M and R when the above equations are solved are $M = 199.33$ and $R = 250.83$.
Therefore Russo is increased by 0.83 units and Masso is reduced by 0.67 units and the change in contribution will be as follows:

	£
Increase in contribution from Russo ($0.83 \times £50$) =	41.50
Decrease in contribution from Masso (0.67×40) =	(26.80)
Increase in contribution	14.70

Hence the value of an independent marginal increase in machine capacity is £14.70 per hour.

Assembly Capacity

With an additional hour of assembly capacity the new optimal plan will be given by the solution of the following equations:

$$M + 2R = 700 \text{ (Unchanged machining constraint)}$$
$$2.5M + 2R = 1,001 \text{ (Revised assembly constraint)}$$

The values for M and R when the above equations are solved are M = 200.67 and R = 249.67. Therefore Masso is increased by 0.67 units and Russo is decreased by 0.33 units and the change in contribution will be as follows:

$$£$$
Increase in contribution from Masso $(0.67 \times £40) = 26.80$
Decrease in contribution from Russo $(0.33 \times £50) = (16.50)$

Increase in contribution   10.30

Hence the value of an independent marginal increase in assembly capacity is £10.30 per hour.

(c) The assumptions underlying the above calculations are:

 (i) Linearity over the whole output range for costs, revenues and quantity of resources used;
 (ii) Divisibility of products (It is assumed that products can be produced in fractions of units);
(iii) Divisibility of resources (Supplies of resources may only be available in specified multiples);
(iv) The objectives of the firm (Assumed that the single objective of a firm is to maximise short-term contribution);
 (v) All of the available opportunities for the use of the resources have been included in the L.P. model.

Figure 1

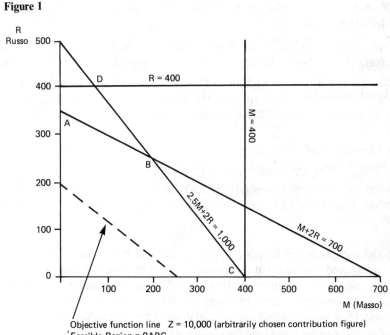

Objective function line   Z = 10,000 (arbitrarily chosen contribution figure)
Feasible Region = 0ABC

Answer to problem 22.10

(a) At a discount rate of 15% the NPV calculations are as follows:

$$(£000's)$$

Project A: $-60+(30\times0.87)+(25\times1.41)$ $=+\;1.35$

Project B: $-30-(20\times0.87)+(25\times0.76)+(45\times0.66)=+\;1.30$

Project C: $-40-(50\times0.87)+(60\times0.76)+(70\times0.66)=+\;8.30$

Project D: $\;\;\;\;0-(80\times0.87)+(45\times0.76)+(55\times0.66)=+\;0.90$

Project E: $-50+(10\times0.87)+(30\times0.76)+(40\times0.66)=+\;7.90$

$$+19.75$$

The firm should invest £180,000 in projects A, B, C, D and E given no restriction in investment funds. As a result the market value of the company should rise by £19,750.

(b) If funds are restricted for 1980 only, the projects can be ranked by the profitability index. The calculations are as follows:

Project	Present value (NPV + Investment cost) £000's	Investment cost £000's	Profitability index	Ranking
A	61.35	60	1.0225	5
B	31.30	30	1.0433	4
C	48.30	40	1.2075	2
D	0.90	0	∞	1
E	57.90	50	1.158	3

Therefore the company should undertake projects D, C, E and this will utilise funds of £90,000. The remaining £10,000 should be invested in project B (i.e. $\frac{1}{3}$ of Project B should be undertaken). It is assumed that projects are divisible.

(c) Let a, b, c, d and e represent the proportion of projects A, B, C, D, and E accepted and x represent surplus funds (in £000's) placed on bank deposit from 1st January in 1980 to 31st December 1980 at 10%.

$$\therefore \text{NPV of £1,000 invested in } x = \frac{£1,100}{(1+0.15)} - £1,000$$

$$= -£43.48$$

LP model

Maximise $1.35a+1.30b+8.30c+0.90d+7.90e-0.043x^*$ subject to:

$60a+30b+40c+50e+x\leqslant100$ (1980 constraint in £000's)

$20b+50c+80d\leqslant90+30a+10e+1.1x$ (1981 constraint in £000's)

a, b, c, d, e, x $\geqslant0$

a, b, c, d, e $\;\leqslant1$

*Note that the model is expressed in £000's. Therefore $-£43.48$ expressed in £000's is £-0.043. Also note that surplus funds are placed on deposit at 1st January 1980 only. After 1st January 1981 capital is available without limit. Consequently it is assumed at January 1981 it is unnecessary to maintain funds for future periods by placing funds on deposit to yield a negative NPV.

In the above model it is assumed that capital constraints can be eased by project generated cash flows. If this is not possible and capital constraints are absolute, the formulation is:

Maximise $1.35a + 1.30b + 8.30c + 0.90d + 7.90e - 0.043x$ subject to:

$60a + 30b + 40c + 50e + x \leqslant 100$

$20b + 50c + 80d \qquad \leqslant 90 + 1.1x$

$a, b, c, d, e \leqslant 1$

$a, b, c, d, e, x \geqslant 0$

(d) The limitations are as follows:

   (i) Divisibility of projects may not be realistic and integer programming may have to be used.
  (ii) Constraints are unlikely to be completely fixed and precise as implied in the mathematical models.
 (iii) Not all the relevant information can be quantified. For example market constraints might exist which cannot be quantified.
 (iv) All the information for the model may not be available. For example it may not be possible to precisely specify the constraints of future periods.
  (v) All the relationships contained within the formulation may not be linear.
 (vi) All the potential investment opportunities may not be identified and included in the analysis.
(vii) The LP formulation assumes that all the project's cash flows are certain and therefore it cannot incorporate uncertainty. The solution produced can only be considered optimal given this restrictive assumption.
(viii) All investments may not be independent of each other. There may be some unspecified inter-dependencies.

Answer to problem 22.11

(a)

  Let x_1 = proportion of project A undertaken
       x_2 = proportion of project B undertaken
       x_3 = proportion of project C undertaken
       x_4 = proportion of project D undertaken
       x_5 = proportion of project E undertaken
       x_6 = cash unused at time 1 and carried forward to time 2
       x_7 = cash unused at time 2 and carried forward to time 3

The L.P. model is as follows:

  Maximise $x_1 + 0.8x_2 - 0.6x_3 + 3x_4 + 0.7x_5$

  subject to $7x_1 + 6x_2 + 2x_3 \leqslant 12$ (Time 0 cash available)

  $-1.5x_1 - 2x_2 - 4x_3 + 8x_4 + x_6 \leqslant 2$ (Time 1 cash available—see note 1)

  $-2x_1 - x_2 + 0.5x_3 + 2x_4 + 3x_5 + x_7 \leqslant 1.08x_6$ (Time 2 cash available—see note 2)

  $-2x_1 - x_2 + 2x_3 + x_4 - x_5 \leqslant 1.08x_7$ (Time 3 cash available—see note 3)

  $0.6x_1 + 0.8x_2 - 0.1x_3 + 10 \geqslant 11$ (Year 1 profit constraint—see note 4)

  $0.6x_1 + 0.3x_2 - 0.2x_3 - 0.3x_4 + 12 \geqslant (0.6x_1 + 0.8x_2 - 0.1x_3 + 10) \, 1.1$

     (Year 2 profit constraint: Year 1 profit plus 10%)

  $1.4x_1 + 0.8x_2 - 0.3x_3 - 0.2x_4 + 1.5x_5 + 11 \geqslant (0.6x_1 + 0.3x_2 - 0.2x_3 - 0.3x_4 + 12) \, 1.1$

     (Year 3 profit constraint: Year 2 profit + 10%)

  $x_1, x_2, x_3, x_4, x_5, x_6, x_7 \geqslant 0$ (Non negativity constraint)

  $x_1, x_2, x_3, x_4, x_5 \leqslant 1$ (Maximum investment constraint)

An alternative presentation is to transfer the negative items which are listed to the left of the $\leqslant$ sign to the right of the sign. These variables will now be entered as positive items.

Notes

		£ (million)
(1) Time 1 cash available = New equity		7.5
	Less loan repayment	5.5
		2.0

(2) Time 2 cash available = Unused cash at time 1 plus interest

(3) Time 3 cash available = Unused cash at time 2 plus interest

(4) Minimum profit target = £10m + 10% = £11m.

(b) It may be rational in the following circumstances to undertake a project with a negative NPV:

 (i) Where the qualitative factors outweigh the negative NPV. For example the building of a works canteen or the provision of recreational facilities for employees.

(ii) A project with a negative NPV which provides large cash inflows in the early year thus enabling an additional project to be accepted with a NPV in excess of the negative NPV of the first project.

(c) *Merits of Mathematical Programming*

  (i) Ability to solve complex problems incorporating the effects of complex interactions.

 (ii) Speed in solving the problem using computer facilities.

(iii) The output from the model can highlight the key constraints to which attention should be directed.

(iv) Sensitivity analysis can be applied. The effects of changes in the variables can be speedily tested.

Limitations of mathematical programming

  (i) Divisibility of projects may not be realistic and integer programming may have to be used.

 (ii) Constraints are unlikely to be completely fixed and precise as implied in the mathematical models.

(iii) Not all the relevant information can be quantified.

(iv) All the information for the model may not be available. For example it may not be possible to precisely specify the constraints of future periods.

 (v) All the relationships contained within the formulation may not be linear.

(vi) All the potential investment opportunities may not be identified and included in the analysis.

(vii) The LP formulation assumes that all the project's cash flows are certain and therefore it cannot incorporate uncertainty. The solution produced can only be considered optimal given this restrictive assumption.

Performance measures and control in divisionalised companies

Details of the questions are as follows:

23.1 to 23.3 Calculation of divisional ROCE for various transactions and a discussion as to whether the divisional ROCE measure will encourage goal congruence.

23.4 Discussion of various divisional performance measures.

23.5 Discussion of suitable measures of performance for each of the stated goals of an organisation which has multiple goals.

23.6 to 23.13 Various questions requiring a discussion of topics covered in Chapter 23.

Question 16.5 from Chapter 16 can be tackled at this stage. This is a management control problem concerning a company with profit centres.

Answer to problem 23.1

(1) It is assumed that bank/cash is controlled by group headquarters. Therefore bank/cash is not included in the ROCE calculations. The ROCE percentages are as follows:

Detail for calculations	1978 Existing basis Division A %	1978 Existing basis Division B %	1978 Proposed basis Division A %	1978 Proposed basis Division B %
(a) Budgeted ROCE (ignoring any of the transactions)	18.00(1)	9.17(2)	29.03(3)	15.28(4)
(b) ROCE resulting from transaction No. 1	19.33(5)	—	27.62(6)	—
(c) ROCE resulting from transaction No. 2	17.25(7)	—	26.73(8)	—

(d) ROCE resulting from transaction No. 3	18.13(9)	8.97(10)	—	—
(e) ROCE resulting from transaction No. 4	—	—	27.94(11)	15.38(12)

Calculations

(1) $\dfrac{£90,000}{£500,000}$

(2) $\dfrac{£55,000}{£600,000}$

(3) $\dfrac{£90,000}{£310,000}$

(4) $\dfrac{£55,000}{£360,000}$

(5) $\dfrac{£81,200}{£420,000}$

(6) $\dfrac{£81,200}{£310,000-£16,000}$

(7) $\dfrac{£90,000+(£15,000-£8,500 \text{ Depn.})}{£559,500}$

(8) $\dfrac{£90,000+(£15,000-£8,500)}{£310,000+(£59,500-£8,500)}$

(9) $\dfrac{£90,000-£3,000}{£500,000-£20,000}$

(10) $\dfrac{£52,000}{£580,000}$

(11) $\dfrac{£90,000+£5,000}{£310,000+£30,000}$

(12) $\dfrac{£55,000+£5,000}{£360,000+£30,000}$

Note that with transaction number 1 (calculations 5 and 6) the loss of sale is offset by the discontinuation in in the depreciation charge.

$£$

(2) NPV: £15,000 × 4.564 = 68,460
      Investment cost   = (59,500)

      NPV   8,960

IRR is where £15,000 × discount factor = £59,500
            ∴ Discount factor = 3.966 (£59,500 ÷ £15,000)
                          IRR ≃ 17%

(3) *Transaction 1:* The company is scrapping an asset and sacrificing profits of £8,800 p.a. The equipment should be retained but divisional ROCE increases under the present basis and decreases under the prosposed basis if the asset is scrapped. Therefore the present system does not result in goal congruence for this transaction as the manager can increase his performance rating by scrapping the equipment.
Transaction 2: The project yields a positive NPV and should be accepted. If the project is accepted then divisional ROCE will decline if either the present or proposed basis is used. Therefore neither approach encourages goal congruence. However, it should be noted that in later years the asset base will decline with the proposed basis and ROCE will increase. If the divisional manager seeks to maximise long-run ROCE then he will accept the proposal.
Transaction 3: The company is obtaining £20,000 additional capital at a cost of £3,000 p.a. or 15%.

The cost of raising additional capital is 12%. Therefore the proposal should be rejected. However, the manager of Division A will improve his performance measure and the manager of Division B will suffer a decline in his performance measure if the transaction is undertaken.

Transaction 4: Ideally the DCF approach should be adopted but insufficient information is given in the question. Assuming that £30,000 can be realised then the proposal is justified. On the basis of the performance measures used the manager of Division B will undertake the investment and the manager of Division A will not undertake the investment.

Answer to problem 23.5

(a)(i) Return on capital employed and residual income should be considered as potential measures. The superiority of residual income over return on capital employed (see chapter 23) should be discussed. The objective is to select a performance measure which is consistent with the NPV rule. Residual income is the long run counterpart of the NPV rule but it may lead to decisions which are not consistent with the NPV rule if managers base their decisions on short-term measures. Problems occur with both return on capital employed and residual income in terms of bases which should be used for asset valuations. Current values are preferable to historical costs.

(ii) Ideally market performance measures should indicate sales achievement in relation to the market, competitors and previous performance. Target market shares or unit sales should be established for each product or product range. Actual market shares and unit sales should be compared with targets and previous periods. Trends in market shares should be compared with overall market trends and product life cycles.

(iii) Productivity is concerned with the efficiency of converting physical inputs into physical outputs. Therefore the performance measure should be a physical measure. Possible performance measures include output per direct labour hour and output per machine hour. Where divisions produce a variety of products, output should be expressed in standard hours. If monetary measures are used then changes in price levels should be eliminated. In addition to *total* measures of output for each division, performance measures should also be computed for individual products. Output measures should be compared with targets, previous periods and with other divisions.

(iv) Possible measures of the ability of divisions to offer up-to-date product ranges include:

    A. Number of new products launched in previous periods
    B. Expenditure on product development

Quality and reliability might be measured in terms of:

    A. Percentage of projects rejected
    B. Comparison of target and actual market shares
    C. Comparisons with competitors' products
    D. Customer surveys

The performance measures should be compared with previous periods, targets and competitors (if this is possible). Some of the measures may be difficult to express in quantitative terms and a subjective evaluation may be necessary.

(v) Responsibility towards employees might be reflected by the following measures:

    A. Rate of labour turnover
    B. Level of absenteeism

Additional information is also necessary to explain the reasons for high labour turnover and absenteeism. Possible reasons might be identified by regularly undertaking attitude surveys on such issues as:

    A. Payment systems
    B. Management style
    C. Degree of participation
    D. Working conditions

Other proxy measures which might be used include:

    A. Number of promotions to different employee and management grades
    B. Number of grievance procedures processed
    C. Number of applications received per vacancy
    D. Training expenditure per employee
    E. Number of accidents reported per period

The above measures should be compared with previous periods and targets.

(vi) It is extremely difficult to assess whether a firm is considered to be a socially responsible citizen within the community. Possible areas of interaction between the firm and the local community include:

    A. Employment
    B. Environmental effects
    C. Involvement in community affairs
    D. Provision of recreational and social facilities

Surveys should be undertaken locally in order to assess the attitude of the population to each of the above areas. Possible quantitative measures include:

    A. Amount of financial support given to charities, sports organisations and educational establishments
    B. Amounts spent on anti-pollution measures
    C. Number of complaints received from members of the local community

(vii) Possible growth measures include comparisons over time (in absolute terms and percentage changes) of the following:

    A. Total sales revenue
    B. Profit (Expressed in terms of residual income)
    C. Total assets
    D. Total employees
    E. Total market share

Price changes should be removed where appropriate. Comparisons should be made with other divisions, comparable firms and the industry as a whole.

Survival in the long-term depends on an acceptable level of profitability. Therefore appropriate profitability measures should be used. The degree of divisional autonomy might be measured in terms of an assessment of the central controls imposed by central headquarters (e.g. What are the limits on the amount of capital expenditure decisions that divisions can determine independently).

(b) A single performance measure underestimates the multi-faceted nature of organisational goals. It might be claimed that a profitability measure is sufficiently general to incorporate the other goals. For example maintaining high market shares, increasing productivity, offering an up-to-date product range, being a responsible employee and growth tend to result in increased profitability. To this extent a profitability measure might best capture the multi-faceted nature of organisational goals. Nevertheless the profitability goal alone cannot be expected to capture the complexity of organisational goals. Firms pursue a variety of goals and for this reason there are strong arguments for using multiple performance measures when evaluating organisational performance. For a further discussion of organisational goals see 'Decision-Making Process' in Chapter 1.

Answer to problem 23.6

(a) If divisional budgets are set by a central planning department and imposed on divisional managers then it is true that divisional independence is pseudo independence. However, if budget guidelines and goals are set by the central planning department and divisional managers are given a large degree of freedom in the setting of budgets and conduct of operations then it is incorrect to claim that pseudo independence exists.

One of the reasons for creating a divisionalised organisation structure is to improve motivation by the delegation of responsibility to divisional managers, thus giving them greater freedom over the control of their activities. Nevertheless complete independence cannot be granted as this would destroy the very idea that divisions are an integral part of a single business. The granting of freedom to divisions in conducting their operations can be allowed only if certain limits are applied within which that freedom can be exercised. This normally takes the form of the presentation of budgets by divisions to corporate management for approval. By adopting this approach divisions pay a modest price for the extensive powers of decentralised decision-making.

As long as budgets are not imposed by the central planning department, and divisions are allowed to determine their own budgets within the guidelines set, then divisional managers will have greater independence than the managers of centralised organisations.

(b) The answer should consist of a discussion of divisional profit, return on capital employed and residual income. A discussion of each of these items is presented in Chapter 23.

Answer to problem 23.7

See 'Responsibility Accounting' in Chapter 16 for an explanation of a cost centre, profit centre and investment centre. For a discussion of the strengths and weaknesses of each organisational unit see Chapter 23.

Answer to problem 23.8

(a) Examples of the types of decisions that should be transferred to the new divisional managers include:
  a. Product decisions such as product mix, promotion, pricing etc.
  b. Employment decisions except perhaps for the appointment of senior managers.
  c. Short-term operating decisions of all kinds. Examples include production scheduling, subcontracting, direction of marketing effort etc.
  d. Capital expenditure and disinvestment decisions (with some constraints).
  e. Short-term financing decisions (with some constraints).

(b) The following decisions might be retained at company head office:
  (i) Strategic investment decisions which are critical to the survival of the company as a whole.
  (ii) Certain financing decisions which require that an overall view is taken. For example borrowing commitments and the level of financial gearing should be determined for the group as a whole.
  (iii) Appointment of top management.

(iv) Sourcing decisions such as bulk buying of raw materials if corporate interests are best served by centralised buying.

(v) Capital expenditure decisions above certain limits.

(vi) Common services which are required by all profit centres. Corporate interests might best be served by operating centralised service departments such as an industrial relations department. Possible benefits include reduced costs and the extra benefits of specialisation.

(vii) Arbitration decisions on transfer pricing disputes.

(viii) Decisions on items which benefit the company rather than an individual division e.g. taxation, computer applications etc.

(c) The answer to this question should focus on the importance of designing performance reports which encourage goal congruence. For a discussion of this topic see Chapter 23 particularly the section 'Factors to be Considered in Designing Managerial Performance Measures'.

Answers to problems 23.9 to 23.13

See Chapter 23 for possible answers to these questions.

Transfer pricing in divisionalised companies

Details of the questions are as follows:

24.1 and 24.2	Calculation and comparison of divisional profits based on different transfer pricing rules.
24.3	Construction of optimum production programmes for the receiving division, supplying division and the group as a whole.
24.4 and 24.5	Make or buy decisions involving inter-company trading.
24.6	Calculation of the profit contribution for various departments where conflicts arise as to what should be the appropriate transfer price.
24.7 and 24.8	Construction of profit statements illustrating sub-optimality when a cost-plus transfer price is applied. Both questions require the selection of an optimal transfer price given that unit variable cost is constant.
24.9	A discussion of the optimal transfer price where there is a perfect market for the inter-mediate product but the buying price includes additional transportation costs. The second part of the question requires the setting of an optimal transfer price when the marginal cost of the supplying division is *not* constant.
24.10 to 24.13	Various discussion questions relevant to Chapter 24.

Answer to problem 24.3

(A)(a) Because each division is an autonomous profit centre it is assumed that White Ltd will rank product profitability in terms of unit contributions. The calculation of the transfer prices and unit contributions are as follows:

	A		B	C
	£		£	£
Variable manufacturing cost	6.00		13	18
Fixed cost (see note 1)	5.00		7	12
Total cost	11.00		20	30
Profit margin (10%)	1.10		2	3
Transfer price	13	(market price)	22	33
Contribution to White	7		9	15
Ranking by White (see note 2)	3		2	1

Note

(1) $\dfrac{\text{Product's fixed production overheads}}{\text{Minimum budgeted volume (45,000 hours)}} \times 3 \text{ hours}$

The total hours available will be allocated as follows:

(2) Ranking in terms of contribution per hour remains unchanged as each product uses three hours.

		£
Product A (Minimum): 15,000 units $\dfrac{45,000}{3}$ at £7		105,000
Product B (Minimum): 15,000 units $\dfrac{45,000}{3}$ at £9		135,000
Product C (Balance): 30,000 units $\dfrac{90,000}{3}$ at £15		450,000
Total contribution		690,000
Less fixed costs		360,000
Profit		330,000

(b) *Rose division*

The manager of Rose Division will calculate the following product contributions:

	Theta	*Sigma*	*Omega*
	£	£	£
Transfer price of A	65 (5 × £13)	39 (3 × £13)	26 (2 × £13)
Transfer price of B	110 (5 × £22)	110 (5 × £22)	–
Transfer price of C	–	66 (2 × £33)	264 (8 × £33)
Rose's added variable costs	30	25	45
Rose's variable costs	205	240	335
Selling price	280	295	340
Contribution	75	55	5
Ranking	1	2	3

Minimum sales of 1,500 units of each of the above products will utilise 135,000 hours of capacity in White's division (each product uses 30 hours in White's division). Rose's output is restricted by the production hours available in White's division. The manager of Rose division should select the following output schedule in order to maximise profits:

	£
1,500 units minimum of Omega at a contribution of £5 per unit	7,500
1,500 units minimum of Sigma at a contribution of £55 per unit	82,500
3,000 units (see note 1) of Theta at a contribution of £75 per unit	225,000
	315,000
Less fixed costs	270,000
Profit	45,000

Note

(1) The balance is restricted by White's capacity of 180,000 hours. A balance of 90,000 hours is available after allocating minimum production of 1,500 units to Omega and Sigma. Therefore a maximum of 3,000 units of Theta can be produced. Note that as each product uses 30 hours in White's division the ranking of contribution per hour in White is the same as the product contribution ranking.

(c) The group planning executive will attempt to maximise the group's profit rather than divisional profits. Therefore the output decision should be based on a comparison of the group's incremental costs with incremental revenues. The comparison is as follows:

	Theta £	Sigma £	Omega £
Variable costs: A	30 (5 × £6)	18 (3 × £6)	12 (2 × £6)
B	65 (5 × £13)	65 (5 × £13)	–
C		36 (2 × £18)	144 (8 × £18)
Variable cost of White	95	119	156
Variable cost of Rose	30	25	45
Total unit variable cost	125	144	201
Selling price	280	295	340
Contribution	155	151	139
Ranking	1	2	3

The optimal production allocation and profit is as follows:

	£
1,500 minimum of Omega at a contribution of £139 per unit	208,500
1,500 minimum of Sigma at a contribution of £151 per unit	226,500
3,000 balance to Theta at a contribution of £155 per unit	465,000
	900,000
Less fixed costs	630,000
Profit	270,000

Note that the contribution which the group obtains from selling the intermediate product A on the external market is £7 per unit. It is more profitable to convert A into Theta and sell as a final product.

The above production plan is identical to Rose's plan but different from that which White would choose to maximise its profit. White wishes to maximise output of product C but the output of Theta should be maximised and Theta does not require any of product C. The group could impose the optimal plan on White. A better alternative is to change the transfer price so that it encourages goal congruence.

(B) An increase in capacity of 9,000 hours will result in an allocation of 3,000 hours to each product. Because Theta, Sigma and Omega each use 30 hours in White Division then this will result in the production of an additional 100 units of each product. Therefore with each 9,000 hours increase in White's capacity the contribution will increase as follows:

	£
Theta 100 × 155	15,500
Sigma 100 × 151	15,100
Omega 100 × 139	13,900
Total contribution	44,500

Therefore the results will be as follows:

Capacity increase (hours)	9,000	18,000	27,000	36,000
	£	£	£	£
Contribution increase	44,500	89,000	133,500	178,000
Additional fixed cost	15,000	55,000	125,000	210,000
Increase in profits	29,500	34,000	8,500	(32,000)

Therefore capacity should be increased by 18,000 hours.

Answer to problem 24.4

(a) *Purchase from British angles*
The following diagram illustrates how the quotation is built up:

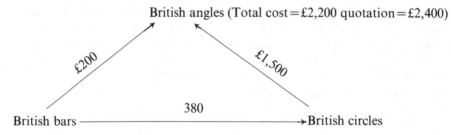

British angles (Total cost = £2,200 quotation = £2,400)

The quotation can be analysed as follows:

		£
(i) British bars		200
(ii) British circles: Ex British bars (1.25 × £380)	475	
(iii) Conversion cost (Balance)	1,025	1,500
(iv) Conversion cost (Balance) of British angles		500
Total cost		2,200
Profit		200
Quoted selling price		2,400

The relevant costs to the BUE group of the above quotation are as follows:

		£	
Item	(i) Incremental costs	150	(75% × £200)
	(ii) Market price	380	(Acceptance will result in a loss of £380 sales revenue)
	(iii) Incremental cost	656	Total cost of conversion work = £820
			Variable cost of conversion work = 80% × £820
	(iv) Incremental cost	300	(60% × £500)
		1,486	

Purchase from Italmet
The relevant cost equals the purchase cost of £1,650.

Purchase from Deutschmet

Acceptance of this contract will involve placing work with British Angles at a price of £550. This consists of £200 conversion plus £350 transfer price from British Circles. The contribution on this work is as follows:

	£		£
Transfer from British Circles	350	Conversion	200
Less profit (25% on cost)	70	Profit ($33\frac{1}{3}$% on cost)	50
Total cost	280	Total cost	150
Incremental cost (80% of total cost)	224	Incremental cost (60% of total cost)	90
Contribution	126	Contribution	110

Acceptance of the contract will result in an additional contribution of £236. This can be offset against the price quoted of £1,800 resulting in a relevant cost of £1,564.

Recommendation

It is in the best interests of BUE if the contract is placed with British Angles. The current transfer pricing system motivates British Dies to purchase from Italmet (the most unacceptable alternative). Also it would not be in British Angles interest to accept the contract at Italmet's price of £1,650 because its incremental costs are £2,000. A transfer price based on variable cost (where spare capacity exists) and market price (where no spare capacity exists) would result in the sum of the divisional costs being equal to the relevant cost of £1,486. Alternatively with a negotiated transfer pricing system managers should trade with each other based on the principle of accepting trade which will provide a contribution to fixed costs. The resulting negotiated transfer prices might result in British Angles quoting the lowest price.

(b) *Assumptions*

(i) British Bars are operating at full capacity in respect of the standard parts and the acceptance of the internal quotation will result in a loss of revenue of £380 per item produced. It is also assumed that customer goodwill will not be affected if British bars devotes some of its capacity to the British dies contract.

(ii) Acceptance of the Deutschmet contract will not result in a loss of sales revenue by British Angles.

(iii) Group headquarters is aware of the problem and has access to the cost information of the subsidiary companies.

Answer to problem 24.7

(a) The contributions for each division and the company as a whole for the various selling prices are as follows:

South division

Output level (units)	Total revenues £	Variable costs £	Total contribution £
1,000	35,000	11,000	24,000
2,000	70,000	22,000	48,000
3,000	105,000	33,000	72,000
4,000	140,000	44,000	96,000
5,000	175,000	55,000	120,000
6,000	210,000	66,000	144,000

North division

Output level (units)	Total revenues	Variable costs	Total cost of transfers	Total contribution
	£	£	£	£
1,000	100,000	7,000	35,000	58,000
2,000	180,000	14,000	70,000	96,000
3,000	240,000	21,000	105,000	114,000
4,000	280,000	28,000	140,000	112,000
5,000	300,000	35,000	175,000	90,000
6,000	300,000	42,000	210,000	48,000

Whole company

Output level (units)	Total revenues	Company variable costs	Company contribution
	£	£	£
1,000	100,000	18,000	82,000
2,000	180,000	36,000	144,000
3,000	240,000	54,000	186,000
4,000	280,000	72,000	208,000
5,000	300,000	90,000	210,000
6,000	300,000	108,000	192,000

(b) Based on the statements in (a) North division should select a selling price of £80 per unit. This selling price produces a maximum divisional contribution of £114,000. It is in the best interests of the company as a whole if a selling price of £60 per unit is selected. If North division selects a selling price of £60 per unit instead of £80 per unit, its overall marginal revenue would increase by £60,000 but its marginal cost would increase by £84,000. Consequently North division will not wish to lower the price.

(c) Where there is no market for the intermediate product and the supplying division has no capacity constraints the correct transfer price is the marginal cost of the supplying division for that output at which marginal cost equals the receiving division's net marginal revenue from converting the intermediate product. When unit variable cost is constant and fixed costs remain unchanged this rule will result in a transfer price which is equal to the supplying division's unit variable cost. Therefore the transfer price will be set at £11 per unit when the variable cost transfer pricing rule is applied. North Ltd will be faced with the following marginal cost and revenue schedules:

Output (units)	Marginal cost (see note i)	Marginal revenue
	£	£
1,000	18,000	100,000
2,000	18,000	80,000
3,000	18,000	60,000
4,000	18,000	40,000
5,000	18,000	20,000
6,000	18,000	Nil

Note

(i) Marginal cost = transfer price of £11 per unit plus conversion variable cost of £7 per unit.

    North Ltd will select the optimum output level for the group as a whole (i.e. 5,000 units) and the optimal selling price of £60 will be selected. A transfer price equal to the variable cost per unit of the supplying division will result in the profits of the group being allocated to North, and South will incur a loss equal to the fixed costs. Consequently a divisional profit incentive can not be applied to the supplying division.

Answer to problem 24.9

(a) The answer to this question can be found in the section headed 'A Perfect Market for the Intermediate Product and the Presence of Selling Costs' in the Appendix to Chapter 24.

(b) *Schedule 1: Calculation of marginal cost, marginal revenue and net marginal revenue*

Output of alpha (units)	Alpha Marginal cost (£000's)		Alpha Marginal revenue (£000's)		Beta net marginal revenue	
0–10	<28		65 (1)*		57 (3)*	
10–20	<28		60 (2)		55 (4/5)	
20–30	<28	see	55 (4/5)	see	53 (6)	see
30–40	<28	note 1	50 (8)	note 2	51 (7)	note 3
40–50	<28		45 (11/12)		49 (9)	
50–60	<28		40		47 (10)	
60–70	28		35		45 (11/12)	
70–80	30		30		43 (13)	
80–90	33		25		40	
90–100	35		20		36	
100–110	37		15		33	
110–120	40		10		30	
120–130	44		5		25	

*The numbers in brackets represent the descending order of ranking of marginal revenue/net marginal revenue for Alpha and Beta.

Notes

(1) The marginal cost per 10 units of alpha increases as output expands. This implies that the marginal cost per 10 units of alpha is less than £28,000 for output of less than 60 units.

(2) The question indicates that the marginal revenue function for alpha decreases in increments of £5,000 for each 10 units increase in sales volume of alpha for output levels from 60–130 units. This implies that the total revenue and marginal revenue function of alpha can be computed from this information on the basis of a £5,000 decline in marginal revenue for each 10 units of output.

(3) The NMR of beta declines as output rises thus suggesting an imperfect final product market. The implication of this is that NMR is in excess of £47,000 for increments of 10 units sales of beta at less than 50 units. The NMR for the first 50 units sales of beta has been estimated based on the information given in the question. We shall see that the accuracy of the estimates for output levels below 60 units is not critical for calculating the optimum transfer price and activity level.

The output of alpha is allocated between the sale of the intermediate product on the external market and the transfer of the intermediate product for sale as a final product on the basis of the ranking indicated in schedule 1. The allocation is presented in the following schedule:

Schedule 2: allocation of output of alpha

(1) Output of Alpha (unit)	(2) Alpha marginal cost (£000's)	(3) Allocation per ranking in schedule 1 (see note 1)	(4) Marginal revenue or NMR (see note 2)
0–10	<28	Alpha	65
10–20	<28	Alpha	60
20–30	<28	Beta	57
30–40	<28	Beta	55
40–50	<28	Alpha	55
50–60	<28	Beta	53
60–70	28	Beta	51
70–80	30	Alpha	50
80–90	33	Beta	49
90–100	35	Beta	47
100–110	37	Beta	45
110–120	40	Alpha	45
120–130	44	No allocation (MR/NMR<MC)	43

Notes

(1) Alpha refers to sale of Alpha as an intermediate product. Beta refers to the transfer of alpha internally for conversion to beta and sale in the final product market.

(2) Appropriate MR/NMR per ranking in schedule 1.

Conclusion

The optimal output level is 120 units. Below this output level MR>MC but beyond 120 units MC>MR. To induce the output of 120 units the transfer price should be set at £44 so as to prevent the receiving division from requesting a further 10 units which will yield a NMR of £43. Examination of schedule 2 indicates that 70 units should be transfered internally for sale as a final product and 50 units of the inter-mediate product sold externally. A transfer price of £44 will result in both divisions arriving at this pro-duction plan independently. Therefore the optimal transfer price is the marginal cost of the supplying division for that output at which marginal cost equals the sum of the receiving division's net marginal revenue from using the intermediate product and the marginal revenue from the sale of the intermediate product. In other words where column 2 equals column 4 in schedule 2.

Answer to problem 24.10

(a) *Advantages of absorption cost*

Provides an indication of the long run production costs of the supplying division. Therefore the receiving department will be charged at the long run cost of production.

Disadvantages of absorption cost

A. Cannot be guaranteed to motivate a divisional manager to make sound decisions. Transfer prices based on absorption cost are not consistent with the optimum transfer price rule outlined in Chapter 24.

B. Transfer prices are imposed resulting in divisional autonomy being undermined.

C. Ignores market prices.

D. Inefficiencies will be passed on to the receiving division if actual cost is used.

E. Zero profits will be earned by the supplying division. Therefore this measure will not be a reasonable measure of the economic performance of the division.

(b) *Advantages of marginal cost*
A. Will motivate sond decisions if set at the marginal cost of supplying division for that output at which marginal cost equals the sum of the receiving division's net marginal revenue from using the intermediate product and the marginal revenue from the sale of the intermediate product.

Disadvantage of marginal cost
A. Imposed transfer prices.
B. May not provide a meaningful performance measure. If variable cost is constant then the supplying division will make a loss equal to the total amount of the fixed costs.
C. Inefficiencies will be passed on to the receiving division if actual cost is used.

(c) *Advantage of cost-plus*
Provides an indication of the long-run production costs of the company and may provide a reasonable measure of economic performance of the supplying and receiving divisions since transfer prices might approximate a fair market price when no external market exists.

Disadvantages of cost-plus
See absorption cost disadvantages.

(d) *Advantages of standard cost*
Ensures that inefficiencies are charged to the supplying division and are not passed on to the receiving division.

Disadvantages of standard cost
Depends on whether standard absorption, marginal or absorption-plus is used. See (a) to (c) above for their respective disadvantages.

Answer to problem 24.11

A sound transfer pricing system should accomplish the following objectives:

  (i) It should motivate the divisional manager to make *sound decisions* and it should communicate information that provides a reliable basis for such decisions. This will happen when actions that divisional managers take to improve the reported profit of their divisions also improves the profit of the company as a whole.
 (ii) It should result in a report of divisional profits that is a reasonable measure of the *managerial performance* of the division.
(iii) It should ensure that divisional *autonomy* is not undermined.

It can be shown that full cost transfer prices may not meet any of the above objectives. Full cost transfer prices contain unitised fixed costs which can easily be misinterpreted as variable costs. This will result in incorrect pricing and output decisions. See 'Effect of Cost-Plus Transfer Prices in Chapter 24 for explanation of how full cost based transfer prices can lead to incorrect decisions.

When *actual* full cost transfer prices are used objectives (ii) and (iii) will not be met as inefficiencies of the supplying division will be passed on to the receiving division. This will mean that actual results will not represent a reasonable measure of divisional performance and divisional autonomy will be undermined. If standard costs are used and there is no external market for the intermediate then objective (ii) above may be satisfied if the transfer price represents the long run cost of supplying the intermediate product.

Answer to problem 24.12

See Chapter 24 for the answer to this question.

Answer to problem 24.13

(a) The answer should include a description of market based, cost based (variable cost, cost-plus etc.) and negotiated transfer prices. For a discussion of these methods see Chapter 24.

(b) For the answer to this question see 'Recommended Procedure for Transfer Prices' in Chapter 24.

(c) The recommended procedure for a market based transfer price might include the following:
  (i) Interdivisional transfers of the intermediate product shall be at market price.
 (ii) Market price is defined as . . . . (The company should define market price).
(iii) The supplying division should give priority to the demands of the receiving division at the prevailing market price and the receiving division should give the supplying division first option on meeting its demand.
(iv) If the receiving division finds a cheaper source of supply it should request the supplying division to meet this price. If it is not prepared to meet this price then head office should be informed. Head office may decide not to interfere in the dispute or may act as arbitrator. The decision of head office shall be binding on both divisions.

not represent a reasonable measure of divisional performance and divisional autonomy will be undermined.
If standard costs are used and there is no external market for the intermediate then objective (ii) above may
be satisfied if the transfer price represents the long run cost of supplying the intermediate product.

Answer to problem 24.12

See Chapter 24 for the answer to this question.

Answer to problem 24.13

(a) The answer should include a discussion of market-based, cost-based (variable cost, full cost, etc.) and negotiated transfer prices. For a discussion of these methods see Chapter 24.

(b) For the answer to this question see 'Recommended Procedure for Transfer Prices' in Chapter 24.

(c) The recommended procedure for a market based transfer price might include the following:
(i) Internal transfers of the intermediate product shall be at market price.
(ii) Market price is defined as ... The company should if the market price)
(iii) The supplying division should give priority to the demands of the receiving division over selling the intermediate and the receiving division should acquire the supplies first option of meeting its demand.
(iv) If the receiving division cannot find a cheaper source of supply it should request the supplying division to meet this price. If it is not prepared to meet this price then head office should be informed. Head office may choose not to interfere in the decision but, if it does so, the decision should benefit both divisions.